Kant and
the Philosophy of History

Kant and
the Philosophy of History

Yirmiyahu Yovel

PRINCETON UNIVERSITY PRESS

PRINCETON, NEW JERSEY

Copyright © 1980 by Princeton University Press
Published by Princeton University Press, Princeton, New Jersey
In the United Kingdom: Princeton University Press, Oxford

All Rights Reserved

Library of Congress Cataloguing in Publication Data will be found
on the last printed page of this book

ISBN 0-691-07225-6
ISBN 0-691-02056-6, pbk.

First Princeton Paperback printing, 1989

Publication of this book has been aided by a grant from The
Andrew W. Mellon Foundation

This book has been composed in Linotype Baskerville

Clothbound editions of Princeton University Press books are printed
on acid-free paper, and binding materials are chosen for strength
and durability

Printed in the United States of America by Princeton University Press,
Princeton, New Jersey

To Shoshana

CONTENTS

PREFACE

This book grew out of over a decade of intermittent Kant studies. As a young undergraduate in Jerusalem, then under strong Neo-Kantian influence (originating in Hermann Cohen's Marburg school), I was led to think that Kant had spelled the doom of all metaphysics, and that his contribution to ethics lay in his formal, all too formal, doctrine of the categorical imperative. As for his essays on history, if they deserved attention at all, they were to be deemed incompatible with the system.

Rereading Kant, however, I have found that, far from abolishing metaphysics, he had set out to renew it; and that beyond his formal imperative he was laying the ground for a second, material stage of practical philosophy, culminating in the idea of moral history. Moreover—and that came almost as a revelation—the two issues, metaphysics and moral history, were closely related in Kant's architectonic. Moral practice was the domain in which those metaphysical interests of the mind that could not be satisfied in the field of knowledge were to be re-channelled and find a valid critical expression. And it was by the moral-historical ideal, set and projected for the world by man's free consciousness, that the existence of the world itself could find justification and a "final end."

To the subject of metaphysics I have devoted an earlier book, *Kant and the Renovation of Metaphysics* (Jerusalem, 1973; now being translated into English), and the subject of history will concern me here. Although independent in content and argument, the two books complement each other and may add up to a reinterpretation of Kant as a whole.

In method, this book is neither a commentary nor a narrative exposition of Kant's overt views. It is an attempt at systematic reconstruction. I do not propose to follow the letter of any particular Kantian text but, combining a number of sources—mainly from Kant's major *systematic* works, like the *Critiques* and the *Religion*—to follow the logical implications and inner architectonic of Kant's position. This will bring out, I hope, the elements of a critical philosophy of history latent in Kant's work and with which he was long grappling, thereby also shedding light on a crucial, if long neglected, dimension of Kant's thought. Another result will be that the short essays Kant wrote explicitly on historical subjects, but which seem "dogmatic" and extraneous to his critical system, will be reintegrated within it. But let me point out that in reconstructing the elements of a critical philosophy of history, I do not claim it is ultimately coherent. In the final analysis it produces an antinomy in Kant's system (I call it "the historical antinomy"); for it can be shown, on different but equally valid grounds, that Kant's idea of rational history is both necessary and untenable in terms of his system. As the Epilogue will argue, Kant could not resolve this antinomy without giving up his radical dualism of reason and nature; this, indeed, led to the breakdown of his position and to Hegel's *Aufhebung*. But recognizing there *is* an antinomy is already important, for it implies the recognition that history is an essential, if problematic, aspect of the critical philosophy.

Earlier versions of a few chapters were previously published as follows: "The God of Kant," *Scripta Hierosolymitana* XX (Jerusalem: The Magnes Press, 1968), 88-123; "The Highest Good and History in Kant's Thought," *Archiv für Geschichte der Philosophie* XI (1973), 238-283; "Rational History and the Cunning of Nature," *Iyyun, A Hebrew Philosophical Quarterly* XXIV (1973), 38-92; "Bible Interpretation as Philosophical Praxis," *Journal of the History of Philosophy* XI (1973), 189-212; "Kant and Rational History," *Philosophy of History and Action*, ed. Yirmiahu Yovel (Dordrecht, D. Reidel Publishing Co., 1979). I am grateful to the publishers of these works for permission to reprint parts of these texts.

Quotations from Kant, except for a few passages in my translation, are taken from the English translations listed in the Table of References. Thanks are due to the Bobbs-Merrill Co. for permission to quote from L. W. Beck's translations of *Idea for a Universal History* and *Perpetual Peace*, included in his edition of essays, *Kant on History* (The Library of Liberal Arts, 1963), and his translation of the *Prolegomena* (The Library of Liberal Arts, 1950). St. Martin's Press, Inc. gave permission to quote from Kant, *Critique of Pure Reason*, translated by N. Kemp-Smith (1929).

In recent years a few books on Kant and history have appeared. The collection of texts in L. W. Beck's edition (*Kant on History*, New York, 1963) has done an immense service in calling attention to this rather neglected part of Kant's work. That it only incorporated Kant's explicit essays on history was unavoidable, as fragments from Kant's more systematic works would not be self-explanatory in the framework of an anthology. K. Weyand's *Kants Geschichtsphilosophie* (Cologne, 1964) will prove a rich and useful auxiliary to anyone working in this field. Galston's *Kant and the Problem of History* (Chicago, 1975) contains detailed commentaries of two Kantian essays, "The Conjectural Beginning of Human History" and, especially, the famous "Idea for a Universal History." Written with a strong political interest, the book limits its scope and approach to Kant's explicit historical texts (along with comparisons to Rousseau and Aristotle). Less traditional is the approach of M. Despland, *Kant on History and Religion* (Montreal and London, 1973) whose great merit is to recognize the importance of Kant's book on religion for grasping his view of history (and thus, also, the moral core of historical progress in Kant). Despland, however, gets carried away in his tendency to make Kant a religious believer despite himself, and in taking Kant's highly ambivalent and metaphorical language in the *Religion* at face value.

For useful comments and objections I am indebted, among others, to Professors Nathan Rotenstreich, Walter Kaufmann, Richard Popkin, Hans Wagner, Werner Becker, Dieter Henrich, David Hoy, Jacob Taubes, Michael Sukale, W. Galston and L. W. Beck. In Professor Beck's own work on Kant, as well as in that of Professor John Silber, I always found a source of inspiration—also for fruitful disagreements. Professor Richard Bernstein, then editor of *The Review of Metaphysics*, encouraged me to develop my primary thoughts into book form. I am particularly thankful to my students in graduate seminars here and at Princeton University for stimulating reactions. To Ms. Eva Shorr I am more indebted than a simple acknowledgement can express; her help was invaluable in all stages of preparing the book. Mr. Edward Tenner, my editor, went meticulously over the text and greatly improved its style; from him I learnt there was an American language (whereas mine was simple English as *lingua franca*). To them and many others who have helped along the way I offer my thanks.

Y. Y.

Jerusalem, The Hebrew University, April 1979

TABLE OF REFERENCES

Kant's works are quoted by the volumes and pagination of the Prussian Academy of Science and their English translations (except the *Critique of Pure Reason*). The following abbreviations are used:

The Critiques

C_1: *Kritik der reinen Vernunft*, first edition: IV (Berlin, 1911); second edition: III (Berlin, 1911).

A: 1781 English: *Critique of Pure Reason*, tr. by N. Kemp
B: 1787 Smith (London, 1970).
Quoted by the pagination of the first (marked A) and the second (marked B) original German editions. (Also referred to as the first *Critique*.)

C_2: *Kritik der praktischen Vernunft*, V (Berlin, 1913).
1788 English: *Critique of Practical Reason*, tr. by L. W. Beck (New York, 1956). (Also: the second *Critique*.)

C_3: *Kritik der Urtheilskraft*, V (Berlin, 1913).
1790 English: *Critique of Judgement*, tr. by J. C. Meredith (Oxford, 1952) (Also: the third *Critique*.)

Other Works

CB: *Muthmasslicher Anfang der Menschengeschichte*, VIII (Berlin, 1912).
1786 English: *Conjectural Beginning of Human History*, tr. by E. L. Fackenheim, in *Kant on History*, ed. by L. W. Beck (New York, 1963).

Contest: *Der Streit der Fakultäten*, VII (Berlin, 1917)
1798 English: *The Contest of Faculties*, in *Kant's Political Writings*, ed. by H. Reiss, tr. by H. B. Nisbet (Cambridge, 1970),

Education: Pädagogik, ed. F. T. Rink, IX (Berlin, 1923).
1803 English: *Education*, tr. by A. Churton (Ann Arbor, 1960).

Found.: Grundlegung zur Metaphysik der Sitten, IV (Berlin, 1911).
1785 English: *Foundations of the Metaphysics of Morals*, tr. by L. W. Beck (Chicago, 1950).

Idea: Idee zu einer allgemeinen Geschichte in weltbürgerlicher Absicht, VIII (Berlin, 1912).
1784 English: *Idea for a Universal History from a Cosmopolitan Point of View*, tr. by L. W. Beck in *Kant on History* (New York, 1963).

L: Logik, ed. G. B. Jäsche IX (Berlin, 1923).
1800 English (1): *Kant's Introduction to Logic*, tr. by T. K. Abbott (London, 1885).
(2): *Logic*, tr. by R. S. Hartman & W. Schwarz (New York, 1974).

LB: Lose Blätter zu den Fortschritten der Metaphysik, XX (Berlin, 1942).

MM: Metaphysik der Sitten, VI (Berlin, 1914).
1797 English: *Metaphysics of Morals* Part I: *The Metaphysical Elements of Justice*, tr. J. Ladd (New York, 1965).
Part II: *The Doctrine of Virtue*, tr. by M. J. Gregor (New York & Evanston, 1964).

Prol.: Prolegomena zu einer jeden künftigen Metaphysik, die als Wissenschaft wird auftreten können, IV (Berlin, 1911).
1783 English: *Prolegomena to any Future Metaphysics*, tr. by L. W. Beck (New York, 1950).

Rel.: Die Religion innerhalb der Grenzen der blossen Vernunft, VI (Berlin, 1914).
1793 English: *Religion within the Limits of Reason Alone*, tr. by T. M. Greene and H. H. Hudson (New York, 1960).

PP: Zum ewigen Frieden, VIII (Berlin, 1912).
1795 English: *Perpetual Peace*, tr. by L. W. Beck, in *Kant on History* (New York, 1963).

TP: Über den Gemeinspruch: Das mag in der Theorie richtig sein, taugt aber nicht für die Praxis, VIII (Berlin, 1912).

REFERENCES

1793: English: *On the Common Saying: "This May be True in Theory, But it Does Not Apply in Practice,"* in *Kant's Political Writings* (Cambridge, 1970).

UNH: *Allgemeine Naturgeschichte und Theorie des Himmels*, I (Berlin, 1910).

1755 English: *Universal Natural History and Theory of the Heavens*, tr. by W. Hastie (Ann Arbor, 1969; parts only).

Verk.: *Verkündigung des nahen Abschlusses eines Tractats zum ewigen Frieden in der Philosophie*, VIII (Berlin, 1912).

WIE: *Beantwortung der Frage: Was ist Aufklärung?* VIII (Berlin, 1912).

1784 English: *What Is Enlightenment*, tr. by L. W. Beck, in *Kant on History* (New York, 1963).

Kant and
the Philosophy of History

THE HISTORY OF
REASON IN KANT'S SYSTEM

Is rationalism compatible with the modern historical outlook? This is perhaps the most challenging problem left by the rationalists of the Enlightenment to their modern successors. The philosophers of the Age of Reason, starting with Descartes and following Plato, saw reason as eternal, non-temporal, and not bound by cultural and sociological factors. Even the limits of reason (when admitted) were to be understood *sub specie aeternitatis.* This led to a view of history as a contingent, empirical affair, without rational import in itself. Whatever is *Geschichte* is thereby mere *Historie.* It consists in the simple accumulation or recounting of facts that per se neither disclose a rational pattern nor are relevant to the growth of rationality. Indeed, the very notion of *growth* in rationality could at best only have a quantitative, not a qualitative sense. Individual men could become more rational, as they complied with the fixed and eternal norms of rationality that as such were independent of man's actual thinking and practical attitudes. But whereas individual men belonged to the world of becoming, reason "itself" was pure being. It was an eternal truth —immovable, *an sich,* and without change.

The nascent historicism of the eighteenth century challenged this classic view. The problem was not just to admit the rational import of history, but to supply it with a systematic *ground.* And this suggested a reappraisal of the nature and status of rationality. For history to have a rational significance, reason itself—so it seemed—must be construed to allow for its possible historization.

It was certainly Hegel who offered the most comprehensive and far-reaching theory in this respect. In essence, Hegel made the historization of reason a necessary moment of its ascent to the status of eternal truth. Seeking to explain the possibility of *absolute* knowledge, Hegel made it conditional upon the process of the *becoming* of reason, and upon the dialectical *Aufhebung* of this becoming. In this way he presented the growth of rationality as constitutive of its rational character.

Even before Hegel, the conflict between rationalism and historicism had arisen within the philosophy of the Enlightenment itself, where it found an interesting expression in Kant's system. While concerned with the pure and transcendental forms of human reason, Kant did not conceive of them as fixed and ready-made but as *constituted* by the rational subject. He thereby introduced what may be called his "Copernican revolution of rationality"—a revolution that affects Kant's view of the nature of reason no less than it does his special doctrines of knowledge and ethics. This revolution rejected the Platonic model of reason and suggested the systematic ground that could eventually account for the historization of reason. In fact, Hegel's theory relied on the same basic revolution. Reason, for Hegel, has a becoming, because it is the product of the rational subject, who has constituted himself through his historical development. The anti-Platonic theory of rationality was thus logically necessary for Hegel's concept of a history of reason. But on this crucial point, Hegel did not put forward an absolutely new principle; he only developed more coherently and comprehensively an idea that Kant had already expressed implicitly and without dialectical logic.

Against this background, it should no longer be surprising that Kant does, in effect, introduce an explicit concept of a "history of reason," a history that is itself rational or "transcendental" and not empirical. This concept is usually overlooked or explained away by Kantian critics, who find it embarrassing. It seems to be at odds with the "pure" character of reason and also with Kant's theory of time. Yet the concept of the history of reason is genuinely Kantian. It pervades Kant's philosophy of ethics and religion; it underlies his theory of scientific revolutions and the history of philosophy; and it has its systematic roots in his meta-philosophy. The extent to which this concept is incompatible with Kant's theory of time, and has a problematic relation to *empirical* history, is an inner difficulty of the system that does not justify dismissing the concept altogether. Systematic difficulties also arise in well-established Kantian concepts, such as the thing-in-itself or schematism, which no serious Kantian critic would dream of overlooking despite their problematic status.

In this introductory chapter I shall therefore accept the prima facie legitimacy of the concept of a history of reason and ask two questions about it, one *quid facti* and one *quid juris*. First I shall outline the main areas in which this concept actually functions in Kant's critical system, as they will be further developed in the various chapters of this book. But secondly, supposing that it does in fact function in the system, we must ask how the use of this concept can be *justified* in terms of Kant's theory of reason. The answer to this question cannot be given in the form of a strict and flawless *deduction*, but at least we may bring out those meta-philosophical elements of Kant's system in which the notion of a history of reason may look for its grounds.

The History of Reason: *quid facti*

Kant's overt statements, including his official essays on history, do not exhaust the role that rational history actually plays in his philosophy. To recognize this role one must use reconstructive analysis, reading the texts against the inner logic and necessary commitments of Kant's position as only later chapters can do. Here I must be somewhat summary and dogmatic, dealing with the question of *quid facti* by listing the main areas on which Kant's concept of a history of reason comes to bear.

Generally speaking, the history of reason has two main manifestations in Kant: one is the history of reason reshaping the *world*, and the other is the history of reason becoming known and explicated to *itself*. The first aspect of the history of reason is mainly practical; it is the process whereby human reason imprints itself upon the actual world, reshaping its empirical organization in light of its own goals and interests. In this practical sense, rational history is an open-ended process, moving toward an infinitely remote ideal. The second sense of the history of reason is mainly theoretical (using "theory" in the broad sense, including the theory of morality); it is the process whereby human reason gradually explicates its latent paradigm, articulating its essential concepts, principles, and interests within a coherent system. This aspect of the history of reason is in principle *finite*; it culminates in scientific revolutions, which elevate the various theoretical disciplines (logic, mathematics, physics, and eventually philosophy itself) to the level of valid science, and thus, in fact, *abolish* their history and give them a final, immutable form.

Let me elaborate a little on each aspect of the history of reason.

The History of Praxis: Reshaping the World

The Highest Good

Kant was interested in history primarily as a moral task rather than as a cognitive object. History is the domain in which human action is supposed to create a progressive synthesis between the moral demands of reason and the actual world of experience. This synthesis should not be confined to singular acts and particular results, but should encompass the whole range of human practical experience. Thus it must serve as a principle of *totalization*, gradually transforming the basic shapes of the moral, political, and cultural world.

As Chapter One will show, Kant calls the highest totality toward which this process is oriented "the highest good in the world." To make coherent sense, this rational ideal should be construed as the regulative idea of history; and correspondingly, Kant's special imperative ("Act to promote the highest good in the world") can properly be called the *historical* imperative. On the other hand, the rational goal of the highest good (the total moral end of humanity) also expresses the supreme interest of reason; and thus rational history is not only integrated into Kant's critical system, but even related to its very architectonic.

The Philosophy of Religion

This conclusion is further corroborated by Kant's philosophy and critique of religion, which is in fact a latent philosophy of history. According to Kant there can be many faiths and churches but only one religion. This is the religion of reason, which the many historical faiths express with varying degrees of vagueness and empirical distortion. The one true religion is basically identical with Kant's moral theory, especially with that part of it that sets the goal of establishing a moral *totality*. The history of religion is thus a latent mode of the history of reason in two respects. On the one hand it is the process in which the rational principle of morality gradually breaks through the diverse historical creeds until it attains clear explication as a pure system of practical reason. But on the other hand, even after the true nature of religion is known in theory, the task of rational religion is not done, but still lies ahead in future history. This task is to establish the "kingdom of God on earth"—a metaphor expressing the secular moral ideal contained in the highest good. In this way the history of religion is a moment of rational history in general, moving towards the same moral totality.

7

The Cunning of Nature

Alongside this view, in a way as its rival, stands Kant's well-known theory of the dialectic of political history. According to this theory, nature itself, even without the rational will, is working according to a hidden design, bringing about political progress by means of violence and passion. It is through wars, exploitation and calculated self-interest that new political institutions, domestic and international, are created, which in effect serve the goals of reason and freedom. This is the main thesis of Kant's explicit essays on history, such as the *Idea for a Universal History* and *Perpetual Peace*, and it also occurs in Par. 83 of the *Critique of Judgement*. Because these texts put forward a principle of blind, natural teleology, which may be called the cunning of nature, they are usually interpreted as dogmatic and therefore as incompatible with Kant's critical philosophy. This is a strong claim, but as Chapter Four will show, it calls for three important modifications. First, in the *Critique of Judgement*, the principle of the cunning of nature undergoes a radical change in its methodological status. It is now conceived only as a "reflective" teleological judgement that carries no ontological commitment,[1] and thus becomes compatible with the demands of critical reason. Secondly, even as a reflective judgement, the cunning of nature applies to *political* history, which is a narrow and subordinate aspect of the complete historical ideal. The major aspect of historical progress lies in the creation of a *moral* community, defined by the rational quality of the *dispositions* of all its members; and this, by definition, cannot be secured by means of passion and self-interest. Finally, ever since the Enlightenment, the cunning of nature does not play an exclusive role even in political progress. After the requirements of practical reason were explicated, it was the rational will and not

[1] A reflective judgement is distinguished by Kant from a constitutive one in that it has no ontological import. For a full discussion see Chapter Four, pp. 130-132.

8

just the cunning of nature that was expected to affect the political world as well, and thus the two rival principles in fact become complementary.

The History of Theory: The Self-Explication of Reason

The History of Philosophy

Further evidence of the genuine position held by the concept of a history of reason in Kant's system is to be found *in* the process by which human reason actualizes its theoretical potential and becomes known and explicated to itself. This includes the history of the sciences and especially of philosophy. At the end of the *Critique of Pure Reason* Kant introduced the concept of a transcendental history of philosophy actually called "the history of reason." This concept is further developed in his posthumous *Lose Blätter*; in the chapter on the "Architectonic" in the *Critique of Pure Reason*; and in the two prefaces to this major work. Kant here offers a theory of scientific revolution and a model of the history of philosophy that bear a striking resemblance to those of Hegel.

Kant conceives of reason as an interested or "erotic" activity moving towards a systematic explication of itself. Underlying this process is a latent paradigm ("schema") that all philosophical systems have been gradually realizing. All the important doctrines in the history of philosophy are thereby tacit members of one systematic whole, each narrowly stressing some particular "interest of reason" and special aspects of the final pure system. This one-sidedness produces antinomies among the historical systems, leading to their breakdown. However, the collapse of historical systems leaves out a multitude of particular concepts, principles, and categories, which gradually accumulate until they find a new systematic organization. According to Kant this process is finite; like the other theoretical sciences, philosophy is expected to undergo a final *revolution*, creating the ultimate system, which resolves the

9

antinomies among historical systems and finally actualizes the latent paradigm of reason in full. This revolution will for the first time constitute philosophy-as-science and bring to an end the historical process in which one can only philosophize and not yet "learn philosophy." (This is similar to Hegel's idea that the final system abolishes philosophy as the love of knowledge and transforms it into actual knowledge.)

This topic will be elaborated in Chapter Six. But a few passages from Kant's chapter on the Architectonic give a first-hand impression of Kant's idea of the history of reason.

> Systems seem to be formed in the manner of vermin, through *generatio aequivoca*, from the mere confluence of assembled concepts, at first imperfect, and only gradually attaining to completeness (*C1*: A 835/B 863).

This confluence is not, however, a mere aggregate but a *latent organic system*. All historical doctrines, Kant adds,

> have had their schema, as the original germ, in the *self*-development of reason alone. Hence . . . *they are one and all organically united in a system of human knowledge, as members of one whole (ibid.)*

Hence the historicality of this process:

> [O]nly after we have spent much time in the collection of materials in somewhat random fashion, *at the suggestion of an idea lying hidden in our mind*, and after we have, indeed, over a long period, assembled the materials in a merely technical manner, does it first become possible for us to discern the idea in a clearer light and to devise a whole architectonically, in accordance with the ends of reason (*C1*: A 834/B 862; italics added).

10

Kant declares that it is "unfortunate" to have to go through this historical process, but as we shall see, we must also conceive of it as inevitable because of the *finitude* of human reason. Recognizing that our reason is finite includes, among other things, the recognizing that it must have a "becoming" of its own.

In summary, Kant presents reason as showing development and a historical goal. It gradually becomes explicated or known to itself in a progressive movement, and it is also expected to reshape the actual world according to its precepts and practical goals, thus promoting the highest good. From these viewpoints, the concept of rational history not only belongs to the critical philosophy but—as the highest good—it is even the supreme goal around which the system is architectonically organized.

The History of Reason: *quid juris*

The results we have attained are somewhat surprising. They suggest, among other things, a close affinity between Kant's philosophy of reason and Hegel's, and they raise a question about Kant's own view of reason as "pure" and transcendental. Having found a case for the history of reason *quid facti*, I must now ask the question *quid juris*.

Since Kant does not develop his idea, it would be too much to expect to find a full systematic justification for it. As we shall see, the concept of the history of reason invokes antinomies within Kant's system. But instead of merely dismissing the concept at the outset for its embarrassing appearance, we must first try to find as many systematic grounds for it as we can in Kant's own theory of reason, even if these grounds are not sufficiently developed to amount to a full and coherent theory.

To construe Kant's conception of reason we shall draw on three main sources. One is Kant's discussion of the "Architectonic of Human Reason," a major text for understanding his meta-philosophy. A second source is Kant's principle of the Copernican revolution, which must be considered not only in its bare formulation but in the way it is actually worked out in Kant's ontology, ethics, esthetics (the theory of the sublime), etc. This idea is central to Kant's critique of reason and includes both his reinterpretation of reason and his account of its finitude. A third source is Kant's various allusions to the functions, interests, tasks, and even "needs" and "aspirations" of human reason that permeate the corpus of his writings.

In order to identify the meta-philosophical grounds in which Kant's concept of a history of reason can be anchored, we have to consider four interrelated main topics: (a) Kant's Copernican revolution in rationality (his *constitution* theory of reason); (b) the *finitude* of human reason; (c) the conception of reason as a system of *interests*; and (d) the *architectonic unity* of reason. For the purpose of analysis I shall focus on these subjects separately before bringing them together again.

The Copernican Revolution in Rationality

Spontaneity

Kant conceives of reason mainly as a spontaneous activity, not as a mere set of forms. Even the objective side of reason—its concepts, principles, etc.—must be construed as subjective functions, by which the human mind or ego structures itself as well as its experience. This *dynamic* conception of reason is radically different from that of Plato and, indeed, breaks away from the whole classic view of the *logos* as fixed and independent, governing the mind and the world as a thing in itself. For Kant whatever is rational depends on the thinking subject. Reason cannot be divorced from the actual operation of thinking or from the practical attitudes of the mind but is formed by them while also forming them. To be sure, Kant does not mean by this the psychological process of thinking, as an empirical event, but the so-called "transcendental" func-

Heraclitus

12

tioning of the mind. But as such, the dynami\
reason belongs to its very definition.

This idea is closely connected with Kant's cc\
autonomy, and with his constitution theory of rat.\
In being autonomous, human reason must abide o\
those universal rules it sets up by itself, and in wh.   ιτ\
can recognize the explication of its own subjective struc-\
ture. Any other attitude will be "heteronomous" and\
thereby non-rational. This view of autonomy is based\
upon Kant's constitution theory of rationality, i.e., on his\
Copernican revolution, as it affects his view of the nature\
of reason itself and not only of knowledge or ethics. Ac-\
cording to this theory, reason cannot be conceived of as a\
system of universal norms that subsist in themselves, but\
must be seen as constituted by the human subject. The\
objective side of reason, as a set of principles, is thus de-\
pendent on its subjective side, i.e., upon the spontaneous\
activity of the rational ego, who explicates his own struc-\
ture in these principles and recognizes them as his own.\
This model of rationality lays down the conditions by\
which both our subjective attitudes and the *objective\
norms themselves* can gain rational status. No set of uni-\
versal norms is rational in itself, except as it is constituted\
by the subject and can be recognized by him as such. And\
correspondingly, we become rational not by complying\
with a system of preestablished norms, but by setting up\
the norms with which we comply.

In this way, *the very status of rationality is not ready-\
made but constituted,* depending on the spontaneous activ-\
ity of the ego, and this supplies a systematic ground for\
assigning reason a "becoming" of its own. This becoming\
must, moreover, assume a specifically historical character\
because of the finitude of human reason.

The Finitude of Reason

As a critic of reason, Kant was concerned with the finitude\
of human reason side by side with its autonomy. Moreover,

an essential aspect of the autonomy of reason is its recognition of its immanent limitations. As finite, human reason is necessarily confronted with the problem of its own historization. It is not an *intellectus archetypus*, in which there is no difference between the possible and the actual. Since it is finite, reason must inevitably suffer from a gap between its limited potential and its actual articulations; and it thus faces the problem or the task of gradually closing this gap. Reason does not immediately possess the full, though limited scope that it can attain in principle, but must be actualized in a progressive move of self-explication; and thus, again, human reason is subject to a history or a becoming of its own.

The finitude of human reason and its autonomy jointly account for the fact that Kant must admit the concept of an ascent of rationality, not as compliance with externally fixed rules, but as the *self*-explication of the human mind.

The finitude of human reason also has a direct bearing on our next topic—the *interests* of reason.

Reason as Interest

Kant describes reason primarily as a *system of interests*. Its basic feature is *teleological* activity, pursuing its own "essential ends" or immanent tasks. This goal-oriented activity is what the "architectonic" of reason basically means. By this Kant does not mean technical symmetry among the different parts of the system but a dynamic harmony of interests. Reason is thus a system of rational interests that complement one another within an organized hierarchy; and rational activity is a goal-setting activity, directed to the attainment of ends not given to it from without but set or projected by reason itself.

This idea is best known from Kant's moral philosophy, but it is equally present in all the other branches of his system, including his definition of reason as such. In saying that reason is architectonic or teleological, Kant asserts the autonomy of rational interests and lays down a neces-

14

sary condition for rationality in general. Rationality cannot, by definition, only be instrumental. It does not consist in the maximization of certain desired values, whose desirability derived from sources other than reason, such as utility, passion, happiness, piety, social benefits, or technological efficiency. For Kant this is the main difference between reason and what may be called mere intelligence. Intelligence is basically instrumental and pragmatic; it uses rational means in order to further ends that are accidental from the viewpoint of reason itself, since they are always taken from the outside. Reason, however, uses its instrumental means in order to further its essential, not its accidental, ends: and these essential ends are set or projected by the rational subject.

We may express the above by saying that reason is a *self-sufficient* teleological system. It sets forth its immanent tasks while serving as a means of attaining them. Moreover, reason is supposed to be sufficient unto itself, even insofar as its motivational power is concerned. Again, this idea is best expressed in Kant's theory of action, but also applies to reason in general. In saying that reason can be "practical," Kant means, among other things, that it is endowed with sufficient motivational power to realize its own prescriptions, regardless of any other interests. Since it is fundamentally an *interest*, reason can spontaneously generate the motivating principle needed for its actualization.

logos and *eros*

By defining reason in terms of its interests and immanent tasks, Kant ascribes to reason a dynamic and even "erotic" nature. Kantian reason is not mere *logos* but a fusion of Plato's *logos* and *eros*. Plato drew a fundamental distinction between the rational and the motivational aspect of the mind. Reason in itself is the pre-established goal of the mind, to which its erotic principle aspires. Kant accepts the basis of this theory, with two modifications. First,

15

the rational goal is not prescribed in advance, but rather projected, or constituted, by the activity that pursues it. And consequently it is *reason itself* that has the erotic side, i.e., the aspect of aspiration and becoming. Thus, in effect, we find that the Kantian texts are studded with expressions that amount to a virtual *erotic glossary* of reason. Reason is not only endowed with "ends," "tasks," and "interests"; it also has "needs," "satisfactions," "aspirations," "strivings," and "affection"; it has a "vocation," a "destiny," a "calling," and an "appellation"; and needless to say, it has "requirements," "claims," and "pretenses"— which Kant portrayed as concrete attitudes. Many of these expressions should certainly be understood as metaphors; but metaphors for what? For, I suggest, certain aspects of the *interest* of reason which, in itself, is no longer a metaphor in the same sense,[2] but rather a systematic concept. It belongs to Kant's meta-philosophical account of the architectonic of reason and thus supplies a ground for assigning reason a processuality of its own and eventually a history.

Despite the clear evidence, Kantian scholarship has tended to disregard the "interested" character of reason, perhaps out of anti-historical bias. It is symptomatic that even a serious lexicographer like Rudolf Eisler, in his well-known *Kant-Lexikon*, virtually passed over the abundant wealth of dynamic (erotic) predicates that Kant attaches to reason; and he mentions even the crucial concept of *Interesse der Vernunft* with extreme brevity, almost as something to get rid of. (By contrast, the computerized *Kant-Index* started by G. Martin renders the number of occurrences of "interest" in Kant's works as over 700, many of which have reference to reason.) Eisler was so hasty in doing away with the entry on *Interesse der Vernunft*, that

2 It might be a metaphor in the deeper sense in which the substantive "reason" itself is a metaphor, or in which such concepts as "ground" or "basis" are metaphoric. But this is a different issue altogether.

he did not even quote the occurrence of this term in such central Kantian chapters as the "Antinomies" and "The Primacy of Practical Reason."

The necessary relation between interest and reason is made unmistakably explicit when Kant says that *an interest "can never be attributed to a being which lacks reason"* (*C2*, V:79/82). An interest is not a mere impulse but the consciousness of an impulse and the ability to serve and satisfy this impulse by taking one's reflective distance from it. In this sense, *an interest is fundamentally a rational phenomenon*, pertaining only to rational beings. But interests can either be autonomous or heteronomous, according to the origin of their goals. A sensuous interest is heteronomous in that it uses the mediation of reason to promote ends that are *accidental* to reason; whereas a proper interest of reason is directed toward the promotion of rationality itself, i.e., to an *essential* end of reason.

At this point the interested character of reason is related to its finitude and subjective constitution, which give the idea of the architectonic, as a teleology of reason, a distinctively Kantian sense.

First, we have seen that Kant ascribes interests only to rational beings. But equally, he says that only finite beings can have interests (*C2*, V:79/82), thus restricting the concept of interest to the domain of finite rational beings— Kant's typical characterization of man. It is because we are finite that our rationality assumes an interested character. Reason sets itself its immanent goals, not as actually accomplished but in the form of a lack or a privation, and makes the pursuit of these goals *a rational requirement in itself*.[3] This point also introduces a distinction between an

[3] This picture of reason includes part of Kant's answer to the question that occupies many contemporary philosophers, Why be rational? To Kant, viewing rationality as an interested activity, pursuing its own immanent ends, is a necessary condition for answering this question. Rationality does not consist in the mere adjustment of means to an end, but in the positing of the end and in its very *pursuit*. (This, however, is only part of Kant's answer; for ultimately, to be rational

"interest" of reason and an "end" of reason. Until now we have used these concepts interchangeably, but now their difference has to be stated. The concept of end does not necessarily indicate a lack or a privation. It is a teleological concept, whose function is retained even after it has been actualized. The teleological form is absorbed into its final product—for instance, into the system of reason—and preserved in its subsisting organization. Therefore, had we been infinite creatures, in whom the archetypal model of rationality is immediately realized in full, we would still have retained the teleological form of our reason. An interest, on the other hand, is related to the *gap* that exists between the abstract goal and its actuality, between the archetypal model of rationality latent in our minds and its full explication. In this way the finitude of reason sheds further light on what we called the erotic aspect of reason, explaining both its motivational principle[4] and its indispensable historization.

Secondly, as interest has to be understood with respect to finitude, so the essential ends of reason must be conceived in relation to its autonomy. From the Copernican revolution, it is clear that the immanent goals of reason must be understood as they are projected by the rational subject who explicates his own structure in them, and not as merely discovered or assumed by him, as ready-made goals. Earlier philosophers also spoke of inherent ends and immanent rational goals, but they gave them a dogmatic status. An immanent rational goal by definition indicates that it should be pursued for its own sake. But who assigns it this value status, as something to be pursued per se? According to Kant's theory of rationality, the answer must

---

we must be able to identify the "ends of reason" as *our own*. This condition, Kant believes, is fulfilled by the Critique of Reason, governed by his Copernican revolution. Through it we become aware that the goals and norms of rationality are constituted by ourselves and, in effect, are the explication of our own subjectivity.)

[4] See *C2* on "The Incentives of Pure Practical Reason."

18

once more be: the human subject, as he explicates his own subjective structure. One cannot coherently say that one ought to pursue a goal for its own sake, but that this attitude itself is somehow prescribed to us from without. In this case we will not pursue the goal for its own sake but for the sake of satisfying whoever prescribed this attitude to us. In this way, Kant's constitution theory of rationality affects his interpretation of the old notion of inherent ends. Strictly speaking, there are no inherent ends, if by this we mean that the end actually inheres in an object as a thing in itself. To be sure, certain ends are teleologically self-sufficient, but not because they are such in themselves, but because they are constituted (or projected) as such by the rational subject who envisages them. If reason itself is subjectively constituted, so are its values and final ends.

The Architectonic Unity of Reason

What are the specific interests of reason? Kant distinguishes between two types of rational interests, which may be called regional and cross-regional. All these interests are modes of pursuing rationality for its own sake, not for the sake of extraneous values. The regional interests correspond to the specific uses of reason, in knowledge, in moral actions, and also in esthetics. The cross-regional interests are at work in all the regions, laying down further rational requirements. These are, for instance, the *critical* interest of reason, cutting through all the regions; the *metaphysical* interest of reason, which operates in ethics as well; reason's interest in *totalization*, operating in the various "dialectics" of the system; and finally, the *architectonic* interest of reason, seeking the harmonious unity of all the others.[5]

---

[5] Kant accepts as a first postulate that reason can achieve systematic unity by its ideal "schema." All its interests are, in principle, harmonizable, in subordination to a supreme end which does not, however, abolish their respective autonomy. This harmony is governed by the

Insofar as the different interest of reason have not attained full explication, they may produce conflicts and
antinomies—as the history of philosophy as well as of
morality had shown. But all are mutually compatible in
principle and, therefore, the supreme architectonic end of
reason is to actualize and bring to light its fundamental
unity. It is precisely in this way that Kant accounts for the
birth of his own critical system and for the philosophical
program that underlies it. Kant has found an unresolved
antinomy between the metaphysical and the critical interests of reasons, taking the form of an opposition between
dogmatic rationalism and skeptical empiricism; and his
major problem in the *Critiques* is to resolve this antinomy,
creating a *critical metaphysics* that could finally count as
science. In this Kant believes that his system will bring
the whole history of reason to an end—in the theoretical
sense—and thus abolish its historicality. But in so doing,
it will also have to harmonize the cognitive and the practical interests of reason, a result attained in Kant's doctrine of the primacy of pure practical reason.

Even before fully elaborating this point, we can see
that from the viewpoint of the architectonic unity of reason, its historicality becomes inevitable; even though, when
the unity is finally achieved, the history of reason is *transcended*.[6] This might seem a proto-Hegelian idea, had it
not a typically Kantian corollary. According to the primacy
of pure practical reason, even when the history of theory is
consummated, the history of praxis is still open. The supreme interest of reason, under which the whole system
of reason is subsumed, is the creation of the moral totality,
named the highest good; and this is an infinitely remote
utopia, defining the perspective of future history. In this

---

primacy of practical reason, which makes practical interest superior to
the others. The supreme end round which the system is organized is
the supreme practical end; and thus (as we have remarked before)
the historical ideal is placed not just within the system, but in fact at
its "architectonic" center.

6 See Chapter Six.

way the architectonic unity of reason, when attained, brings the history of theory to a close, while opening an infinite perspective for the history of praxis.

The Historical Antinomy and Historical Schematism

Having shown the role that Kant's concept of the history of reason plays in both his substantive and his meta-philosophical doctrine, I shall now point out its major difficulties, which might be called *the problem of historical schematism* and the *historical antinomy*.

The problem of historical schematism follows, like other problems of schematism in Kant, from his unbridgeable dualism. Although Kant must admit of a non-empirical history of reason, he cannot explain its relation to *empirical* history. Being finite, and being related to thinking subjects, reason operates "in" and "through" empirical individuals, all of whom participate in the world of experience. Human reason does not have a history independent of Plato, Luther, Newton, or even Robespierre; it is carried out by concrete men and is supposed, in the field of praxis, to affect the organization of the empirical world. How can a bridge be built between the history of reason and empirical history? I think that Kant does not and cannot have a sufficient answer. Reason is to grow, mature, and affect the world in and through empirical history, which goes on in time and is bound by natural laws. How can the correspondence between real states in experience and the stages in the evolution of reason be accounted for? Since no intrinsic ground can be found within the system, Kant must resort in the field of practical reason to a transcendent postulate, "God"; but even this postulate does not *explain* the correspondence. It only asserts and, in the final analysis, *presupposes* it.

Moreover, the problem of historical schematism ties up to a real antinomy, for on the basis of Kant's theory of time, no mediation between reason and empirical history is conceivable. For reason to be a historical principle, it must be embodied in actual time. Yet time, according to Kant's Transcendental Esthetics, is merely a "form of intuition" that cannot apply to reason at all, only to empirical data categorized by the forms of the understanding. Yet both theories are equally necessary to Kant's philosophy. They both stem from Kantian presuppositions, the denial of which would incur an intolerable price. For this reason, in showing that the concept of history of reason is *indispensable* to Kant's theory, I have not at all shown that it is ultimately *coherent*. Quite the contrary: despite its logical roots in one part of Kant's philosophy, it is incompatible with another essential part of his philosophy —the theory of time—and so it constitutes a genuine antinomy within the system.

However, asserting the existence of an antinomy is to imply that both principles are equally necessary to Kant; this is all I wished to do, and all that a reconstructive analysis of the text can yield.

A distinction can be made, to be sure, between processuality and time, as philosophers formerly distinguished between *duratio* and *tempus*. Using this device, one might argue that Kant must admit of some form of non-temporal processuality in reason, a kind of "transcendental" becoming which involves *duratio* but not *tempus*. There certainly are some indications for this view in Kant; for instance, in his Transcendental Deduction it turns out that the identity of the thinking ego is not given in advance but is being actualized in the process whereby the ego unifies the manifold of representations, constituting an objective world of experience, and *re*constituting itself, as an identical "I think," in and through this activity. Here we have a dynamic model, in fact a pure processuality that does not take place in time and yet is necessary for the self-constitution of the rational ego. Similarly, one might argue, some concept of a "transcendental" processuality may be ascribed to reason in its cultural march toward maturation. But this solution not only goes beyond what may be attributed to Kant without stretching his theory too far; it is also not a solution at all, because the basic incompatibility of the two systems, empirical history as a form of experience, and rational history as a non-temporal processuality, remains intact.

However, these objections provide no grounds for disregarding the genuine place that rational history occupies in Kant's system. The concept is not sufficiently coherent; but so, as I noted above, are other Kantian concepts like the thing in itself. Were we to dismiss as illegitimate all the concepts that give Kant trouble, or even only those related to his dualism, we would not, indeed, have very much left.

Kant and Hegel

Since my discussion of Kant has brought to light many similarities between his theory and Hegel's, I wish to conclude by pointing out the main differences.

It goes without saying that Kant's conception is only rudimentary in comparison to Hegel's, and that Kant did not admit of a dialectical logic, as a way of reconciling rationality and empirical history. The latter point accounts for the fundamental dualism in Kant's position, which had led most of his critics to opt for pure reason and to dismiss its history. In a sense, if a choice has to be made, I think they have made the right one; but I contest that such a choice is necessary, as long as we are dealing with pure interpretation. A better and more faithful method is to show the inner difficulties without resolving them in a one-sided way. These difficulties arise from the fact that, contrary to Hegel, Kant did not view the history of reason as necessarily mediated by empirical history. Hegel, indeed, saw reason as constituted, not by the pure ego in its pure self-explication, but by the concrete subject, immersed in the *empirical* process of his historization. Therefore, whereas for Kant empirical history is a challenge and a difficulty vis-à-vis the history of reason, for Hegel, empirical history is the medium, or the moment, in which the history of reason can alone take place. This also explains the second major difference. For both philosophers the history of reason implies its becoming explicated and known to itself. Yet the self-explication of reason applies in Kant only to the subject, not to the object; whereas in Hegel it is equally the self-explication of the object (the world, the Absolute), that actualizes its rationality and becomes known to itself in history. Kant could not accept this daring view, among other things because he rejected the dialectical logic that underlies it. Therefore, the history of reason is for him the self-explication of the subject alone, who subsequently ought to *imprint* his rational forms upon the object rather than to explicate them from the object itself.

It may well be that Hegel not only presented a more comprehensive and developed, but also a more coherent theory. Yet Hegel achieved this by a number of unacceptable presuppositions, especially that reason is infinite, and has even actualized itself in history. For this reason, his more coherent theory is attained at the price of being ultimately false. Kant's great achievement seems to me to be his realization of the finitude of reason, and any further correction of his stand should be made upon the basis of this recognition, rather than upon its rejection.

Finally, however, there is a crucial presupposition that Hegel and Kant share. This is the idea that the history of reason can in principle be sublated, by attaining a final, immutable system. In contrast, I think that it should follow from the "erotic" aspect of reason, and its self-structuring activity, that rationality is an open-ended enterprise, capable of permanently transcending the forms and structures it assumes. Reason should not be equated with some latent, pure, and final paradigm that awaits explication once and for all. Rather, as the reflective articulation of our actual experience, it must be conceived, first, as embedded in all the forms of our knowledge and opinion, and secondly, as an ever self-transcending activity, finding no rest in a "pure" system. The history of reason has no end, except—one might say—in the end of man himself.

PART I

History as the Moral Totality

CHAPTER I

THE HIGHEST GOOD
AS THE IDEA OF HISTORY

Kant scholars have not yet given the concept of the highest good (*summum bonum*) all the attention it deserves. The responsibility rests largely with Kant himself, who never attempted to delineate a comprehensive and unified doctrine of the highest good. This led many of his interpreters to regard the concept of the highest good as marginal, or to concentrate on a single aspect of its complexity, usually interpreting the *summum bonum* as a semi-theological supplement to ethics.[1]

The result is a one-sided picture of Kant's practical philosophy, that becomes restricted to the realm of personal, internal morality. Its further implications as a philosophy of practice—such as the *realization* of morality in the realm of nature, the *totalization* of single moral works within a new system, and in general, the reshaping of given empirical orders to fit moral demands—are generally disregarded or shunted aside. A major purpose of this chapter is to study these further implications and show how they suggest a reinterpretation of the highest good as the regulative idea of history. In so doing I shall depart

[1] This situation was partly set right by Silber: "Kant's Conception of the Highest Good as Immanent and Transcendent," *Phil. Rev.*, LXVIII (1959), 469-492, and "The Importance of the Highest Good in Kant's Ethics," *Ethics*, LXXIII (1962-63), 179-197; by M.-B. Zeldin, "The *Summum Bonum*, the Moral Law and the Existence of God," *Kant-Studien*, LXII (1971), 43-54; and by Klaus Düsing, "Das Problem des höchsten Gutes in Kants praktischer Philosophie," *Kant-Studien*, LXII (1971), 5-42. They did not, however, do full justice to the concept of the highest good and especially did not attempt to analyze all its levels of meaning, starting from its relevance to personal ethics and proceeding to its broader aspects in the framework of history.

from the view that restricts the highest good to the sphere of internal morality alone, and from another current interpretation, which regards Kant's doctrine of history as extraneous to his critical philosophy.[2] The latter finds support in Kant's ambivalence about the origin of historical progress and in such texts as *Idea for a Universal History from a Cosmopolitan Point of View, Perpetual Peace,* and the *Critique of Judgement,* where history is dealt with in dogmatic terms, as a hidden, independent purposiveness of nature. My aim, however, is to expose a competing trend in Kant's thought, which regards history as a rational and conscious moral endeavor, and reinstates it in the framework of the critical philosophy. A reevaluation of the highest good in light of the idea of history is also a reinterpretation of the idea of history as an integral part of the critical philosophy.

The current approach to the highest good tends to reduce its empirical aspect to the concept of happiness or "reward" alone, and gives the idea a decidedly ahistorical connotation, as if it were a rationalized or critical version of the notion of the other world. This interpretation finds support in Kant's early thought, especially in the Methodology of the first *Critique,* but also in the Dialectic of the second *Critique.* However, later Kantian texts,[3] and even certain passages in the second *Critique* itself, reveal important departures from this approach. (a) The highest good is no longer a separate, transcendent world, but becomes the consummate state of *this* world, to be realized through a concrete development in time. (b) The pro-

---

[2] Here I share the general thesis of E. Fackenheim in "Kant's Concept of History," *Kant-Studien,* XLVIII (1956-57), 381-398, although we differ in the way it is worked out. I must disagree completely, however, with T. Ruyssen, who dismissed the possibility of explaining Kant's views on history within the framework of the critical system. (See his article in the anthology *La Philosophie politique de Kant,* Paris, 1962, 34.) A much more promising approach is offered by L. Goldmann, *Introduction à la philosophie de Kant* (Paris, 1967).

[3] Most parts of *C3*; also *Rel.,* and such political writings as *PP* and *TP.*

gressive power of history is ascribed not only to a hidden "cunning of *nature*," but also to the conscious work of practical *reason*. And (c) the concept of happiness loses its central position and is replaced by nature in general as the empirical component of the highest good. The highest good remains a "synthesis" of moral and empirical elements, but not of virtue and happiness alone, but of "freedom" and "nature" at large; and to realize it now means to imprint the demands of the moral idea upon the whole range or totality of our empirical environment, transforming the patterns of our psychological dispositions, our social and political institutions, as well as the surrounding physical and ecological systems—insofar as they relate to the sphere of human needs and moral interests. These changes are due partly to logical requirements implied in Kant's point of departure, and partly to his shifts of interest. Combined, they allow us to see the highest good, in Kantian terms, as the regulative idea of history, actually as the end concept that defines it. History is the process in which the highest good should be realized, and in which the free, formative activity of practical reason remolds the given world into a new, moral world. The historical end also serves as a focus which unites or "totalizes" the intentions and actions of all individual moral agents and all areas of collective creativity such as law, politics and education. History is thus the process where the required "synthesis" of freedom and nature should occur. Moreover, Kant ascribes to reason a metaphysical interest striving for the absolute and the total. Having been denied fulfillment in the field of knowledge, it now finds positive satisfaction in the field of moral-historical action. The result of the whole critical system is to transport the metaphysical interest, in its search for ultimates and totalities, from the deviant cognitive path to its genuine expression in moral history. Thus the ideas of the highest good and history, far from being marginal, become the systematic apex of Kant's whole critical endeavor.

True, the historical meaning of the highest good is not the only one, but it is the most comprehensive and includes if not "sublates" all the others. It also sheds new light on Kant's conception of God, and foreshadows ideas in Hegel, and especially in Marx. However, to prevent an inverted one-sidedness, I plan to discuss *all* the levels of the concept's pertinence in Kant. First I shall outline the basic structure of the highest good, a structure that remains fairly constant in all the variations in the meaning of that concept. Then I shall examine the different meanings the concept assumes, concluding with its historical level.

To begin with, we must show that the concept of the highest good, in all its meanings, defines the boundaries of a second stage of Kant's philosophy of practice, lying beyond the formal ethics of the categorical imperative.

The Two Stages in Kant's Practical System

Kant's practical philosophy is based upon the theory of the categorical imperative but not exhausted by it. Of crucial importance is the dialectic of practical reason, or the doctrine of the postulates and the highest good, that complements the formal ethics with a material element and presents human practice with its ultimate objective. Kant's practical system should be thus divided into two parts or stages, the formal and the material, or in Kant's terms, the absolute and the comprehensive.[4]

The first stage is discussed in the *Foundations of the Metaphysics of Morals*, as well as the Analytic of the second *Critique*. It examines the structure of the good will and establishes its absolute principle, including the negative and positive freedom of the will, its special power of motivation, the universal form which governs its legislation, and the subjective initiative of the moral agent in making

[4] Or the unconditioned and the whole (total). Cf. *C2*, V:108, 110/ 112, 114.

this law and in acting from it. The second stage, on the other hand, fulfills the need "to conceive of some sort of final end for all our actions and abstentions, taken as a whole" (*Rel.* VI:5/5). It does not merely determine the absolute principle of the moral will but goes on to define its *total object*. Its axis is the formulation of a new imperative with a definite content—"act to promote the highest good in the world"[5]—to Kant a more complete and comprehensive imperative than the basic categorical one. The latter tells us how to act, while the former tells us in addition *what* should be realized, as the final outcome of moral action. It is concerned not with the specific "what" of particular actions, which obviously depends on contingent circumstances, but only with that fixed, total object to which all moral actions should ultimately aspire. Thus it responds to the double "need of reason" (a crucial if ambivalent Kantian concept): first, to the *logical* requirement of reason that the sphere of action be "totalized," i.e., systematized synoptically; and secondly, to a *subjective* or psychological condition of the human mind, to "our *natural* needs" as humans, since "in the absence of all reference to an end, no determination of the will can take place in man" (*Rel.*, VI:4/4).

Priority and Inclusion

While maintaining the necessity of the second stage, Kant asserts the priority of the categorical imperative over that which refers to the highest good. Such a hierarchy is for Kant fundamental. "So much depends, when we wish to unite two good things, upon the order in which they are united!" (*Rel.*, VI:179/167); and here, as elsewhere, the right order is the priority of the formal principle over any content. The material imperative includes the formal (categorical) imperative as an absolute condition and adds to

---

[5] Sometimes he says: "act to realize the highest good," but this is not an exact formulation. Man can act to realize the ideal only by means of a partial contribution, so that he can only promote it.

it a necessary complement. Without the second stage the moral system would remain pure, absolute, and incomplete.

Kant provides several interpretations to the priority of the formal imperative. The most common[6] is the representation of the final end not as a determining ground of the will, but only as an accompaniment. It is a regulative idea that lacks constitutive (motivational) power over the will but places the isolated acts in a broader perspective and allows the agent to see them as contributing to the moral progress of the universe. In one place, however, Kant does allow the final end to directly determine the will ($C2$, V:110/114). He argues that this does not necessarily break morality or involve heteronomy, since the specific end is not particular and circumstantial but comprehensive and "objective," and that this goal contains the principle of morality and is recognized *a priori* by it. But Kant always adheres to one basic interpretation of priority: the categorical imperative conditions the *way* in which the ultimate goal should be realized, for the notion of an end sanctifying the means is self-contradictory.[7]

Relevant Texts

A division of Kant's practical system into these two stages, and their linkage of priority and inclusion, find support in almost all of Kant's practical works. The second *Critique* expresses this in the relation of the Dialectic to the Analytic in general, and specifically in a different type of imperative that stands at the center of each; by the distinction between the good and the highest good; In *Religion within the Limits of Reason Alone*, the greater part

---

[6] E.g., *Rel.*, VI:4-5/4-5; *C3*, Par. 87; *C2*, V:109/113.

[7] This is important for our discussion because Kant recognizes nonmoral processes that promote the highest good. But, given the priority of the Categorical imperative, no action that, in itself, may further the highest good (say, a certain political action, or revolution) can be sanctioned *a priori* if its execution involves transgression of the formal imperative.

of the preface to the second edition explains the transition
to the highest good in a slightly different way; and in *The
Doctrine of Virtue*, the same structure is retained (*MM*,
VI:379-386/36-44). Kant analyzes here the transition from
the formal duty to the "end which is in itself a duty," and
defines the distinction and the relation of priority between
the two parts of ethics, the one concerned with duty and
the other with end duty. The concept of an end duty is
confined here to the doctrine of virtue but in other works
it also appears in the context of the theory of law and politics, as in "Against Hobbes" in *Theory and Practice*. The
last part of the third *Critique* is devoted to the idea of
a moral teleology of the universe, to be promoted by human action. Kant here concentrates on the second stage
of his practical system. Distinguishing repeatedly between
the two stages,[8] he argues that failure to believe in the moral perfectibility of the universe or in the existence of a
"moral author of the world" is detrimental only to the
second part of ethics, namely, to the intention of promoting
the highest good—but it must not affect the fundamental
formal law. The more common interpretation, which restricts Kant's ethics to its first stage alone, is the outgrowth
of reading Kant's ethical theory through the narrow outlook of the *Foundations*. But this book only lays the foundations for Kant's practical philosophy and, true to its
name, does not claim to cover its whole range. And even
here we find a "kingdom of ends" and the notion of a
correspondence between morality and nature (happiness)
as a supreme moral objective (*Found.*, IV:391-392, 438-
439/54, 95-96).

The *complete* practical system of Kant thus tries to determine not only the absolute form of moral action but
also its supreme content, in two stages related by priority
and inclusion. These two stages are expressed by the two
central imperatives of the system, one demanding action

[8] *C3*, V:447-448, 451-453/II:114-116, 119-121.

only from maxims that can be universalized, the other the promotion of the highest good. They are not two separate entities, for the first is included in the second as an absolute condition. Neither is the second imperative just an example of the use of the categorical imperative, like the duty to repay a loan. In every instance the form is necessary and determined, the content being contingent and variable, while in the second imperative the content is necessary and determined as well, "totalizing" the particular contents in one final end. The material imperative is more comprehensive, since it includes the first as the form of the will, while adding to it a new element—the total object of the will.

Kant expressed the relation between the two stages and the two imperatives thus:

> The moral [categorical] law is the formal rational condition of the employment of our freedom and, as such, of itself alone lays its obligation upon us, independently of any end as its material condition. But it also defines for us a final end, and does so *a priori*, and makes it obligatory upon us to strive towards its attainment. This end is [the *summum bonum*, as] the highest good *in the world* (*C3*, V:450/II:118).[9]

The Systematic Functions of the Concept of the Highest Good

Our central problem, however, is a systematic one: the relocation of this vision of moral nature in the framework of the critical system. The systematic functions of this concept, or the problems it has to solve within the critique of practice, may be outlined under three headings: (a) synthesis, (b) totalization, (c) provision of an objective final end.

[9] This is also a brief account of the preface to the first edition of the *Religion* and the essence of the transition from the Analytic to the Dialectic in the second *Critique*.

All are interconnected and are resolved in a single object: the total synthesis of the practical sphere is at once the final end of all action. Yet the initial problems as distinct; moreover, Kant emphasizes different aspects at different times.[10] These aspects deserve separate analysis.

Synthesis, or the Reunification of the Moral and the Natural

Synthesis, in its broadest sense, is one of the pivotal problems in Kant's thought, perhaps the most difficult of all. The radical *separation* of the spontaneous (*a priori*) and receptive (empirically given) principles of thought and action seemed to Kant to be a necessary condition for his critical approach. How, then, could he reunite them to provide for concrete cognition and practical behavior? Essentially, this is one problem, but its expression varies according to the systematic context. In the practical field it is generally revealed by the opposition between freedom and nature, first on the level of intention or project, and later on the level of action.

On the level of intention, the pure will is confronted by its own given or receptive elements, natural drives and inclinations, whose general principle is the aspiration for happiness. Both exist in man necessarily: the pure will is a "fact" of his moral consciousness; the quest for happiness a datum of his natural existence and, being a dual creature, he cannot dissociate himself from either one. Man's willing is split into two heterogeneous principles and into two corresponding heterogeneous *objectives* or "goods"— the moral good and the natural good (called *das Gute* and

---

[10] In *C2* the need to unify man's moral with his natural aspirations is emphasized. In *C3* the emphasis is rather on the unification of the noumenal legislation and "the external possibility of its realization," as well as on the need to move toward a total moral cosmos. The preface to *Rel.* emphasizes the need for continuity of intentions and consequences and man's natural need to consider the final consequences of his acts. However, all the aspects appear in every one of these works.

das Wohl),[11] and this raises the problem of their reunification in one comprehensive good.

On the level of action the will is faced with the external world, in relationship to which it must act. The question of synthesis here assumes a different form. If the source of moral intent is assigned to the internal freedom of the will, how can such projects affect the independent realm of nature and become exhibited or embodied (*dargestellt*) in empirical systems and occurrences? This issue has a broader aspect, which deserves special attention. The moral will, as practical reason, is dissatisfied with only a segment of reality; it wants to affect it in its entirety.[12] Reflecting "on the course of the world from a moral standpoint" (*C3*, V:449n./II, 117n.), it wishes to reidentify itself in it and to see its intent embodied and its laws prevail in the very *organization* of the empirical world.[13] This phase of the problem is intimately tied up with the question of totalization. Here the will faces not an accidental set of natural causes, but "the totality of objects in experience"—i.e., in Kantian terms, the whole system of nature—which it wishes to reorganize to fit moral laws.

[11] As against *das Übel* and *das Böse* (*das Weh*).

[12] Ideally such an intent is already present in the basic categorical imperative, since according to its second formulation (in *Found.*, IV:421/80; *C2*, V:45/46) the right action is one that can constitute a universal order of nature without contradiction. This point becomes more pronounced when Kant explains that the categorical imperative is applied to concrete action by *representing* a complete moral world which that action as it were establishes (see *C2*, V:69-70/72-73 and *Reflexion* no. 5612, [XVIII]); see also R. Daval's interpretation in *La Métaphysique de Kant* (Paris, 1951). With the appearance of the material imperative, however, it is no longer the *representation* but rather the reality of such a world that counts; it is not enough to act as if our action has established a moral world but to concretely work towards its realization (see also first preface to *Rel.*).

[13] "Albeit, then, between the realm of the natural concept, as the sensible, and the realm of the concept of freedom, as the super-sensible, there is a great gulf fixed . . . still the latter *should* influence the former, that is to say, *the concept of freedom should actualize in the sensible world the end proposed by its laws.*" (*C3*, V:175/I:14; italics added.)

In a word, the moral will faces a problem of synthesis with empirical nature, both in its "internal" and "external" sense. One of the reasons for the shift in the meaning of the highest good is that Kant attached growing importance to the problem in its second sense, even as a way of solving the first.

Totalization, or Material Continuity of Intentions and Consequences

Synthesis means uniting *heterogeneous* elements, but Kant must also face the problem of the sequential integration of separate items of the *same* kind. In the sphere of practical reason this problem results from the fact that the formal principle of morality relates to single acts and fails to provide a theoretical framework to deal with the continuity of actions—both subjectively (from the viewpoint of their implied intentions or dispositions) and objectively (from the viewpoint of their real consequences).

Subjectively, volition has a discontinuous structure, since freedom is to Kant an absolutely spontaneous power, self-generating in each act and independent of anything that occurred in the past or will occur in the future.[14] The moral subject performs a multiplicity of single acts that do not necessarily form a continuous process. And objectively, too, every act initiates its own chain of natural causes, without a guarantee that the consequences of one act can combine with those of another into a coherent and meaningful process. Since the formal stage of morality is based only on the absolute condition of the will, it must thus ignore both the continuity of intentions and the progressive control of effects. Yet Kant believes such a diffuse situation incompatible both with the structure of human reason and with the "*natural* characteristics" of Man. To the activity of human reason it is essential to aim at growing systematization and the creation of totalities; therefore, even when the absolute condition of the will is fulfilled, reason

---

[14] Cf. *C2*, V:98/101-102; *Rel.*, VI:40-41/35-36.

still demands the integration of all discrete acts in one ultimate object (*C2*, V:108/112). And man's natural condition, too, prevents an *a priori* futile action, making it necessary for all human activity to consider its outcome—if not as a direct motive, at least as an accompanying representation (*Rel.*, VI:6n.-7n./6n.-7n.). In addition to the categorical imperative the practical system requires a regulative idea, in the form of a final end, to totalize the multiple intentions of all moral agents and the chains of objective consequences in one coherent process, leading to a final synthesis.[15]

The Need for an End

Kant sometimes treats the need for an end independently of other problems, explaining that "in the absence of all reference to an end, no determination of the will can take place in man." This crucial sentence, beside repeating the structural truism that every choice is a choice of something, also makes a non-trivial comment on the anthropology of moral decisions and the limitation of human nature.

The pure principle of morality demands that man act without regard to consequences. He ought to do his duty regardless of circumstances, even if he has good reason to believe that the consequences of his act will be lost in a hostile or indifferent nature. As far as the formal law is concerned, a man can act in a vacuum, without contributing to any real change in the world. However, Kant regards such a situation as incompatible with human nature. Man is not pure reason but a dual creature, involved and interested in his environment. Therefore, even when he acts from duty, disregarding his self-interest and thus becom-

---

[15] For the first task, the totalization of the intentions, the idea of the highest good in itself is sufficient; for the second, the totalization of the consequences, there is a need for a guarantee through the postulate of God's existence.

ing *subjectively* moral, he still wants objective results that contribute to the implementation of a moral project in the world. Man is naturally incapable of intending to perform futile—in the terms of an opposite doctrine we might say: Sisyphean—deeds but constantly demands to know "what is to result from this right conduct of ours" (*Rel.*, VI:5/4). The idea of the highest good answers this demand by defining "a special point of focus for the unification of all ends" (*Rel.*, VI:5/5), and by presenting the desirable objective outcome of all moral and historical efforts of mankind.

This is a different reason for the appearance of the idea of the highest good. It too is bound to man's natural consitution: not to his desire for happiness but to a different and more complex type of need, independent of the first. This point should be made at the outset, for it bears on the meaning of the highest good and the concept of hope connected to it (i.e., the hope for happiness-for-the-worthy assimilated to the hope for a successful realization of morality in the world), as well as on the basis for postulating the existence of God.

But do we not have a problem here? How can Kant reconcile this new principle—that the will cannot be determined without an end-concept—with the more fundamental ethical principle, that a will determined by an end is "heteronomous" (*C2*, V:21-39/19-41)? Kant struggles with this difficulty in various ways. He emphasizes the uniqueness of the highest good as an end projected by morality itself and *a priori* recognized by it. Kant also shows that unlike any particular goal that is altered according to circumstances, this is the only total and comprehensive end that remains constant in all actions as their ultimate objective. Yet Kant seems to feel that as long as the end is permitted to determine the will directly, the danger of heteronomy remains. He therefore takes another route as well, stating that "this idea arises *out of* morality and is not its basis" (*Rel.*, VI:5/5, italics added), i.e., the end concept necessarily accompanies the moral act without determining it. The act is determined by the formal moment of the imperative, while the representation of the final end only places my particular act in a broader context, together with other particular acts (mine, and other agents') that are supposed to contribute to the same ultimate result. The danger of heteronomy is avoided in that the vision of the final end is not a direct motivation but an accompanying idea.[16]

In summary, the concept of the highest good is designed to fulfil a variety of systematic functions, most of them interconnected and some more independent than others. It should cover all types of syntheses in the practical field, particularly between virtue and happiness, between intention and consequences, and in the last analysis, between the moral idea and the totality of human experience. It attempts to provide all actions with a final, objective end-concept, but only as an accompanying idea and not as a basis for motivations, and it focuses the multiplicity of subjective intentions and objective consequences of each individual and of humanity. This complex of issues accounts for the fact that Kant's discussions of the highest good take different directions, at times relating to a partial aspect of the concept, at times attempting a fuller account, yet without explicating all its implications and achieving a clear synopsis. To carry Kant's thought further, we must examine the transition to the highest good before discussing its various meanings. From a systematic point of view, how did Kant pass to the "second stage" of his practical philosophy? What made this passage necessary? And, was it continuous or did it involve a systematic "leap?"

---

[16] Nevertheless, Kant himself is not too careful about these distinctions. The moment he establishes the highest good as an object of duty, he allows it to determine the will directly. When all is said and done, the problem that morality includes at least one *a priori* content remains in Kant's system.

The Problem of Transition and the Duality
in the Moral Will

The problem of the transition from the formal law to the end-concept of the highest good raises a special difficulty. Kant insists that it is the moral law that establishes the final end, doing so *a priori*.[17] Yet the idea of the highest good is clearly not derived from the concept of the pure will as such. It emerges rather from a philosophical reconsideration of various *empirical* factors, such as man's natural aspiration for happiness; his equally natural interest in the effect of his acts; and more generally, the empirical conditions of the world upon which the will must act. In establishing the *fundamental* principle of morality these elements were ignored, but in order to provide a comprehensive theory of practice (and hope), they must be reintegrated into the system and, under definite conditions, even be recognized as relevant to morality itself. However, if one maintains Kant's claim that it is the moral law that grants such recognition, then the moral law cannot be identified with the mere categorical imperative. It *already* must be this higher type of law, embodied in the imperative to realize the highest good, that transcends the boundaries of the former and cannot be reduced to it.

Hence the transition between the two stages of the practical system is not continuous. There is no contradiction here, as some have claimed,[18] because happiness, included in the highest good as "reward," does not become the motive (*Triebfeder*) of action. There is also no necessary "hypocrisy" here, as Hegel charged,[19] for intervention in the external world does not *ipso facto* impair the purity

---

[17] Cf. *Rel.*, VI:4-5/4-5. Elsewhere Kant presents the highest good as the necessary object of the moral will (*C2*, V:122/126), being an "object . . . of the pure will" (*ibid.*, 109/112), which "we are determined *a priori* by reason to further" (*C3*, V:453/II:122).

[18] For example, T. M. Greene and A. Seth Pringle-Pattison.

[19] Phenomenology of Mind, VI, C b, tr. by J. B. Baillie (New York, 1967), 628-641.

of the will.[20] But clearly there is a lack of direct or intrinsic transition from the concept of the pure will to that of the highest good. The former is defined through strict exclusion of any empirical consideration, ignoring happiness as well as consequences, while the latter restores these considerations and puts them in a broader moral context, even making them the elements of a new *imperative*.

The absence of an inherent continuity between the two stages also indicates the duality in Kant's concept of "moral will." To him a moral imperative is a projection or explication of the structure of the moral will; and since both stages involve an imperative, each implies a different type of moral will. The will that has the highest good as its object (or more specifically, that gives the highest good its value by willing it) remains no longer the pure, empty moral will of the *Foundations* and of the Analytic of the second *Critique*, but becomes enriched, though only externally, by more concrete constituents. It formerly willed only its own purity, ignoring the natural aspirations of man and the shape of the reality he faced; now it gives human aspirations for happiness moral legitimization under well-defined conditions and is concerned with reshaping the totality of experience to fit its projects and moral lawfulness.[21]

The Good *versus* the Highest Good

The duality in Kant's concept of moral will can explain an apparent inconsistency in the text of the second *Critique*.[22] Here the problem of identifying the "object" of

[20] The compromise frequently required in such an intervention may affect the purity of the will, but not the fact of particularization *per se*.

[21] In one place Kant admits that "practical reason does, indeed, extend itself therein beyond the [categorical] law"; yet he argues that this extension is due to "the strictest obedience to moral laws" and is therefore "*a priori*" (*Rel.*, VI:7n./7n.).

[22] I am referring to a dualism within the moral will itself, not to the distinction between *Wille* and *Willkür*.

the moral will is twice discussed with different results. If in the Analytic Kant identifies the object with the mere *form* (or manner) determining the will,[23] naming it the good (*C*2, V:57-65/59-67), in the Dialectic he identifies the object with a specific content, naming it the highest good. The good of the Analytic is not a "usual" object; it fails to indicate what precisely the will is willing, and in particular does not provide the will with something beyond itself at which it should aim. This good only reformulates the structural conditions on which the autonomy of the will depends and in fact makes this autonomy its object. If we insist upon knowing what the will is willing here, the only answer is: itself. In willing *the good*, the will is relating to *itself* as object, wishing to realize its own autonomy and subjective worth; while any particular object or content only serves as means to that end, lacking moral value *per se*. In the Dialectic the object is presented as a synthesis of moral and empirical constituents, furnishing the will with a specific content. In willing this object the will is concerned with something other than itself, namely with an objective reorganization of the world. Moreover, the new organization of the world now acquires *moral* value as such —not, to be sure, as something prior to the will, which externally determines it, but as posited or projected by the will itself. This twin interpretation of its object is not accidental in Kant, for it depends on the duality of the concept of the moral will itself. If we remember one of Kant's pivotal principles, that the good is not prior to the will but derived from it as its object,[24] it will be clear that two definitions of the moral will must produce two parallel definitions of object (or good), and vice versa.

[23] Here to be an object means "only the relation of the will to the action whereby it or its opposite is brought into being" (*C*2, V:57/59). Accordingly this object "could not be a thing but only the manner of acting" (*ibid.*, 60/62).

[24] Cf. *C*2, V:62-63/63-65 and J. Silber, "The Copernican Revolution in Ethics," *Kant-Studien*, LI (1959/60), 85-101.

The Source of Moral Contents

The two types of moral will invite further comparison. In either case Kant says that a moral action requires some end or content to be added to the pure form of the will. So does an action resulting from the formal imperative, for one cannot perform a duty "as such" without doing something specific. Morever, in each case Kant states that the content is appended to the will without conditioning it.[25] But if we ask for the *source* of this content the difference will appear. In the first case the content is contingent on the will, depending on external circumstances: either on a natural drive, whose acceptance or rejection passes the test of universalizability, or on a concatenation of events, which obliges a man to take a stand. This content is neither posited by the will itself nor really willed by the pure will. The latter wills only itself, i.e., the fulfillment of duty for its own sake; and the content serves only as a necessary means to that end. The second case marks a radical difference. Here, the content is yielded by the will itself (it is the product of an *"a priori* synthesis"); and far from being accidental to the moral will, it constitutes its genuine object.

Reaction *versus* Initiative

There is another aspect to this difference. When the moral agent is guided only by formal law, he must remain in a passive position. Although his actions originate in freedom, their content is dictated by circumstances. Such a man does not initiate, he only reacts; lacking the binding conception of a better world, he must confine himself to the existing system, attempting to preserve the purity of his will by responding correctly to given situations. Politically, too, this must lead to a passive and conservative position. By

25 On the question of the formal imperative see *C*2, V:33-34/33-34; on the question of the material imperative see *ibid.*, 109-110/113-114 and the first preface to the *Rel.*

contrast, the material imperative becomes a source of positive initiatives, enriching the concept of freedom. It no longer suffices to respond to circumstances; one has to change them in light of an *a priori* moral scheme, thereby creating new orders and systems, such as moral education, free political institutions and a "rational" church. The one moral will initiates; the other merely responds.

The source of discontinuity between the two stages is not the introduction of the concept of the highest good itself but the *imperative* to realize it. Analytically there are two steps in Kant's passage to the second stage. One is the formation of the concept, the other its moral legitimation (to be referred to below as the "descriptive" and the "normative" levels respectively). In the first stage the empirical factors, excluded when establishing the basic ethical principles (e.g., happiness, consequences, "nature" in general) are reintegrated into a broader concept of action and disposition, which takes into account the practical nature of man. The idea of the highest good, with all its meanings and implications, summarizes this concept. While transcending the limits of the formal imperative, this level remains compatible with it and, more importantly, does not yet suggest a new concept of moral will. In the second stage, however, the whole synthesis of the highest good becomes the object of a new *imperative* or moral duty. The empirical elements mentioned above are now included in a *morally desirable* goal and thus are recognized as relevant to morality itself.[26] To be sure, this recognition is given

---

[26] This is particularly pronounced when Kant states (while discussing the human interest in ends and consequences) that "it cannot be a matter of unconcern to morality as to whether or not it forms for itself the concept of a final end" (*Rel.*, VI:5/5); or when he argues, with regard to man's aspirations to happiness, that "certainly our weal and woe are very important in the estimation of our practical reason" (*C2*, V:61/63); or when he states (in all three *Critiques*) that the demand for reward is justified by the judgement of impartial reason (cf. *C1*, A813/B841; *C3*, V:458/II: 129; *C2*, V:110/114-115). That vague *instantia*, in whose eyes reward and consequences carry moral weight, can be identified with the moral will in its second meaning.

under strict conditions, laid down by the basic moral law, included in the concept of the highest good as its "synthesizing" rules. But the point is that now—and only now—a new concept of moral will is constituted by implication. For this new will there is already a moral necessity, an ought, that happiness be attained by the ethically worthy and that morality be embodied in the systems of the world at large. Yet the transition to this new and enriched moral will fails to represent any moral necessity, taking "moral" in the sense of the original formal imperative.

We should now examine the changes and the consecutive strata in Kant's theory of the total object of the will, and how the latter turns into the Idea of History.

The Variety of Definitions of the Highest Good

The ambiguous character of Kant's discussions of the highest good has already been examined. No single text is an adequate summary, and some texts provide varying definitions of the concept[27] or reduce it to a single aspect[28]; and Kant's terminology also changes frequently.[29] Clearly he was not expressing a finished theory but searching for it. There are four major groups of definitions. First: "Vir-

[27] For example, in C_3 once the highest good is identified with "the existence of rational beings under moral laws" (C_3, V:444/II: 111) and another time with "the union of universal happiness with morality" (C_3, V:453/II: 122). In C_2 Kant talks about the highest good of "one person" and about the highest good of "a possible world" (V:110/115) and so on. There is a connection and an order of development among the various meanings of the highest good.

[28] For example, "Mankind . . . in its complete moral perfection" (Rel., VI:60/54); "the highest good as a social good" (ibid., 97/89); or "one's own perfection and the happiness of others" (MM, VI:385/44). While the term "highest good" is not mentioned in the last instance, highest good is clearly a variant of the same concept.

[29] The non-empirical constituent of the highest good is called "freedom," "morality," "virtue," "moral laws," "the good." The empirical constituent is called "nature," "happiness," "well-being," "physical good," "world," "the totality of objects of experience." And the connection between the two parts is expressed, inter alia, as "synthesis," "harmony," "coordination," "totality."

48

tue and happiness together constitute the possession of the highest good for one person" (C2, V:110/115).[30] Here the highest good has a personal meaning. It is the highest good of *somebody*. The moral constituent is described as virtue (*Tugend*), which is a characteristic of an individual, and the happiness is his private happiness.

Second: "[This *summum bonum* is formed by] the union of the greatest welfare of the rational beings in the world with the supreme condition of their good, or, in other words, [by] the union of universal happiness with the strictest morality" (C3, V:453/II:122). Here the highest good appears as a *universal* system of morality and reward, which embraces all of humanity. It is an idea that unifies the ends of all possible *wills*. However, in the *Religion* it is expanded and becomes a "special focus for the unification of all ends"; and if we include here not only the subjective ends of the will but also those of the world that responds to it, we shall reach a third and broader view of the highest good, as "the union of the purposiveness arising from freedom with the purposiveness of nature" (*Rel.*, VI:5/5).

In Leibnizian terms this same idea was expressed in the second *Critique* as "the exact harmony of the realm of nature with the realm of morals" (C2, V:145/151). The world in which this harmony prevails is the "highest derived good (the best world)," or also *natura ectypa* (C2, V:43/44). The notion of a copy or derived replica relates to the speculative idea of a *natura archetypa*, a pure supersensible world (the "intelligible substratum of creation" known also from the third *Critique*). This is a transcendent ideal that lacks reality but serves as a background and a pattern to be followed when reshaping *this* world. The derived or copied character of the highest good means that

---

[30] There are echoes of the Greek and Augustinian traditions in this definition. The highest good of a person is a combination (in Proclus a fusion, what Kant would call heteronomy) of the good of the soul and the good of the body. Cf. St. Augustine, *Confessions*, Book 19, Ch. 4.

it is the embodiment of the transcendent model within the sensible world, with all its empirical systems.

Despite the Leibnizian undertones, crucial differences exist. Kant's "best world," unlike Leibniz's, is not *actual* but yet to be realized; and "the harmony between nature and morality" is a product of *human* action and not that of God; the *natura ectypa* is "a nature in which reason would *bring forth* the highest good were it accompanied by sufficient physical capabilities" (C_2, V:43/45). This capability is guaranteed by the postulate of God's existence; and man exploits it by giving "to the sensible world as sensuous nature . . . the form of supersensuous nature without interfering with the mechanism of the former" (C_2, V:43/44).

There are terminological and conceptual differences between the definitions, but they all occur within the framework of one general problem. The highest good has one invariable definition (the total object of practical reason) and the systematic functions analyzed above; it is always connected to the imperative to realize it and to the postulate of God, which guarantees its possibility, thus delineating the second stage of the practical system. Therefore we may regard all the variations analytically as stages in Kant's search for "that whole which is no part of a yet larger whole of the same kind" (C_2, V:110/114) or the ultimate object of the will.

These stages, moreover, are suggested by the groups of definitions we have detected: (a) the highest good as the unification of the objects of the individual will (virtue and private happiness), (b) the highest good as a universal system of morality and empirical welfare, (c) the highest good as an *overall* harmony of experience and morality, or as moral nature. And since this harmony should be created by human action (by man's reshaping of the sensuous world in light of a supersensuous idea, and by his creating new social and ecological systems) the moral nature suggests (d) the idea of history.

The Personal Highest Good

"Virtue and happiness together constitute the possession of the highest good for one person" (C2, V:110/115). Here the highest good designates the integral final-end of the individual. Man's "dual nature" accounts for his quest for moral perfection as well as for the satisfaction of his desires. The personal highest good is the "synthesis of concepts" (C2, V:113/117), each of which generalizes a different type of goal. One is "happiness" (Glückseligkeit), a vague empirical concept signifying the complete and constant satisfaction of all natural inclinations. Its empirical nature denies this concept an a priori determination, for its content varies according to the person and the situation. The second is virtue (Tugend), a well-defined a priori concept signifying the permanent disposition to act from respect for the moral law during one's whole lifetime. Both these concepts have a unifying function in their respective domains. The concept of happiness generalizes all hedonistic desires, while the concept of virtue (the comprehensive moral disposition) integrates isolated, independent acts of duty into a continuity of character and a way of life. The concept of the highest good, as the combination of both, constitutes the inclusive goal of the whole person.

Virtue

Kant's interpreters tend to stress only the innovation, some say the contradiction, in the recurrence of the concept of happiness in the moral objective. However, the concept of virtue, too, represents a new element in comparison with the formal stage of morality. This new element is totalization. In a way, the concept of virtue serves as a model for the concept of the highest good in its full (historical) sense. In both cases man is offered a final-end that unifies the totality of his moral effort, and in both there is a graduated process, in which natural factors (whether "internal" or "external") are being reorganized

51

in light of the moral idea. The individual's progress towards virtue on the microcosmic level is analogous to the macrocosmic (macrohistorical) progress of the world towards the highest good.

What, then, is virtue? The formal principle of morality relates only to isolated acts which are mutually independent. Each of them has a determining ground (*Bestimm-ungsgrund*) and a moral value of its own; one cannot be the cause of the other, nor impair its purity (if it is good), or "atone" for it (if it is evil). The result is a diffuse picture of the will, which ignores such problems of continuity as the moral value of a *character*, a *personality*, and a *way of life*. But the moral subject, like the subject of knowledge, does not consist of a series of isolated acts; he exists as a reidentification of himself in the multiplicity that constitutes his conscious life, and as constantly ascribing it to himself, either as its knowing subject or as its morally responsible agent. This means that some moral quality must be ascribable to him as an entire person, a global meaning underlining all his acts.

Kant describes virtue as a fundamental disposition or resolution, the maxim of maxims,[31] which forms the background of all particular moral acts and unifies or totalizes them in one meaningful context. Kant introduces here the complex notion of a "free character"[32] (not dissimilar to Sartre's notion of *projêt fondamental*). On the one hand, the particular acts are not causal outcomes of the fundamental resolution but always involve new, spontaneous initiatives. On the other, these are no longer totally arbitrary and contingent, for they are taken in the light of a global choice, which they implement and at the same time renew or reconfirm. The tie between the fundamental maxim and its particular expressions is one not of deter-

[31] Also, "the ultimate subjective ground of the adoption of maxims" (*Rel.*, VI:25/20).

[32] Or alternatively, the notion of free habit (*habitus libertatis*), as opposed to a semi-deterministic view of habit and character. See *MM*, VI:407/68-69.

mination but of logical implication, requiring the free subject to draw this implication and implement it. For each situation the global maxim intimates the right choice, but man must still make it; thus renewing his global resolution each time he realizes it in a particular situation. This scheme, however, also allows for deviations from the basic choice, and even for its complete reversal or "conversion."

Hence the attainment of virtue depends first on the adoption of the fundamental maxim of morality (the disposition to disregard natural inclinations in all morally relevant cases), and secondly on its implementation in every case. However, Kant believes that man's limited nature allows only imperfect implementation. Moral progress for the individual consists of strengthening his free character to such an extent that his deviations tend to zero. The theory of virtue thus proposes both a totalizing principle of personality and an infinitely distant moral objective.[33]

Happiness

To avoid much of the confusion created by this topic it should be emphasized at the outset that on the personal level of the highest good the concept of happiness is purely descriptive. It is part of the explication of the structure of human willing and does not yet involve duty.

When Kant speaks of the imperative to realize the highest good, he is already transcending the personal level of this concept and posits, by definition, its impersonal or universal level. As duty, the highest good refers to human-

---

[33] This discussion is based mainly on Kant's later ideas, in the *Religion*, which presents a new and more coherent moral theory and realizes explicitly the problem of moral continuity. *One* of the changes relating specifically to virtue is that in *C2* the virtuous disposition is supposed to be achieved only at the ideal end of the process (thus requiring the postulate of immortality). In the *Rel.*, on the other hand, the global virtuous disposition is created by a "revolution" at the *beginning* of the moral process, whose goal is to close the gap between this general disposition and its phenomenal manifestations.

ity in general; it binds the individual not as considered in his isolation but as a member of the human community, sharing a common human goal, to which he can only contribute; thus the highest good can no longer mean the individual's private virtue and happiness. The duty to realize it necessarily means that each individual work in cooperation with others to create a new world-system that combines universal morality and welfare, i.e., in which the morally worthy will attain happiness through the laws of the system itself. However, this duty cannot require each individual to worry about his own happiness or reward, not only because of a concern about mixed motives but primarily because the desire for happiness exists anyway, making an ought meaningless.[34] The duty to realize the highest good pertains only to the concept's universal level, and, indeed, constitutes this level. On the personal level only a descriptive analysis of human willing is given, tied to a systematic attempt to combine its heterogeneous goals in a single objective without creating a moral contradiction or heteronomy.

The Readmission of Happiness

How then, does happiness appear in the highest good? The morality of duty, even in its perfected form as the morality of virtue, relates only to man's rational essence. Without always insisting on the repression of his natural inclinations,[35] It is utterly indifferent to their satisfaction. But man himself cannot be indifferent to that. As a creature

---

[34] Cf. *Rel.*, VI:6n.-7/6n.-7; *C2*, V:25/24; *Found.*, IV:416/75.

[35] I disagree with a reading of Kantian ethics that requires the permanent suppression of the inclinations. When duty and inclination happen to suggest the same course of action, it is indeed difficult to know which is the actual motive (*Bestimmungsgrund*) of the act. But this impairs the *ratio cognoscendi* of the moral act, not its *ratio essendi*. Morality requires not action counter to inclination but complete disregard of inclination at the point of decision, and this is feasible according to Kant's theory of motivation (*Triebfedern*) (see *C2*, V:71-83, 93/73-85, 96; *Found.*, IV:400/61). The possibility of pure rational motivation is a major condition for the possibility of Kantian ethics and one of the senses in which reason is practical.

of needs and desires, he has an aspiration to happiness as an inherent part of his nature. It can be denied a role in his actual motivation (i.e., be excluded from the determining ground of the will), but not abolished altogether. A man who bars the desire for happiness from affecting his decisions will nonetheless continue to desire happiness and feel its absence, and thus his morality will make him at once good and ungratified.

Although moral perfection has its own form of satisfaction, described as a kind of "intellectual contentment" (C2, V:118/122) and even as "apathy," (MM, VI:408/70), Kant emphasizes that it is unlikely to replace empirical gratification. The sense of fulfillment and liberation in moral perfection is the possession of the "moral ego" alone, and not of the individual as a whole. The "sensuous ego" does not participate in it, and, moreover, moral contentment is often attained at its expense.

This is a peculiarly Kantian version of the problem of the suffering of the just or of moral theodicy. Even before it assumes cosmic and historical dimensions, the issue arises in the very structure of the individual will.

The problem stems from the will's division into two heterogeneous principles under which moral fulfillment must ignore, and frequently frustrate, the wish for natural gratification. But since the "empirical" self and its goals is also a necessary part of personality, Kant holds that practical philosophy, as a theory of action and of will, must account for these factors and define their place within a unified system of goals of the moral man. (Note that we are not speaking of duties and legitimations as yet; we are only examining the question of what the complete goal of a concrete man is and how this goal is possible.)

Worthiness and Reward

Simple as this argument may seem, it represents a turn in the development of Kant's doctrine. On the descriptive level the switch is suggested and even made necessary by the very nature of Kantian morals. Centered on the concept of duty or the ought, Kantian ethics presuppose the heterogeneity of the good; as against the moral good that man ought to do (*das Gute*), there is the natural good that he desires as a matter of fact (*das Wohl*). But this very division, which alone makes morality possible, means that morality in itself is incapable of fulfilling the *whole* end of a limited rational being (*C1*: A 813/B 841). Morality is only the supreme (*supremum*) good of the will but not its total (*consummatum*) good (*C2*, V:110/114), thus raising the problem of how the latter is conceivable.

Here Kant examines several possibilities. (*C2*, V:111-113/115-117) *Renunciation* of one of the components cannot take place and would not solve the problem. Man will persist in desiring happiness and in recognizing the validity of the moral law even after denying one of them a determining role in his behavior. His willing will retain its dual character, even if only one of them becomes a source of action. The *reduction* of one good to the other is not a solution either (a mistake Kant attributes both to the Stoics and to the Epicureans), since the two are absolutely heterogeneous. Unity can be achieved only through a *synthesis* of the elements, each preserving its peculiar quality while consolidating with the other by an *a priori* rule. This rule combines the elements hierarchically, since only one of them may form the ground for motivation, while the other must be related to it as a neutral corollary. Due to the *a priori* character of the moral law, it also supplies the rule for linking itself to the hedonistic goal of happiness.[36] Virtue becomes the absolute condition for the satisfaction of desires, and even though man continues to want happiness, *now he does so only under this condition*. Happiness takes on the character of reward, and its relation to morality becomes one of worthiness (*Würdigkeit*). Only by being moral can man regard himself as worthy of having his desires satisfied, and the categorical imperative now acquires the following form: "Do that, through which thou

[36] In this it resembles the category, which is both a constituent and a condition of the cognitive synthesis.

becomest worthy to be happy" (*C1*: A 808-809/B 836-837).
This new formulation goes beyond the standard categorical
imperative, since to define a moral man as worthy of something is an admission that morality is only a partial good,
which invites supplementation by another type of good.
The new formulation, however, makes morality not only
a component of the total good but also its rule and precondition. In the highest good *the moral good* and *the
natural good* are combined according with the rule of
worthiness to form the entire good of the moral man.

This specific form of the imperative, "Do that through
which thou becomest worthy to be happy," substantiates,
I think, our analysis of the descriptive level. On the one
hand, this is not yet the *material* imperative of Kant's
system, since it does not include the *duty* to promote
the highest good. On the other hand, this formulation is
not analytically derived from the basic categorical imperative, since the latter does not include the concept of happiness, and does not imply that a man fulfilling it will
become entitled to reward. The present formulation corresponds to the transition-point between the two stages; it
fits the *personal* and *descriptive* level of the highest good
with which we are concerned.

Worthiness and reward convey a special meaning in this
context. Man becomes worthy in his own eyes and not
from the viewpoint of external authority from which he
expects reward. He himself sets his morality as a precondition for satisfying his desires. At this point worthiness
is only a negative condition, which limits the individual's
willing, and not a positive right or claim vis-à-vis someone
else.

Morality a "Passport to Happiness"?

Here a crucial problem arises. If the will to become moral
is a will to be worthy of happiness, one could think that
morality serves only as a "passport to happiness."[37] Since

[37] See A. Seth Pringle-Pattison, *The Idea of God* (New York, 1920),
33.

this issue attracted a great deal of criticism, it calls for a detailed analysis.

It cannot be denied that in his earliest text on the highest good Kant once referred to the hope for happiness as a condition for leading a moral life ($C1$, A 812-813/B 840-841). Yet philosophers sometimes say things that seem (or are) inconsistent with their own systems. The question is not whether Kant actually made this isolated statement but whether, on the logic of his position, he was *committed* (or even permitted) to make it; and the answer to both parts of this question is clearly negative.

The "passport to happiness" thesis suggests that morality is not sought for its own sake but ultimately for attaining utilitarian goals. This claim is not only unfounded but *meaningless* in Kantian terms. Given the fundamentals of Kant's ethics it is logically impossible to use morality as a means; and whoever intends to be moral in order to gain happiness does not, by definition, aim at morality at all, but aims directly at the satisfaction of his inclinations.

One could alter the criticism and say that the inclusion of happiness in the overall object of the will leads to heteronomy. In this form the claim will be meaningful but, in my view, it does not apply to Kant's theory. Kant may avoid this criticism by his special theory of motives (*Triebfedern*),[38] and his principle that the moral value of man lies exclusively in the effective motive of his action: in "the determining ground of his will." This enables the creation of the following model. The man who wants to be worthy of happiness acts on the basis of duty, and this aim alone *determines* his will, i.e., becomes his effective motivation.

[38] On Kant's theory, both the empirical *and* the rational will have sufficient motivational power to produce a decision (followed by an action) in complete disregard of each other. It is true that the *observer*, including the agent himself in self-observation, may have difficulty in knowing which type of motive has the upper hand when both recommend the same course of action. But this is a problem of *ratio cognoscendi*, not of *ratio essendi*. In itself, an action can be rationally motivated even when its external or behavioral side happens to correspond to the one which utility, too, would have preferred.

The aspiration to happiness persists, but it is denied any influence over the decision making. Such a mute desire, which only accompanies the determination of the will without interfering with it, assumes the form of *ex post facto* hope. The moral man wills (actively) the fulfillment of his duty, and hopes (passively, without being motivated by it) for happiness. He does not do good to profit by it, but having done good he hopes to attain happiness as well. Hope is not a heteronomous factor, because it is an *ex post facto* wish. It arises because one has already chosen morally, rejecting the quest for happiness from among the motives of his behavior and at times even acting against it and, therefore, all one can do is *hope* that eventually it, too, will be satisfied. Thus the appearance of happiness in the highest good as an object of non-motivating, *ex post facto* hope is compatible with the Kantian theory of morality.

Whether this hope is founded or vain is a question in its own right. The moral man hopes for happiness. But, asks Kant, is he also *entitled* (*darf*) to expect it? In other words, does his hope have a ground in reality, or is it just a delusion of the imagination and the faculty of desire? This question, which concerns man's subjective consciousness no less than the system's logical construction, is not answered by Kant in the theory of the highest good itself but in the supplementary theory of the Deity. The function of postulating the "existence of God" is to provide this hope with a foundation (*Grund*) *in the structure of reality itself*, thus transforming it from an absurd to a rational hope.

Much of the objection to making happiness a component of the highest good is summarized by T. M. Greene's remark that the introduction of happiness either leads to heteronomy or is superfluous.[39] The above discussion has shown these criticisms to be unfounded. The reintroduction of happiness is a crucial complement of the theory of will, while heteronomy is avoided by the Kantian doctrine

---

[39] See his introduction to the English edition of the *Rel.*, lxiv.

of motives. Moreover, at the descriptive level one cannot argue against an alleged "introduction" of happiness into the object of the will, since it has been there all along.

Points of Criticism

The vulnerable points of the arguments are found elsewhere. First, the doctrine of motives is itself an implausible and undemonstrated metaphysical postulate. Kant argues that it is necessary to assume it just as one must assume freedom itself (C_2, V:72/75); and in view of the radical dualism of reason and inclination, it follows that Kantian ethics stands or falls with the doctrine of motives. But this may be an argument against such radical dualism. Second, the extreme heterogeneity of the components of the highest good leaves the problem of *one* object of will unsolved. The connection is artificial, and the impossibility of uniting them within the determining ground of the will (since *this* would be heteronomy) maintains the duality intact. Third and correspondingly, it is difficult to determine who is the *one* man that wills the highest good, since the same dualism persists in dividing the moral from the empirical subject. Thus Kant fails to achieve unity with respect either to the subject or the object.

All valid criticisms revert to one fundamental difficulty: the radical division between spontaneity and receptivity. This problem occurs in almost every branch of Kant's system, and in the final analysis it is solved only by recourse to such transcendent assumptions as the postulate of the existence of God and the reflective idea of the "supersensible substratum of creation."

The Personal Highest Good as a Descriptive Explication

To summarize, the personal meaning of the highest good can be defined as the combination of the objects of the intention (i.e., *active* willing) and the hope of the moral man. On this first level the concept appears only as the explication of the complete structure of human willing and as yet introduces no new imperative. The novel elements over and beyond the Analytic or the *Foundations* consist at this stage of (a) drawing attention to the fact that acts of duty, too, are accompanied necessarily and without heteronomy by the aspiration to happiness (as mere hope), and (b) the addition of a totalizing principle. At this point the concern is not with a particular intention and hope, which have combined in a single act, but with the ultimate intention and hope of the whole person.

But Kant goes even further by making the highest good an object of *duty*, and the hope for happiness a *right* to it.[40] Only now, and not in the alleged introduction of happiness into the highest good, does the major shift from the first to the second stage of the system occur. With this transition happiness loses its hedonistic character of immediate, individual satisfaction; and hope, too, ceases to be bound to the individual's happiness and is directed to broader (historical) perspectives.

The Highest Good as Duty

The moral imperative to realize the highest good is emphasized several times in Kant and appears in almost all his practical works. It also serves as a first premise in the "moral proof" of the existence of God. However, as many critics have pointed out, Kant fails to account for the alleged necessity of this duty.[41] We have seen that it does not evolve out of the formal stage of morality, since the categorical imperative demands only that man act from rational motives, ignoring the question of the agent's hap-

[40] This happens in the same text and, sometimes, even in the same sentence, e.g., *C2*, V:110-111/114-115. Yet the distinctions I make here are, as noted above, the result of a conceptual analysis and neither they nor the relation between them always appear explicitly in Kant.

[41] See L. W. Beck, *A Commentary on Kant's Critique of Practical Reason* (Chicago, 1960), 244-245; J. Guttmann, *Kants Gottesbegriff in seiner positiven Entwicklung* (Berlin, 1906), 65; J. Silber, "Kant's Conception of the Highest Good," *Phil. Rev.*, LXVIII (1959), 469-492; G. Simmel, *Kant* (Leipzig, 1905), 127.

piness. How, then, do reward and the highest human good in general become a *moral* end?

Since Kant does not discuss this question explicitly, his view must be reconstructed from statements of striking similarity scattered in his works. In the second *Critique* Kant declares that reward to the worthy is required

> not merely in the partial eyes of a person who makes himself his end but even in the judgement of an impartial reason which impartially regards persons in the world as ends in themselves. For to be in need of happiness and also worthy of it and yet not to partake of it could not be in accordance with the complete volition of an omnipotent rational being, if we assume such only for the sake of the argument (*C2*, V:110/ 114-115).

A similar statement can be found in the first *Critique*:

> To make the good complete he who behaves in such a manner as not to be unworthy of happiness must be able to hope that he will participate in happiness. Even the reason that is free from all private purposes, should it put itself in the place of a being that had to distribute happiness to others, cannot judge otherwise (*C1*, A 813/B 841).

And again, in the third *Critique*:

> It could never be that the issue is all alike, whether a man has acted fairly or falsely, with equity or with violence, albeit to his life's end, . . . his virtues have brought him no reward, his transgressions no punishment. It seems as though they perceived a voice within them say that it must make a difference (*C3*, V:458/ II:129).

The three Critiques only reassert in different ways that reward is a moral claim, without supplying a reason why. The contention that man is "worthy" of happiness is useless, since the question concerns the way in which "worthiness," which was first a self-imposed limiting condition of the will, becomes a positive right or claim addressed to some other authority. It is significant that all three texts use obscure images and metaphors (an "impartial reason"; an "inner voice"; an "omnipotent rational being" that is assumed "only for the sake of the argument") precisely at the point that needs explanation, i.e., *who* determines the moral necessity of reward. The categorical imperative is incapable of doing this, since it disregards happiness in *any* form, including that of "reward."

The inevitable conclusion is that on this crucial issue, extraneous moralistic considerations are brought in, deriving probably from a vague feeling of justice, but not rooted in Kant's basic ethics. The above-quoted images and exclamations reinforce the impression that this is an external viewpoint that Kant attributes to the moral law itself, without being able to show its derivation from it.[42]

This is an outstanding illustration of the discontinuity between the two stages in Kant's practical system. It is also an example of the *way* in which the transition occurs: Under certain conditions (here: worthiness), the relevant empirical factor (here: happiness) is recognized as morally desirable and thus is included in the object of a new, broader moral will. The new will determines the moral necessity of reward; but it could not have been constituted

[42] The non-systematic considerations which influence Kant at this point are not ultimately as accidental as it would seem from Simmel and Beck. Simmel says that Kant was influenced here by the mechanistic conception of justice "common in the eighteenth century" (*ibid.*, 127). Beck explains that Kant was influenced primarily by the image of the impartial observer taken from English philosophy. It seems, however, that Kant's position derives from an older and more profound source: historically it dates back at least as far as the Bible, and subjectively, Kant manifests a zealous concern for the problem of reward and punishment and a deep sensitivity to the phenomena of the suffering just and the prosperous sinner. The interpretation of Simmel and Beck deprives Kant's view of its genuine pathos; yet notwithstanding its presence and authenticity, this Kantian pathos should be seen as external to his system and not properly integrated into it.

in the first place without involving a systematic discontinuity.

Our problem now is to see what meaning the concept of the highest good must assume, if it is to be understood, as it should, as a human duty.

The Universal Highest Good

As duty, the highest good must alter its meaning and lose its purely personal character. The concept of duty implies the ability of the content of man's willing to be universalized; moreover, whoever acts from duty does not aim merely at some particular state of affairs, but at a whole world order—a "universal law of nature" (*Found.*, V:436/ 93)—that is desirable from the viewpoint of any possible moral will. It follows that, as duty, the highest good incorporates not only my personal final end (my private happiness and virtue), but an ultimate design for the entire moral universe. It is now defined as "the highest good that reason presents to *all* rational beings as the goal of *all* their moral wishes" (*C2*, V:115/119): a universal human system that will combine the greatest and most widespread happiness with the strictest morality of all rational beings.[43] Thus the material imperative establishes a single teleological system that totalizes, through the reciprocal relations of duty, the personal highest good of every man.[44]

We should notice that a new factor was introduced here.[45] The formal stage of morality already entailed an

[43] *C3*, V:453/122; cf. also *C2*, V:129-130/133-134, where the universal highest good is described as "a whole wherein the greatest happiness is thought of as connected in exact degree to the greatest degree of moral perfection." (Incidentally, Kant's frequent use of the expression "rational beings" instead of "human beings" stems from his conjecture—as an astronomer—that rational and sensuous beings may be found on other planets as well. Thus, the highest good will ideally have cosmic perspectives!)

[44] In his analysis of this idea Guttmann notes in *Kant's Gottesbegriff* (61-62) without further explanation that Kant takes a new turn here. In terms of our conceptual reconstruction this "turn" is more precisely, the making of the highest good into a duty.

[45] By "new" I mean *systematically* new, not an idea at which Kant

act of universalization, establishing a unity of the many wills;[46] and in it, too, the will intended to create an entire world-order, valid for all rational beings (*Found.*, IV:438/ 95). However, the reciprocal system of wills, established through the formal imperative, concerns only the rational will of each individual, leaving the empirical will in its particularity. Although it neutralizes the natural conflict between the many empirical wills,[47] the system falls short of establishing a positive common object. Under it, each man wills the same universalizable goal that can and should be the object of every other rational will, bearing with him also a passive hope for private happiness. The universal highest good, on the other hand, integrates natural desires, too, in one *moral* object. The universalized factor of happiness is now conceived as a *world order*, in which the worthy attain reward, and thus is included in the common end of the *moral* will. On the level of the empirical

---

had arrived later in his career. (Let me stress again that my present analysis is structural, not historical, and as my choice of quotations will show, many of the basic themes are already present in such early works as *C1* and *Found.*)

[46] Universalization is not merely a logical calculus, but an actual subjective attitude, in which the individual will is actively disposed to recognize the freedom and value of others and to act out of this recognition. This establishes an ideal totality of wills and partly explains Kant's transition to the new formulation of the imperative in terms of "man as an end."

[47] The good will relates to itself by recognizing all other free wills, whereas the empirical will relates to itself by its rejection of other wills, which it views either as a means or as an obstacle to its own happiness, and to which it does not grant equal status. Since other "empirical" persons relate to me in this way, the reciprocal relation between us is one not of recognition but of conflict. This struggle need not express itself in practice, for it exists as the structure of the relationship, a structure that can be concretely manifested any time. Even when we both enjoy bringing happiness to one another, we are still in a state of tension, because each wants to make the other a means of achieving pleasure. The harmony in this situation is imaginary, since the moment pleasure ceases, we will not be able to obtain anything from one another except by competition or violence. (This is also Kant's reinterpretation of Hobbes's "*bellum omnium in omnes*," cf. *Rel.*, VI:97n./ 89n.)

will, happiness is a principle of conflict and division between men, and on the level of the formal imperative it has no function in their relations; but here it participates in the common final end that unites them all.[48]

The "Self-Rewarding System"

The ultimate goal is conceived by Kant as a "self-rewarding system" ($C1$: A 809-810/B 837-838), in which happiness accrues to the worthy from the immanent order of things and not from a particular divine or human intervention. Originally, this was a Leibnizian idea which Kant adapted to his doctrine of the highest good and kept as a permanent principle in all the versions of this concept. The highest good is always conceived as a harmony of heterogeneous systems, where exact correspondence between the different constituents (virtue and happiness, *Moralität* and *Legalität*, disposition and consequences, or freedom and nature in general) takes place *by the autonomous laws of each system itself*.

Kant has never discussed in detail the mechanism of such a self-rewarding system, and again, his view must be reconstructed from scattered hints. Kant believes that universal happiness or welfare presupposes universal morality not only as a *moral* but also as a real *historical* condition. When discussing universal morality, Kant at first meant only pure, subjective (or intersubjective) morality in the sense of the "kingdom of ends." But in his later political works, and in the *Religion*, he realized that the moral administration of happiness also depends on creating *objective* institutions, which reflect the laws of morality in the external world of *Legalität*. Among these are freedom and equal opportunity,[49] just political constitutions,[50] criminal justice with

---

[48] A rudimentary form of *Aufhebung* seems to be implied here, justifying Guttmann's use of this term in the present context (*op. cit.*, 62).

[49] *TP*, VIII:290-298/74-80. One cannot constitute a state on the principle of happiness (utilitarianism) but only on the principle of freedom; yet since freedom means, among other things, the right of every individual to seek his happiness without infringing on that of others,

sanctions and rewards,[51] and a world confederation that leads to peace and to the well-being that goes with it (*PP*, VIII:378/125-126). Moral legislation must first be implemented in the ethical or intersubjective relations between men and be embodied (*dargestellt*) in political and jurisprudential institutions; only then can universal welfare be attained as well.

Heteronomy Reconsidered

Have we not returned to a heteronomous stand? On the personal level, this difficulty could be avoided by making a distinction between active volition and inactive aspiration (mere hope). But at this stage the question recurs, since happiness is now included in the object of man's *active* will. Kant tries to answer the question by claiming that this willing follows from duty and not from interest. The happiness included in the object of my willing is not my private interest but something universal and objective that the moral law demands of me. It is true that the realization of the ideal will also bring happiness to the individual, yet "not happiness, but the moral law . . . is proved to be the ground determining the will to further the highest good."[52] My private happiness remains the object of an unmotivating hope, whereas the happiness I seek actively is that of mankind in general.[53]

This argument is sufficiently supported by Kant's doctrine of motives (*Triebfedern*), according to which one can, *with-*

a state constituted on the principle of freedom will also lead to the increase of happiness, that is, to a sort of automatic reward.

50 Cf. *Idea*, VIII:22/16-17.

51 Cf. *MM*, particularly VI:331-337/99-107, where the retributive principle is made the principle of these sanctions.

52 *C2*, V:130/134; cf. V:109-110/113-114.

53 To emphasize this point or, perhaps from caution, Kant speaks about "one's own perfection and the happiness of others" (*MM*, VI:385/44). Yet contrary to Silber's view, this definition does not cover the scope of the concept of the highest good, but only a narrower aspect of it, falling between the personal and the universal levels in the present analysis.

out heteronomy, intend to do something which one also desires. But Kant can rely on still another point. The realization of the highest good is an infinitely remote ideal, and man is aware of it. He acts, then, with the knowledge that his goal of universal happiness is not a personal interest but a universal world order, to be established by the cumulative work of generations.

The Changes in the Concept of Happiness

From a particular (lucky) set of events, related to one person, happiness thus becomes a universal order; from immediate gratification it becomes the deferred satisfaction which is always projected into future generations. In both ways its hedonistic character is superseded. Included in the highest good as duty, happiness itself becomes a moral principle ("reward to the worthy"), destined to be instituted in the world by human actions and presupposing as a real and historical condition the creation of a ethically and politically rational society.

The Highest Good as Moral Nature

Until now we were engaged in a step-by-step analysis of the highest good in its *narrow* sense, as a synthesis of morality and happiness. But Kant has also a broader conception, in which happiness is secondary, and its place is taken by nature in general as the empirical constituent of the highest good. (Kant means primarily human and social nature, i.e., civilization; but he also includes physical nature, in so far as it enters the range of human action and control.)

Although this change reflects a shift of emphasis in Kant's intellectual interests, it is not completely arbitrary. The new conception of the highest good embraces the old and is related to it first, because the problem of synthesis in the practical sphere has more than one expression and second, because reward is an *empirical* event occurring according to moral *laws* and so exemplifying the general idea of a "moral nature."

The inclusion of reward within the moral end enables Kant to use a new definition of the highest good, i.e., "the existence of rational beings under moral laws" (*C3*, V:444/ II: 111).[54] This seems a narrower definition at first, since it omits happiness. However, the definition appears in close textual proximity to the usual one, which does include happines (*C3*, V:450/II:118), and Kant must have seen them as congruent. Indeed, the inclusion of reward within the object of the will made reward itself a moral law. Therefore, the moral laws to which men are subject, according to the new definition, are of two kinds: the internal, rational laws of the categorical imperative and the external, natural laws of the reward mechanism. The "existence of rational beings under moral laws," with which the definition is concerned, means existence under these *two* systems of laws, governing both moral behavior and the attainment of happiness.[55]

Further, since "existence under . . . laws" is the standard Kantian definition of nature,[56] the new definition makes clear that the highest good, at which the will aims, signifies an organized system or *a whole world*. Regarded according to the dual meaning of moral laws mentioned above, the nature in question is neither empirical nature alone, nor supersensible nature, but their synthesis. The highest good, says Kant in the same context, is a world in which both what *initiates* behavior and what *results* from it are "ordained according to moral laws" (*C3*, V:449n./II:117n.). Moral

---

⁵⁴ Cf. V:448-449/II: 116-117.

⁵⁵ In this I disagree with Albert Schweitzer, who interpreted the new definition as an unexplained reduction of the previous one. See A. Schweitzer, *Die Religions-Philosophie Kants* (Leipzig, 1905). Hugo Bergmann, too, in Ha'Filosofia shel Immanuel Kant (*The Philosophy of I. Kant*, Jerusalem, 1928) is inclined to accept Schweitzer's interpretation.

⁵⁶ Cf. *Prol.*, IV:292/52; *C1*, A 216/B 263, *Found.*, IV:421/80; *C2*, V:43/44. In the last citation Kant distinguishes between two kinds of nature: archetypal nature and *natura ectypa*. The former is a pure noumenal world, "the supersensible substrate of nature" that appears in *C3*; while the latter, its "copy," is as the "derived" highest good that has to be produced by man in and out of the sensuous world.

ɪlness in its broadest sense thus establishes a world that ᴜdes both a system of intersubjective attitudes and a ɛem of empirical events, both of which are subject to the rules of morality and are therefore in complete harmony.[57] Thus the highest good becomes an ideal of a coordination between the natural order and moral legislation. However, as long as only the mere idea of reward to the worthy is considered, the coordination in question has a very narrow basis. To complete the description of the new meaning of the highest good, we must include some additions and changes of emphasis made by Kant, particularly beginning with the third *Critique*.

From Happiness to the Objectification of Morality

We saw that the moral will faces the problem of achieving a synthesis not only with the object of inclination but also with the external world upon which it has to act. Therefore, *the coordination of nature and morality is required not only from the narrow viewpoint of reward, but also from the viewpoint of the realization of morality itself in the world.* If "the concept of freedom is meant to actualize in the sensible world the end proposed by its laws" (*C3*, V:175-176/I:14), then a harmony between the two must be created, both from the standpoint of nature's *responsiveness* to moral activity, and from the viewpoint of its being *actually* reshaped by it.[58]

This form of synthesis can be described as the embodiment (*Darstellung*) or externalization of morality in the

---

[57] It should be noted that the idea of "moralizing nature" much preceded Kant's critical period. It is present, in fact, ever since his early writings, such as *UNH*, and may be seen as a major theme that links his philosophical concerns throughout his periods. (For an elaboration see Chapter Three.)

[58] The moral reshaping of nature is the act of man alone, while nature's initial *responsiveness* to the act of reshaping is guaranteed by God's existence. Yet this responsiveness can itself be reinforced by the human act, since a partly civilized and moralized world is better equipped to respond to new moral praxis and to facilitate its objective institutionalization.

natural world. It includes the narrower form of synthesis present in the concept of reward but generalizes it beyond the narrow scope of happiness. Thus the emphasis within the empirical component of the highest good, and the very concept itself, changes in Kant according to these two forms of synthesis.

In the first *Critique*, in the *Foundations*, in most of the relevant parts of the second *Critique*, and in paragraphs 87 and 88 of the third, Kant concentrates on the question of happiness, describing the synthesis between morality and nature primarily from the viewpoint of reward; whereas in other parts of the third *Critique*,[59] in the *Religion*, in the political works, and in important discussions of the "typic" and the "natura ectypa" in the second *Critique* itself,[60] Kant emphasizes the generalized problem of consequences and especially the embodiment of morality in the empirical world. Here reward becomes *only* one of the manifestations of the overall correspondence; while those empirical systems, which participate in the structure of the highest good, are now considered in the first place as *objectifications* of morality itself, in law, in a state, in the rational church, etc.[61]

Correspondingly, the object of *hope* also changes. Hope, too, is no longer concerned with happiness alone, but first with an adequate fulfillment of moral intentions and the successful realization of moral nature in general.[62]

To conclude, the highest good is the name of a *world*, in which moral lawfulness governs both the subjective atti-

59 Especially, Introd. Sect. II (V:174-176/I:11-14); also in Pars. 83, 86, 87.
60 See *C2*, V:68-71/72-73 for the "typic," and *ibid.*, 43-44/44-45 for *natura ectypa*.
61 This is the sense in which one must construe the definition of the highest good as "the existence of rational beings under moral laws" and as "mankind . . . in its complete moral perfection" (*Rel.*, VI:60/54). Both relate not only to internal morality but also to its objectification in the institutions of society. And accordingly, Kant adds that the final outcome in both cases will include well-being.
62 This is a major change with respect to the narrow conception of the first *Critique*, which states that "all hoping is directed to happiness" (*C1*, A 805/B 833).

71

tudes of all individuals, thus constituting a universal ethical community, as well as the objective, empirical sphere in which they live and act. In this world, maximal well-being prevails, too, since the law of reward has become part of the ruling moral lawfulness. This kind of world—"the best world" (*C2*, V:125/130)—should now become the guiding ideal that "totalizes" human action.

The Highest Good as the Regulative Idea of History

In the first two *Critiques*, Kant tends to think of the highest good as a separate world, transcendent to our world and, in fact, a sort of critical and rational version of the notion of the next world.[63] In this sense of the concept, as Guttmann has said,[64] one wonders how there can be a *duty* to realize the highest good. However, from the third *Critique* on, Kant's conception changes. The highest good becomes the "final end of creation" itself, i.e., the consummate state of *this* world. Its realization is conceived as "the kingdom of God on *earth*";[65] and despite its infinite remoteness, it involves a concrete synthesis, to be realized *in time*, between the moral will and empirical reality. The highest good and the given world no longer signify two different worlds but two states, present and ideal, of the same world. In other words, the highest good becomes a historical goal.

Only in light of this change can the human duty to realize or promote the highest good become meaningful. The highest good is our own world brought to perfection. It is not the transcendent world of God, but like the given world it has temporal existence and empirical constituents. But if at present the systems of nature and morality are separated, in the highest good complete harmony is to prevail between them. As known and given to us, nature is alien to the laws of morality and even frustrates them. The duty to realize the

[63] A similar conception is found in the fragments of the *Opus Postumum*.

[64] Guttmann, *Kant's Gottesbegriff*, 67-68.

[65] *Rel.*, VI:134/125, italics added; cf. *ibid.*, 122-123, 133-135/113, 124-126.

highest good means, therefore, that we should overcome this alienness[66] by impressing new patterns on the ways of nature and by reshaping its empirical elements into such systems as will manifest and promote the moral laws. In Kant's characteristic formula, we must "impart to the sensuous world the form of a system of rational beings" (C2, V:43/ 45). This certainly does not imply the abolition of the empirical laws, which are *given* to us. But these laws must be put to uses of a higher order, serving as the empirical substratum for a new world that will be a copy or a manifestation of the moral idea. In this ideal human world causal laws and human passions will certainly persist, but their course will be governed by morally significant patterns: both by the subjectively free dispositions of all individuals and by objectively rational institutions of society as a whole. The duty to realize the highest good calls us to imprint upon "the sensible world . . . the form of supersensuous nature, without interfering with the mechanism of the former" (C2, V:43/44). Using as a basis the course of the world, and the given empirical laws, man must create, in his history, a new "nature" which embodies a moral and human meaning.[67]

[66] Alienness should not be confused with alienation. In Kant the ontological structure of nature is initially alien to freedom but it is not alienated (or self-alienated) from it. The work of moral history is to overcome this alienness of nature by imprinting human patterns and ends upon it. The modern problem of alienation, i.e., that these human ends and creations confront man and pervert instead of develop his essence, was not discussed by Kant as such (although a theoretical model of alienation may be found, *mutatis mutandis*, in Kant's theory of the sublime and in the evaluation of dogmatic metaphysics that must stem from his Copernican revolution).

[67] There is an interesting parallel, in this point, between the work of moral history and that of the genius in art: "The imagination (as a productive faculty of cognition) is a powerful agent for *creating*, as it were, *a second nature out of the materials supplied to it by actual nature* . . . and we even use it to remodel experience, always following, no doubt, laws that are based on analogy, but also following principles which have a higher seat in reason . . . *the material can be borrowed by us from nature . . . but be worked up by us into . . . what surpasses nature*" (C3, V:314/I: 176, italics added). It is thus not accidental

In this historical sense, the highest good is the principle of the most comprehensive type of totalization and extends the boundaries of the individual's duty. In the formal stage of morality, the individual is obliged to perform isolated acts. Virtue is introduced to integrate these acts in the framework of the whole personality, and a *personal* moral end is established. On the other hand, the highest good is also the virtue of humanity and nature in general. The individual required to promote the highest good cannot be satisfied with acting on the formal basis of the categorical imperative while rejecting nature and ignoring the world. He must intervene in them and concern himself with their perfection. The duty to promote the highest good no longer means that a person should make himself good, but that he should also make the *world* good. He ought to transcend the limits of his private morality and posit to himself, as the subject of moral progress, not only his own personality, but also the entire world.[68]

How, more specifically, should we understand this "synthesis" which bestows "supersensuous form on sensuous nature without interfering with its mechanical laws"? In principle, it is recreated in every *individual* moral act whose consequences are manifested in the empirical world.[69] Yet,

---

that the work of art served Kant as a symbol or analogy for the moral enterprise (*C3*, Par. 59).

[68] This idea—the humanization and reshaping of nature by means of *praxis*—contains the nucleus of ideas later developed by Hegel and Marx. Decisive differences do exist. In Kant the transition to empirical realization involves a systematic "leap" while in Hegel it follows conceptually. Moreover, Hegel and Marx do not relate the historical synthesis, which gives nature a human meaning, to morality, which to them is internal and subjective. In Kant the postulate of an external mediator (God) is required to guarantee the possibility of the synthesis, while in Hegel the possibility is guaranteed in principle, since nature is not heterogeneous to reason but a moment of the spirit itself. In Hegel and Marx these problems are dealt with explicitly, while in Kant they have to be reconstructed from fragmentary discussions. These differences, however, and others which have not been mentioned here, should not obscure the debt of Hegel and Marx to Kant.

[69] How such a manifestation is possible is a question apart, which the

such acts indicate only a fragmentary synthesis, whereas the creation of a moral *world* requires their integration in one comprehensive synthesis. Of necessity it transcends the bounds of a single act and can only be created by a cumulative and cooperative effort of humanity. The highest good as moral nature will thus become the regulative idea of History, and of culture which serves it. In Kant's view this is the sphere where an interrelation between the phenomenal world and the will which reshapes it is created and preserved (*Idea*, VIII:24-28/18-23). Culture is the product of man "employing nature as a means in accordance with the maxims of his free ends" (*C3*, V:431/II,94); and, included in it, are political, educational, scientific, esthetic, economic, and also technological institutions. History is a broader sphere, in which culture figures both as means and as manifestation; essentially, history is the growing perfection of internal and external *morality* or, as Kant sometimes puts it, of the internal and external *freedom* of all mankind. Culture itself does not guarantee ethical progress (*Idea*, VIII:27/21-22), but it is a necessary auxiliary (*C3*, Par. 83); and, also, accumulates and preserves past achievements.[70]

The highest good is thus the summit of the historical enterprise. In itself, it constitutes a unity of an internal and external system, and its attainment presupposes the work of culture while going beyond it.

Physical and Social Nature

The extraction of the concept of history from that of moral nature may become clearer by taking note that nature is conceived here more in the psychological and sociological sense than in the physical one. The empirical nature that should embody the moral idea is, first of all, the world of interpersonal relations and social institutions. Physical objects participate in this nature only as mediated by human

---

theory of the typic and the postulate of God's existence attempt to answer.

[70] For a discussion of culture see Chapter Four.

ends and interests, thus duly acquiring a new meaning as "property," "climate," "technology," etc. This restriction of the notion of moral nature is obviously necessary, since morality has meaning only in relation to man, and, therefore, "moral nature" can thus be only that nature that enters the context of human actions and interests or praxis. Accordingly, the crux of the Kantian highest good is the moral *society*, conceived under the dual aspect of inner disposition and external institution: It is first, a system of subjective attitudes, in which all members recognize each other's freedom and equal status as ends in themselves, and second, a system of external institutions, comprising legal and educational systems, international bodies, a rational church, and the products of culture in general. Both systems are essential components in the Kantian ideal. The supreme value, indeed, lies in the system of inner dispositions (*Moralität*) without which the entire enterprise would be a spiritless mechanism. Yet the external systems of *Legalität* are also necessary, both in their own right and as a means for the former. Kant's ethical community can be founded only within a political structure that secures and organizes the necessities of life; while its *extension* requires a free and rational state embodying the laws of morality and the principle of autonomy in its political institutions.[71] But the external systems are also required for their own sake, since the rational will is concerned not only with its own purity but also with its objective manifestation in the world. As the historical ideal the highest good must thus be conceived as the reciprocal relation between these two systems and not as exhausted by either one.

An important change in Kant's view of the operative power in history completes this picture. Kant consistently argues that history is not an accidental accumulation of events, but a meaningful process leading towards the development of freedom. While the *Idea for a Universal History*

[71] *Rel.*, VI:93-94/85-86; *Idea*, VIII:26/21.

conceives instincts and violence rather than rational action as the principle of progress, later discussions like *Theory and Practice, What is Enlightenment,* and *Religion* emphasize the role of the moral will as a generator of history. It is man's conscious freedom, not the inherent powers of nature, that creates his own image and the shape of the world.[72] This novel conception, together with the transposition of the highest good from the transcendent sphere into the "end of creation" (two philosophically parallel changes, reinforce the new function of the highest good as the end-concept of history. Early works like the first *Critique* (1781) and the *Idea* (1784) imply that the progress of history is controlled by empirical forces alone and project the object of the moral will beyond this world. However, the above changes leave no doubt that Kant considers history a field of conscious rational action and the object of the will a real historical state.[73]

Kant and Leibniz

More light can be shed on this issue by comparing Kant with Leibniz. Kant is Leibniz's successor in his desire to make the mechanical science of nature compatible with a moral-teleological view of the universe. More specifically: the theory of the highest good is Kant's version of the Liebnizian harmony between the realms of nature and grace. However, in Leibniz this harmony exists *actually.* It is a *pre-established* harmony, belonging to the eternal and unchangeable structure of the universe. Accordingly, Leibniz's world is *already* "the best of worlds," established as such by

[72] There is a striking correspondence between the moral realization of the individual and that of historical humanity. In both cases freedom exists at first only as a potential that has to realize its essence through its own power. The result, with respect to the individual, is autonomy or virtue; with respect to humanity at large, the highest good. In both cases freedom is the point of departure of the process, as well as its medium and ultimate goal.

[73] For a detailed analysis of this issue, see Chapter Four.

the original will of God. For this reason, history in the strict sense has no systematic footing in Leibniz, much as he ascribes progress and dynamism to the individual monads.

In Kant, by contrast, history is defined by the gap that separates the actual world from the best, and by the task— which now reverts to man—to close this gap and bring about the desirable harmony between the realms of nature and freedom. This harmony is no longer pre-established but referred to the remote future; and from the eternal work of God it becomes the historical task of man. God, as we shall see in the next chapter, only serves as an ontological "guarantee" that man can perform his historical role.

These differences between Kant and Leibniz also clarify the historical character of such Kantian notions as "the final-end of creation" and moral teleology in general.

History acquires a genuine ontological task by becoming the medium that should link the existing world with its (moral) end. The structure of creation (in the broadest sense, which includes both nature and reason) is neither static nor perfect but progressing toward essential innovations. Man becomes a sort of demiurge[74] who creates a moral world within the given world and thus translates the end of creation from potentiality to actuality.[75]

---

[74] In Kant's phrase, *Weltbaumeister*, "the architect of the world" (*CI*, A 627/ B 655). He cannot create the world; he can only reshape it, since "he is always much hampered by the adaptability of the material in which he works" (*ibid.*).

[75] This also implies that Kant and Leibniz differ on the issue of evil. In Leibniz evil is part of the harmony which persists even in "the best of all worlds." In Kant it belongs to the period prior to the creation of harmony, and will ideally be eliminated in the "best of worlds." Since Leibniz's world was prearranged and predetermined, he has to find fundamental metaphysical reasons for the existence of evil (theodicy). Kant, by viewing the world as historical and developing, also uses history to effect the abolition of evil itself: evil is not necessary and will abolish itself in the historical process. (Kant also put an end to all possibility of theodicy in his essay *Über das Misslingen aller philosophischen Versuche in der Theodicee*.)

Retrospect

Although Kant's vision of a moral nature preceded the critical system, it was reintegrated within the conceptual framework of the latter. In the spirit of the Copernican revolution, the creation of a moral nature (the highest good) is conceived as a task of the free will, not as a merely natural process. This gives the moral will a well-determined and comprehensive content, binding in one (historical) consciousness all isolated acts of duty. Correspondingly, the practical system is transferred from the stage of morality of intention to that of objectified moral praxis, including such systems as politics, jurisprudence, education, etc. In Kantian terminology the highest good becomes the regulative idea that guides the work of synthesis and totalization in the sphere of practice. This presupposes the cognitive synthesis that forms the empirical world of phenomena but completes it with a higher form of synthesis, whose goal is to unify the realms of freedom and nature and to embody the moral idea in the totality of relevant experience. This further reshaping of the world is to be accomplished in time and through the cooperation of generations; it is the final end of history and equally that of creation or existence itself. If Kant's philosophy can furnish existence with an ideal meaning or a justifying *telos*, it can do so only from the viewpoint of moral history and not as part of the world's actual ontology. The final end of the world is not inherent in it *per se*, as in a thing in itself; it is projected on it by man's moral consciousness and is realized by his praxis in history. The process of moral praxis unites man and nature by both remolding and transcending their actual existence in light of a rational ideal, thus introducing into human experience the only possible justification of existence. The universe or "creation" does not exist for its own sake, as in Aristotle and, fundamentally, in Spinoza; nor for the sake of any actual existent within it, like the empirical being of man;

or beyond it, like God. It exists for the sake of the moral system that it has yet to become. And man preserves his privileged position in creation not as the inherent goal of everything else, but as the dynamic, historic creature that gives meaning to the world by projecting its final end and by gradually bringing it about.[76]

[76] This point is elaborated further in Chapter Four.

CHAPTER II

GOD AND HUMAN ACTION

The concept of God is presented by Kant as a "postulate" lacking content and status of its own. It derives both meaning and validity from the function it fulfills in the system: to guarantee the possibility of the highest good. But since the Kantian concept of the highest good is ambiguous, the meaning of the concept of God in any particular context depends on the meaning of the highest good in that context. Thus when the highest good is understood as the combination of virtue and happiness, God is understood as the power that guarantees the possibility of that particular combination, namely of the full self-realization of the individual, including natural satisfaction taken as reward. On the other hand, when the highest good signifies a universal ethical community (das ethische gemeine Wesen; Rel., VI: 96/88), God is conceived as the power that makes it ontologically possible to overcome what Kant calls "the ethical state of nature" (Rel., VI:95/87), to achieve a universal propagation of morality in a fundamentally indifferent and frequently hostile world, and more particularly, to succeed in the historical process of rational education and enlightenment (Aufklärung). Again, the highest good is also understood as the synthesis of the moral idea with empirical reality, that is, as a perfect world in which moral laws are exhibited in the intentions and personalities of all individuals, as well as in their objectified creations: judicial and political institutions, culture in general. In this context, God must be conceived as the power that guarantees historical progress in the full sense, namely the ability of human praxis to embody its intentions in the given world and to reshape it as a good world ("the best world"; C2, V:125/

130). We have seen that the last is the most comprehensive meaning of the highest good and includes all the others; and that the duty "to promote the highest good in the world" comes to mean that the human race, in its history, is called upon by its own reason to use the empirical world and its given orders as means for the progressive creation of a new world, which will be a copy (*ectypus*) or embodiment (*Darstellung*) of the moral idea. From a synoptic view of the Kantian practical system and its implications, the concept of God must also be understood in relation to the problem of historical realization. In the last analysis, the idea of God guarantees not merely that the just will be rewarded, but primarily that mankind is capable of fulfilling its supreme task: to act as a new kind of demiurge, who creates a moral world within the given world, thus translating the final end (*Endzweck*) of creation itself from potentiality to actuality. The duty to promote the highest good is also the systematic ground for the postulation of the existence of God.

The Problem of Possibility

A basic principle of the Kantian ethics is that *sollen* is meaningless without *können*, or that ability is a necessary condition of duty (*ultra posse nemo obligatur*). Duty is by its concept a *free* necessity, which stems from spontaneous reasoning and not from external causes; it presupposes responsibility, which in turn implies open possibilities. But in the absence of ability there is no responsibility either, and the free necessity of the act is replaced by coercion or prevention from without. The relation between *sollen* and *können* is therefore analytic. Just as it is meaningless to oblige a man to do what he would anyway be driven to do by the necessity of his nature (e.g., to desire happiness), so it is meaningless to demand from him what he is unable to do because of physical or metaphysical limitations. He would do the first and abstain from the second for reasons that have nothing to do with moral decisions and so cannot be related to an *imperative*. This argument applies to the formal, "categorical" imperative as well as to the historical imperative to promote the highest good. "Reason," says Kant, "cannot command one to pursue an end that is recognized to be nothing but a fiction" (*C3*, V:472/II:147), and therefore without knowledge, or at least without "rational faith," that the highest good is possible, the imperative to promote it will collapse.

By using the concept of ability (*posse, können*) Kant draws a distinction between what is morally possible and what is possible in reality, thus raising, this time in the most comprehensive way, one of the basic questions in his practical philosophy: "the reciprocal relations subsisting between the world and that moral end and the possibility of realizing it under external conditions" (*C3*, V:447-448/II: 115). To know whether the highest good is possible not only morally but also as a historical reality, one must see (a) whether the world actually responds to moral demands, or at least (b) whether it can lend itself to a formative action on men's part, which would *bring* its orders into harmony with morality.

The first question is given a negative answer by our physical and historical experience and by the principles of the critical philosophy. The way of the existing world is indifferent to moral laws and even obstructs them. Its empirical laws depend upon contingent data not subject to our theoretical determination or practical control. Hence it not only fails to reward the worthy and to foster the propagation of the ethical community, but it frequently frustrates the execution of our intentions and produces results harmful both to the individual and to society. Occasionally the natural and the moral courses may converge, but they diverge far more frequently; and in any event, from the viewpoint of natural laws, the human or the moral meaning of a given event (or whether it has such a meaning at all), is a matter of chance and indifference. "The action, with its absolute necessity of the moral order, is looked on as physically wholly contingent" (C3, V:403/II:58), and the moral agent may therefore at most "expect to find a chance concurrence now and again, but he can never expect to find in nature . . . a consistent agreement according to fixed rules" (V:452/II:121).

Does this mean that the highest good is not possible? Not necessarily. All that we have learned thus far is that the moral nature does not exist in fact, but not whether it is possible to bring it into existence. This raises the second question. The imperative to realize the highest good in the world demands that we eliminate the contingency in question and introduce a moral and a human meaning into the fixed rules of experience itself. Its demand is, as Kant says, "to impart to the sensuous world the form of a system of rational beings," though "without interference with the laws" of the former (C2, V:43/44). In other words, on the basis of the given nature and by using its prevailing laws, we have to create a "second nature," which will exhibit moral ideas. But this is possbile only if the given nature can lend itself to moral reshaping, and if the free activity of man is capable of carrying this out. Thus the highest good sets a new problem of bridging or of "schematism," this time on the practical level. Freedom and nature, spontaneity and receptivity, are for Kant completely heterogeneous. If they ought to become components of a single synthesis, then there must be something in us or in nature which can bridge that "great gulf" which, according to Kant, "is fixed between the realm of the natural concept . . . and the realm of the concept of freedom" (C3, Intro., Sec. II, V:175-176/I: 14).

Schematizing Attempts

In a chapter entitled "The Typic of Pure Practical Judgement" (C2, V:67-71/68-72), Kant was looking for the mediating factor in the form of law that is inherent in morality as well as in the empirical world. Since both domains display a system of universal and rationally necessary determinations, they share the same logical form that may serve to bridge between them. But this solution is still inadequate, since the common factor it stresses is no more than an abstract form. In their concrete contents, however, a moral law may still clash with a natural law, even though each may be universal and necessary in its own domain. It is precisely the *law-abiding*, "nomic" course of nature that will thwart the demand of the moral law—a recurrent event of which Kant is well aware. The typic furnishes only a minimal correspondence,[1] namely a common formal structure; but it cannot guarantee the approximation of a material harmony any more than it can prevent a setback.

In the second part of the *Critique of Judgement*, Kant tries to supplement the typic with a kind of teleological schematism. One manifestation of finality in nature is that its *particular* laws, as Kant believes, form a coherent system. Since the specific content of each such law depends on contingent (receptive) elements, their coherence is rather surprising; and in any case it shows that even the given and contingent elements of nature display an affinity with rational structures. In addition, the "internal" finality found in living organisms also testifies that nature is capable of embodying some ends of reason. This kind of schematization is richer and more concrete than the typic, yet it, too, is insufficient. In the first place, the teleological determinations have no constitutive value. They belong not to the object, to nature itself, but only to our subjective or reflective judgement of it, while the initial problem is whether a moral goal can find support in the real structure of nature. Secondly, the rational pattern found in teleological phenomena is of a *cognitive* type, which differs from the practical type of legislation and manifests no moral intention. From this viewpoint the teleological schematization re-

[1] Cf. N. Rotenstreich, *Experience and Its Systematization*, 2nd ed., enl. (The Hague, 1972), 28.

sembles that of the typic. It states that in addition to the form of law, the form of finality is also common to morality and to natural phenomena. But just as before we were dealing with different kinds of law, so now we have to do with different senses of finality (*C3*, V: 180-181/I: 80-20); and in neither case do we go beyond merely formal analogies.

These attempts have failed because the possibility of the highest good requires a richer schematization that would establish the affinity of moral action not only to the *a priori* form of natural phenomena but also to their given content. If man ought, through his historical activity, to produce a synthesis between nature and the moral idea, then the particular, material, element in the world must also depend on his free determination and be subject to his complete control. But to assert this would violate the principles of the critical philosophy and reach far beyond the autonomy of human reason as Kant understands it. The world that confronts us as given in our historical activity is already a synthetic product of our *cognitive* activity, operating in accordance with the principles of the critical view. This view, which denies man the capacity of intellectual intuition (*intellektuelle Anschauung*), makes *him* dependent on the contingent, external data that determine the content of the objects he knows, of the *particular* laws of nature, and of the phenomenal results of his action. Although his understanding legislates for the world, this legislation only places the data in systems of external relations without thereby overcoming their alienness. Even after the constructive task of cognition has been completed, man is still confronted with an external datum; only it is no longer the manifold of sense impressions in time and space, but nature as a whole, with all the ramifications of its particular laws, that now confronts him as this datum. Both the duality of the "I" and the world and the alienness of the content persist in the cognitive synthesis, which is therefore unable to open the world to human praxis or ensure the adequate realization of its end.[2] It follows that while relying on his limited autonomy alone and without assistance from a higher source, man can only determine some formal similarities between the realms of freedom and nature, while the problem of material reshaping remains unsolved.

The Practical Antinomy

This gives rise to the "antinomy of practical reason," which expresses the opposition between the consciousness of our duty to realize the highest good and the awareness of our inability to show that and how this realization is possible. Men find out that "a final end within that is set before them as a duty, and a nature without that has no final end, although in it the former end has to be actualized, are in open contradiction" $(C_3,$ V:458/II:129).[3] A duty implies the possibility of fulfilling it, but in the case of the highest good this possibility is not guaranteed. While Kant ascribes this state of affairs at times to a lack in nature and at times to a lack in man,[4] the latter is the crucial point; for in the

---

[2] This may suggest the failure of theory, since one purpose of knowledge is to make moral use of experience (cf. C_1, A 816/B 844). (I am using "theory" or "theoretical" in the Kantian sense, which is very close to "cognition" and "cognitive.")

[3] The practical antinomy is expressed here more precisely than in the chapter so entitled in the second *Critique* (V:113-114/117-118). There, the careless formulation of the antinomy gives the impression that it is construed as follows: thesis—"happiness cannot constitute the cause of virtue"; antithesis—"virtue cannot constitute the cause of happiness." But as L. W. Beck has shown in his *Commentary on Kant's Critique of Practical Reason* (Chicago, 1960), 247, this is not an antinomy at all. The two propositions are not contradictory; they do not stem from a "necessity of reason"; and the problem is not resolved by their simultaneous acceptance or rejection. The real antinomy which Kant has in mind, however, is this: thesis—"the highest good is not possible, since we do not see how either of its heterogeneous constituents can cause, or be synthetized with, the other"; antithesis—"the highest good is possible, since it is a duty and duty implies possibility." What seems to be the whole antinomy is only the proof of the thesis in the actual antinomy.

[4] From man's standpoint, Kant represents this failure either as a flaw in knowledge (our inability to foresee the results) or as a flaw in

last analysis, all the varieties come back to the limitations of human reason. If we do not discover a factor in nature that guarantees the possibility of its moral reshaping, it is because we ourselves, who determine the structure of nature, but do so from a dualistic and finite position, cannot legitimately assert the existence of such a factor. On the other hand, we find in ourselves the duty to realize the final end; and the resulting tension cannot be resolved except by postulating indirectly what one cannot determine directly. The practical antinomy, then, comes from the same source that gave rise to the speculative antinomies, namely the demand of reason to transcend the legitimate limits of its knowledge; and one can already see that the solution of this antinomy—the postulate of God's existence—will have no other function than to help man to overcome his limitation and subordinate nature to his human ends.

The Two-Stage Argument for God's Existence

As a limited rational being, man is unable to regard the highest good as possible. Consequently, since duty presupposes ability, the imperative to realize the highest good would become "fantastic, directed to empty, imaginary ends, and consequently inherently false" ($C2$, V:114/118). Yet this imperative is no less valid than the basic categorical imperative: it is also a *fact* of moral consciousness, and it, too, may be used as a *ratio cognoscendi* for the acquisition of further knowledge. Just as the categorical imperative indicates the existence of freedom, namely of the capacity to fulfill it, so the imperative to realize the highest good indicates that it *is* possible through our action. But since we do not see what within our own resources can explain or

---

the power of action (our use of particular laws of nature for our purposes), or again as a speculative limitation (our inability to establish a link between the kingdoms of nature and of morals; $C2$, V:114/118). But the postulate of God's existence is primarily connected with the third which includes the first two.

guarantee this possibility, Kant draws the conclusion that we must see it is guaranteed by some transcendent power. If the possibility lies neither in nature nor in reason alone, it is justifiable to postulate as their common origin a third power, beyond and above man, that embraces both and establishes a basic affinity between them. This power is conceived as the primordial unity of all those dualities which fall within the human sphere, such as spontaneity *versus* receptivity or the practical *versus* the theoretical; and as such it constitutes the metaphysical ground for the possibility—that must be there—of bringing morality and nature together and of realizing the highest good.

It is important to note that this procedure of postulation consists of two distinct stages. At the initial stage, which alone has logical necessity,[5] all that we postulate is a vague and indefinite principle: *"something* that contains the ground of the possibility and practical reality, or practicability, of a necessary moral final end" (*C3*, V:457/II:127; Kant's italics). Of this something we know nothing, except that it is there, and that it fulfills the function described. Kant even adds that from a purely objective or logical point of view, it makes no difference how we represent this factor to ourselves; he makes it "subject to our own choice" (*C2*, V:145-146/151; also *C3*, Pars. 87, 88, 89). But here our subjective limitations come into play, forcing us to *imagine* this factor with the aid of metaphoric, anthropomorphic imagery and by way of analogy with our human faculties.

[5] I say "logical necessity" only to differentiate it from natural or empirical necessity; but it is clearly a special and unusual kind of logical necessity. Taking its departure from the analysis of normative concepts, the logical procedure in question arrives at conclusions concerning the actual *structure of the world*. This method which, indeed, claims for its conclusions not the status of scientific judgements but only that of rational moral postulates—is based on the principle of the primacy of pure practical reason. Although I regard this principle as unacceptable, I shall not criticize it here, since my present aim is to show that this method, for all its faults, is designed to demonstrate the existence not of some overwhelming superior being, but only of the ontological possibility of a strictly human goal. (For my criticism of the primacy principle, see Epilogue, pp. 287-298.)

In this way we draw a "second inference" (*C3*, V:455/II: 125),[6] whose nature is psychological rather than logical, and regard that "something" as a supreme personal being, endowed with understanding and will, who is the "moral author of the world," that is, as God.

The Speculative Background of the Postulate

A combination of several texts[7] furnishes a good idea of the speculative scheme to which the human mind is driven, according to Kant, in this "second inference." It can be summarized as follows: God is represented as an archetypal intellect (*intellectus archetypus*), that is, as the union of "intellectual intuition" with a self-particularizing "holy will," whose thinking, intuiting and willing are one, and at the same time his creativity. This creativity constitutes the inward object of God and, at the same time, "the supersensible substratum" of our own world; it is the *original* highest good, or the *natura archetypa*, whose copy has to be produced in the human world as a "*derived* highest good" or as a *natura ectypa*. The archetypal nature, however, is not only the model that man has to copy but also the origin or the point of unity from which our faculties emanate, and as such the guarantee of human capacity to succeed in the

---

6 Meredith translated this as "a further inference"; but Kant says very clearly: "ein zweiter Schluss," which should be rendered as "a second inference." This is not a mere nuance. "Further" may create the impression of one continuous argument, whose parts have the same nature and logical validity. But it is a major point of this chapter that Kant's postulate must be analyzed in *two different stages*, of which only the first (which attributes to the world a principle of moral finality) is regarded as logically valid and as having "objective reality from a practical viewpoint"; the second stage, which goes on to imagine a personified God as the author of this finality, is merely subjective and psychological, even from a "practical viewpoint."

7 Especially *C3*, the discussions of the archetypal intellect, the supersensible substratum of creation and the moral proof of God's existence (Pars. 76, 57, 77, 78, 82, 87). Cf. also the discussions of intuitive intellect in *C1* and in the *Dissertatio* of 1770, the discussion of the *natura archetypa* in *C2*, 44 and in *Lose Blätter* 5.612, and numerous references in passing.

act of copying. For if, beyond the position of duality or dualities in which we find ourselves, there is a *single* principle for all possible modes of legislation and of content-particularization, then the encounter between the rational and the empirical and between reality and the *sollen* is no longer contingent, and their virtual unification has found a metaphysical ground.

It should be noted that this heavily laden scheme, influenced by the terminology and by the ideas of the school metaphysics and also by the writings of Leibniz,[8] is not confined by Kant to his doctrine of the deity. In a less elaborate form it had already appeared in the groundwork for the critical philosophy, Kant's Latin *Dissertatio* of 1770, and from that time it figures permanently in the background of all the parts of his growing system. But within the context of the highest good, this scheme appears in subordination to the primacy of pure practical reason,[9] and

[8] Kant was open to several suggestions from the Leibnizian school, especially to those discussions of the relations between God's faculties and the world, between God and His "inner object," between possibility and necessity in God, etc. It might be added that the highest good, too, is described by Kant in Leibnizian terminology—as the best world, as a harmony of nature and morality (nature and grace), as a system that combines the mechanical with the (morally) teleological outlook, and so on. The most important difference is that in Kant, Leibniz's idea is historicized: the harmonious, best world does not actually exist as the product of divine goodness, but should be realized progressively by human praxis.

[9] The principle of the primacy of pure practical reason states that, within the *total* context of human activities, the theoretical interest is subordinate to the practical and subject to its demands. As long as theory (or art) is taken in isolation, each should be governed only by its own immanent criteria. But when each is considered in relation to praxis, it becomes subordinate to higher criteria. These criteria justify the assertion of propositions which transcend the limits of the theoretical domains under the following conditions: (a) they fulfil a "pure need" of reason; (b) they are taken not as scientific judgements but only as "postulates" which make the realization of morality possible. In this way Kant frees human knowledge from the authority of the church, the state and other external interests, only to subordinate it to a higher rational interest, which is that of morality. Reason as a whole remains autonomous, but its two major expressions are hierarchically ordered. This, as Kant says, "is the only case where my interest

as such it acquires a new status. In the groundwork for the critical system it was only a negative representation, the background against which our *limitation* is determined. In the teleological discussions of the third *Critique*, the speculative scheme was further assigned the positive though nonconstitutive role of directing our *reflection* on nature. Now, however, it is actually given a *constitutive* function, as an element that contributes to our *action* on nature. To be sure, even now there are several reservations to make concerning this set of representations. For one thing, we do not really *know* it, but (according to the famous Kantian distinction) only *think* it, and that in subordination to a context of moral action. Also, the representations that it contains (like understanding, will, omnipresence, intentional creativity, common origin, and so on) are explicitly declared to be merely subjective symbols and extrapolated analogies with the human mind, and as such have no objective import. Finally, the idea retains a regulative value in relation to the historical enterprise which it serves to guarantee, but whose climax is perpetually postponed to infinity. But there is nonetheless one *decisive* respect in which the idea now "becomes also constitutive, in other words . . . practically determinant" (*C3*, V:457/II:128), and this refers to "our own selves and our will" (*C3*, V:457/II:127, a few lines earlier): on grounds of the postulate we confirm that we are able to endow nature with moral meanings, and that the duty to do so is, therefore, accompanied by a real possibility.

The Objective Kernel of the Postulate

"In this manner . . . the moral law leads to religion" (*C2*, V:129/134; *Rel.*, VI:6/5); but, in spite of the traditional

---

inevitably determines my judgement" (*C2*, V:143/149) but he does not consider this a kind of rationalization or mere ideology, since we have to do with "one and the same reason" (*ibid.*, 121/125), whose inner and genuine structure is expressed by the doctrine of the primacy of pure practical reason.

terminology of the discussion, the "God" here attained has no theological meaning. He is neither the author of moral precepts nor an object of love, of awe, or of any religious experience. He cannot intervene in nature or break its laws, nor does He have any value superior to that of an individual man or to that of historical humanity. God is a "moral author of the world" whom neither the world nor morality needs in itself, and both speculative and practical reason cannot, and should not, presuppose. He, or rather, it, is only a set of speculative representations, by which we add a semi-theoretical "explanation" to the statement, "it is in our power," which previously we have derived from moral concepts alone. The first and absolute point is the duty to realize the highest good, from which one may validly infer the ability to do so: this, and only this, is the objective kernel of the Kantian postulate. But, since the postulate already expresses a theoretical judgement, Kant thinks that it should be supplemented by an independent theoretical account, which will start from the fact of ability and refer it to certain preceding speculative principles (the "common origin") that are supposed to explain it. This leads him to present as the origin of our faculties a Supreme Being, endowed with analogous faculties and uniting in itself all those cognitive and practical elements that for us, as limited beings, are split into dualities.

This scheme is not really an explanation. Kant himself stresses its purely subjective nature, although he presents it as "inevitable." The problem, however, is that he attempts at the same time to give a systematic import to what was initially only a psychological necessity, by fitting it (not with complete success) into the "architectonic" model of the antinomies of reason, and by presenting it as a condition for the solution of the practical antinomy. This solution, which is also modelled on the familiar pattern of the theoretical antinomies, consists in accepting both the thesis and the antithesis as true, while distinguishing between a transcendent and an immanent sphere of applicability. The thesis states, in essence, that "the highest good is possible through human action, since it is our duty to realize it," and it is true in every case. The antithesis, which counters that "according to the nature of *our faculties of knowledge* we are unable to conceive of the highest good as possible," is also true so long as one observes the reservation expressed in its opening clause.[10] But by the speculative appendix of the postulate we get a new judgement that cancels the reservation mentioned, stating that, if we abandon the limited, immanent viewpoint, and refer the duality in our faculties to a common origin beyond them, then we shall be able to regard the highest good as possible. In that case, the heterogeneity of human faculties, and consequently of the realms of nature and morality that they constitute, will no longer be considered as an ultimate metaphysical datum, but only as the bifurcation of a more fundamental unity. Consequently, we shall be justified in assuming that in view of the primordial affinity of the diverging elements, they can be virtually reunited in a single moral world. This change of viewpoint, justified in concrete moral situations by the primacy of practical reason, is the only meaning of the representation of God in this context; and it is noteworthy that no direct influence upon nature or history, such as miracles or providence, is ascribed to Him. The only change is that *human powers* are now conceived as richer and greater than they were before the postulation of the common origin.

In this light one can also understand the sense of the assertion that God is "a moral author of the world," or "the ultimate cause of nature and morality" (*C2*, 125, 145/129, 151; *C3*, Pars. 88, 90, 91). Kant does not mean that God is the direct author of the world, or that he interferes with its orders, or, again, that he imposes the decrees of morality upon Man: such a view, to his mind, would spell the doom

10 It might be observed that the antinomy is not really contradictory even in this form, since the antithesis is not the negation of the thesis but only a suspension of judgement with regard to its content.

of practical and theoretical philosophy alike (*C1*, A 4/B 8; *Prol.*, §44; *Rel.*, VI:121/111). But while human autonomy suffices for determining the systems of nature and of morality separately, for the purpose of their *unification* it must postulate a "divine assistance," namely the archetypal origin of human faculties.[11]

Man, Not God, as the Historical Agent

At this point we should consider the argument of those interpreters who maintain that the antinomy has not been solved even after the postulation, since the capacity to realize the highest good was ascribed to God alone, while the human duty to do so remains meaningless.[12] Our analysis makes clear that this does not reflect Kant's way of thought with its explicit though problematical distinction between the source that establishes or ensures the capacity on the one hand, and the agent who has this capacity, as well as the duty, on the other. In God, he maintains, lies the ontological ground (*Grund*) of harmonizing nature and morality; but, once this ground has been established, the harmonization itself will be brought about "through the application of our powers" (*C3*, V:450/II:118).[13] What God

[11] As a matter of fact, human autonomy needs assistance even to determine nature, for a synthesis of heterogeneous elements is involved here, too. But, since no moral interest is concerned, the success of the cognitive synthesis cannot be attributed to any transcendent source, and it thus remains a "happy chance."

[12] Cf. Beck, *A Commentary*, 244-245.

[13] Cf. Par. 88 of the third *Critique*: the possibility of the final end is postulated "for the direction of our energies towards [its] realization" (V:455/II:124). Also, the highest good is "practical for us, i.e., one which is to be made real by *our* will" (*C2*, V:113/117; italics added). Again: "moral teleology is thus of immanent use only; it enables us to fulfil our vocation in this present world" (*C1*, A 819/B 847). In the *Religion* Kant denounces those who rely solely on divine assistance as showing "*a slavish cast of mind*" (VI:184/173; italics added), and again makes similar points in 51-52/47; 53/48-49; 57/50; 132/123; 139/130. The passages in which he repeats that the highest good is the content of human duty are innumerable.

guarantees is not the realization of the highest good but only its ontological possibility; and this guarantee, moreover, is furnished not by special action on God's part, but by his very existence. Since there is a God (and thus, a "supersensible substratum" of the whole of creation), the synthesis of the highest good is possible. But the realization of this possibility, its translation from potentiality into actuality, is the duty of man and not the action of God. At most, God helps us to help ourselves. The solution that Kant suggests to the antinomy is to be found in the ability not of God but of man, although man's ability presupposes the existence of God and cannot be deduced from his own immanent characteristics.

Promotion vs. Full Realization

On the other hand, the fact that man's primacy as a historical agent cannot be determined without a transcendent support is a sign of man's limitation and the reason why the *full* realization of the historical ideal always remains at an infinite remove. From the strict point of view of criticism we must assert a radical split between the given and the *a priori* elements of our theoretical and practical experience, as well as between the various *a priori* modes of legislation, the cognitive and the moral. The postulate of God's existence suspends these critical assumptions, assuring us that, ultimately, all the heterogeneous elements have a common source and a basic affinity, and hence they can be virtually reunited by our work. But even as—and precisely because—their common source lies beyond our constitutive knowledge, so their virtual reunion, too, must have a trancendent feature, by always lying in advance of our concrete historical situations. For having recourse to a transcendent principle man thus pays with postponement of the desired realization to infinity; and the human enterprise remains in the intermediate sphere of approximation and progress. Accordingly, both the duty and the ability ascribed to man refer not to total realization of the highest good, but only to its promotion or approach (*Annäherung*)—a term that Kant takes care to use in most of the relevant contexts. On several occasions, when he stresses the difference between promotion and realization, Kant assumes a certain residue that cannot be taken care of by man alone, but must be referred to the mystery of a "divine action."[14] This surplus indicates the gap between any achieved stage and infinity, and as such it is a necessary part of the view under consideration. Since there must always be such a gap, there will always be a surplus of *abstract* possibility, which will remain a *mere* possibility forever and therefore does not constitute a part of human duty. But gradual realization, at any stage, is a real possibility and a duty imposed upon man; and only after we make our utmost contribution to the *promotion* of the highest good are we entitled to hope for its total realization. The divine sanction thus seems to be assigned a further function: besides ensuring human ability of partial realization, it also provides the grounds for the agent's hope of a future completion. Yet both these modes of divine assistance serve to sanction and encourage *human* activity.

It should be recalled that Kant regards the idea of direct intervention by God in nature as the "*salto mortale* of human reason" (*Rel.*, VI:121/111). His references in our context to "divine assistance" and "providence" should therefore be understood as mere figures of speech. In fact, Kant says that one does not know whence the hoped-for completion will come, and that the whole matter remains "an abyss of mystery": not only is it unclear *what exactly* God will do, but even "whether [He will do] *anything at all*";[15]

[14] The particular content of this surplus varies with the context. Sometimes it is absolute personal perfection, sometimes atonement or grace, sometimes the completion of the system of rewards of the ethical community, and so on. All these are partial aspects of the highest good, but the point applies to the highest good as a whole too.

[15] Greene and Hudson translated this as "anything in general," but the German *überhaupt* is better rendered here by "at all."

and "meanwhile man knows . . . *nothing but what he must himself do* in order to be worthy of that supplement, unknown, or at least incomprehensible, to him" (*Rel.*, VI:139/130; second italics added).

The last points may be illustrated by another quotation from the *Religion*, dealing with the ethical community:

> To found a moral people of God is therefore a task whose *consummation* can be looked for not from men but only from God Himself. Yet man is not entitled on this account to be idle in his business and to let providence rule, as though each could apply himself exclusively to his own private moral affairs and relinquish to a higher wisdom all the affairs of the human race (as regards its moral destiny). Rather *must man proceed as though everything depended upon him*; only on this condition dare he hope that higher wisdom will grant the completion of his well-intentioned endeavors (*Rel.*, VI:100-101/92; italics added).

The Change in the Object of Hope

The quoted statements reflect also the changes in Kant's later writings concerning the nature of the highest good and the answer to the two fundamental questions, "What ought I to do?" and "What may I hope for?" In the view of the first two *Critiques*, man had to be concerned with his personal moral perfection, through which he became worthy of happiness, and (postulating the existence of God) rationally justified in his hope of attaining it. Whereas now it is said that he should extend the dominion of morality over his whole race and over nature in general, thereby becoming worthy of, and rationally-justified in hoping for, *the success and the completion of his endeavors*. Duty is no longer restricted to the cultivation of one's moral personality but is extended to the promotion of a moral world, while hope refers no longer to personal happiness, but to the *com-*

plete realization of this moral world. These changes greatly reduce the eudaemonistic element that characterized Kant's early doctrine of the Deity, shifting the axis of his mature doctrine from the problem of personal reward to the problem of the concrete outcome of moral action.

Human Action and Divine "Assistance"

The systematic position of the divine guarantee can now be summarized. Kant conceives of it as a kind of metaphysical potentiality, as a ground for possible development, and not as actual reality. As such, *it establishes the potential existence of a moral world order, and the power of man to translate it gradually into actuality.* Man is both the author of the supreme laws which govern nature and morality separately, and the active, historical being that promotes their union. To fulfil the first two functions we do not need God and may not presuppose Him. To fulfil the third, however, we must and may postulate a "divine assistance," both as the source of our ability to promote the highest good, and as the (unknown) ground of our hope that it will be completely actualized.

Kant's doctrine of the Deity thus serves not to belittle the image of man in comparison with some Supreme Being, but rather to exalt him in his own eyes by attributing to him powers of cosmic creation and shaping. In this it completes and enriches the idea of the "Copernican revolution" that lies at the basis of Kant's philosophy, as well as his concept of human freedom, itself an extension of that revolution.[16] For human spontaneity is now conceived not only as freedom *from* the processes of the world, not even as the ability of occasional interference in them, but also as a creative power in respect to their morally defined *totality.*

The preceding discussion also makes clear that within the Kantian system the concept of God occupies a position anal-

16 See Chapter Three.

99

ogous to that of schematism in its various forms. Both are intended to overcome, even if from opposite directions, the duality of the spontaneous and the receptive elements of the world that man constitutes and works upon, and to make possible their encounter. The schematism (in the broad sense, which includes the typic and other bridging factors)[17] is supposed to do this *post factum*, presupposing the fact of duality and seeking a *tertium comparationis* to mediate between them. This *tertium*, although it originates in spontaneity itself, makes possible only an *external* synthesis, namely a mere *combination*, in which the ingredients preserve their mutual heterogeneity and do not penetrate or imply one another. Since there is no principle as ground even for the possibility of that external correspondence, its occurrence remains utterly fortuitous and—as Kant calls it—"a happy chance." On the other hand, the concept of God is supposed to indicate a common source underlying these factors, and thus to set the possibility of their harmonization upon a *fundamental* ground. It, too, affords only a coordinated action of inherently heterogeneous systems and not an internal synthesis; but at least it implies that this coordination, if it should occur, would not be merely accidental but would have a metaphysical ground and explanation.

In this respect, Kant's doctrine of the Deity carries on the tradition of making God the mediating term between the fundamental dualities in reality. No less than the God of Descartes, of Geulincx, or of Leibniz, the God of Kant, too, is a systematical device and a *deus ex machina*; and considering his "postulated" status he is even more that. And yet, besides his role as "the God of the philosophers" (to use Pascal's term), the Kantian God is supposed *also* to play a role in respect to the feeling and the assurance of the individual. The importance of this role is accentuated by expressing it in the form of a special "proof of God's exist-

[17] For a detailed survey of other problems of schematization, see R. Daval, *La Métaphysique de Kant* (Paris, 1951).

ence," or more precisely, as a special ground for postulating that existence.

The Anthropological Argument for God's Existence

Thus far, the "proof" of God's existence (that is, the justification of the postulate) has been based on the argument that duty presupposes ability. But ability has for Kant a second sense, concerning not only the *execution* of the end but also the *intention* to do so; and he thinks that without an assurance of our ability to execute the duty, we shall be unable even to will it. This gives rise to a somewhat more complex argument for God's existence, which gives systematic import to some special features of human nature and may, therefore, be named anthropological. The crux of this argument is that the power of execution is not only a logical condition of duty, but also a psychological condition of the "inner act" of intention. In the previous analysis we saw that the *concept of* duty cannot be reconciled with empty goals, and now it is added that the human mind, too, is incapable of aspiring to them. Thus the existence of God, which guarantees the possibility of execution, is here postulated primarily to make possible the very intention.

Futility and Productivity

In a rough and distorted form, this particular argument has already appeared in the "Methodology" of the first *Critique* (A 812-813/B 840-841). A corrected formulation recurs in a central chapter of the second *Critique* (V:143/148) and in several passages of the third (Pars. 86, 87, 88); but its clearest and mature expression is offered in the beginning of the *Religion* (VI:4-6/4-6).[18] Here Kant maintains that man is

---

18 This is partly because when writing the *Religion* Kant had already made the shift in the meaning of hope and the empirical component of the highest good: it is no longer happiness alone, but the realization of morality and its adequate *Darstellung* in the empirical world. For a fuller discussion, see Chapter One, "The need for an end."

by nature incapable of intending to do what one may call Sisyphean deeds, but demands that his actions integrate in a productive and meaningful continuity or totalization within the concrete world.[19] His action must, therefore, be accompanied first by a *representation* of a final or total end, and, secondly, by the assurance that it can be realized. So long as he feels that his deeds are insignificant for the course of the world, he cannot find full satisfaction in his action, and this may become "a hindrance to moral decision" (*Rel.*, VI:5/5). Man knows, of course, that his moral deeds do contribute to the formation of his *inner* worth; but this cannot make up for the sense of emptiness and futility that the same deeds may invoke by their fruitlessness in the outside world. It is precisely this dual result that may intensify the consciousness of a barrier between the inner self and the world, suggesting to the potential agent that his moral efforts would accentuate, not diminish, his alien and impotent position. This, Kant holds, would produce an attitude of passivity and retreat, undermining the psychological possibility of intending to promote the highest good.[20] Yet,

[19] His meaning should be understood as follows: an imperative that commands a vain action cannot become a subjective motive. Although the individual would continue to acknowledge its validity, he would be powerless to decide to carry it out. The consciousness of duty would thus lose its motivational force, and "transcendental freedom" itself would be put in question.

[20] It may be noted here that the satisfaction to which Kant refers in this context is of a kind that can be reduced neither to the "empirical ego" nor to the "intelligible ego." On the one hand, it is not the satisfaction that comes from the fulfillment of inclination but of duty; on the other, it is not the pure satisfaction, respect, that derives from the autonomous act as such (*C2*, V:80-81/83-84), since the problem is presented precisely by the *inability* of the autonomous act as such to arouse the kind of satisfaction that Kant has in mind. What we have, then, is a third type of satisfaction, connected with the fulfilment of duty, though from the point of view not of the internal act but of the external results. To put it another way, this is a form of satisfaction which originates in the shaping and influencing of the real world, a pleasure in creation, as it were. In stressing the importance of this matter, Kant attains a deeper anthropological insight than that reflected in the theory of the categorical imperative, breaking through the

since the duty to do so remains, in his view, unshakeable, he concludes that there must be something in the structure of reality itself that can remove man's fear of barrenness and reassure him that there is a *well-founded* hope for the productivity of his endeavor. This "something," represented as "the existence of God" is thus postulated not only to sustain the logical meaning of duty, but also to enable the human mind to pursue its goals.

Possible Objections

Does not this amount to a projection of a lack, or still worse, to a philosophical self-deception? An unsympathetic critic, taking an extrinsic view, could raise these objections with justification. Even from a viewpoint that tries to get closer to Kant's terms without psychoanalyzing his philosophy, one must challenge the principle that for moral-practical purposes, legitimizes an inference that reasons from the sphere of *sollen* to the ultimate foundations of the sphere of *Sein*. Consequently, one may deny the alleged "objectivity" of the ensuing postulate—even in its basic and reduced form, as analyzed above—and say that, in effect, although not in theory, it resembles the "articles of faith" of a Spinoza, whose sole task is to mobilize man's mental powers in the service of a desirable practical end.[21] Yet all these objections are not specific to the "anthropological argument" alone: they apply equally to the conceptual argument that we have examined, as well as to *all* other forms of

---

limits of the simplified dualistic scheme on which he had modeled his division of human reality.

[21] At the same time, two obvious differences must be borne in mind. Whereas Spinoza regards the articles of faith as false (or as ambiguous statements that are, at least in their literal or *prima facie* sense, false), Kant presents them neither as true nor false but as undecided from a cognitive, viewpoint. According to Spinoza, the articles of faith are designed to make man *obey*, that is, to derive a pattern of conduct from imagination and fear that resembles the one that originates in freedom; for Kant, however, the postulates are designed to promote free and rational conduct *par excellence*.

postulation under the principle of the primacy of pure practical reason. On the other hand, if that principle is accepted for the sake of the analysis, then one has to agree with Kant that the anthropological argument is no less objective than the conceptual one, since it depends on it and is mediated by it. For the anthropological proof, too, is ultimately based on the principle that duty presupposes ability, but it extends the notion of ability to the mental sphere as well. Hence it has the same validity as the conceptual proof and cannot be regarded as a merely subjective projection.[22]

[22] The diverse elements of Kant's "moral argument" may be combined as follows:
Part I
1. It is our moral duty to promote the highest good in the world.
2. Fulfilment of this duty requires: (a) the psychological ability to intend to do it (to commit oneself to it) and (b) the practical ability actually to do it. Psychological ability presupposes faith in practical ability, and practical ability implies that the world is liable to respond to human action.
3. Where there is a moral duty, [there is rational justification for believing that] one has whatever ability is requisite for its fulfilment. Therefore, by (1), (2), and (3),
4. [there is rational justification for believing that] one has (a) the psychological ability to intend to promote the highest good (to commit oneself to it) and (b) the practical ability to actually do it.
Part II
5. But in what can be *known* about the world and about man, according to the critical philosophy, there is nothing that can explain the ability described in (2)(b) and (4)(b). Therefore,
6. the ability described in (2)(b) and (4)(b) must be regarded as grounded in "something" that transcends our *knowledge*.
Part III
7. Our subjective limitation forces us to imagine the "something" posited in (6) by human analogies, and to present it as an extramundane "moral author of the world."
8. Since this is the traditional idea of God, we thus postulate God's existence.
The purpose of this outline is neither to formalize Kant's argument nor to analyze its fallacies, but only to list the *diverse* elements in his postulation of God and to show how he correlates them. For further clarification, it may be noted:
(a) Proposition 1 serves as the absolute starting point of the whole discussion. To Kant, it represents a "fact" of moral consciousness, whose validity cannot be challenged by any posterior considera-

This special relation between the conceptual and the psychological consideration affords an important key to Kant's doctrine of the Deity. An essential feature of the doctrine is that it is meant to meet the demands of the individual consciousness not in an immediate or romantic way, but by the mediation of a rational argument. Closer consideration of this point calls for an analysis of its expression in three central themes of the doctrine of the Deity, namely, need, faith, and hope.

Need, Faith, and Hope

In a well-known and controversial passage of the second *Critique*,[23] Kant presents the postulates as objects of a "rational faith" that stems from a "need of pure reason." Rational faith satisfies this need of reason by confirming the possibility of the highest good.

Thomas Wizenmann objected that the existence of a need does not imply the existence of the object which satisfies it. To this Kant makes an obscure reply (*C2*, V:143n./149n.) which his critics find inadequate. I think that Kant's meaning will become clearer if one notices that he conceives the relation between need and faith in a *double* sense—psychological as well as logical—and that the first is mediated by the second.

In the logical sense, "a need of reason," is a metaphorical way of denoting a flaw or an inconsistency in a given system

---

tion. Whatever is found to be incompatible with this proposition should be appropriately modified.

(b) Proposition 3 represents the principle of postulation based upon the primacy of pure practical reason. The clause in square brackets indicates that we have to do not with ordinary knowledge but with "rational faith."

(c) In proposition 2, requirement (a) and its dependence upon requirement (b) represents the premises of the "anthropological argument."

(d) Kant himself assigns logical validity only to Parts I and II, Part III being a subjective surplus.

[23] "On Assent Arising from a Need of Pure Reason," *C2*, V:142-146/147-151.

of propositions. Since reason discovers in itself the practical antinomy, it has a need of the reconciling supplement that would eliminate the contradiction. This it finds in the postulate of God's existence, which becomes the object of the so-called rational faith. In this sense rational faith means not a merely psychological state of mind but a *logically grounded belief in a theoretical judgement, i.e. a kind of quasi-knowledge*. This particular judgement cannot appear in any theoretical *science*, since it does not cohere with other theoretical judgements, either in following from them or in helping to furnish grounds for them. Its sole validation being derived from moral concepts and precepts, it has no cognitive value and serves our action in the world rather than our comprehension of it. Yet this is still a judgement of a theoretical type (as is also stated in Kant's definition of a postulate; cf. *C2*, V:122/127), and therefore may be regarded as a special and subordinate piece of knowledge.[24] The term "faith" only serves to prevent the impression that this is an ordinary cognitive proposition; but it is far from denoting a subjective experience or a merely personal arbitrary conviction.

In a *psychological* sense, the need may be taken literally. It is the need of the individual consciousness, which relates both to one's overall world-picture and to the integration of one's particular actions in it. In the first place, man needs the assurance that the world itself is not altogether contingent but is a meaningful system or process. Secondly, he needs assurance that his own active life can contribute to the historical end, and that he may expect nature to be cooperative and responsive. Neither need is merely intellectual; both involve emotion and the inner life, which also explains their relevance to religion. Yet it is not by any inner experience that the needed assurance is attained but by a purely

24 Cf. "Is our *knowledge* really widened in such a way by pure practical reason . . . ? *Certainly*, but only from a practical point of view." And again: "There remains, then, a *knowledge* of God, but only in a practical context" (*C2*, V:133, 137/138, 142; italics added).

rational consideration. The point of departure is the *logical* need, from which one infers a factor that makes the highest good possible. This knowledge, in its turn, evokes a psychological response and thus satisfies the subjective aspirations as well; yet the foundation of the postulate lies not in man's aspiration for assurance but in the *systematical implications of the concept of duty*, namely, in the logical and not in the psychological need.

This may help us complete and reformulate Kant's answer to Wizenmann. It is certainly true that the existence of a subjective or merely psychological need does not imply that the object which would satisfy it exists. But the existence of God is inferred not from a psychological need but from a systematical (logical) one. The former is satisfied only indirectly, by the mediation of the latter, namely, by the fact that the legitimate satisfaction of the logical need produces an adequate repercussion in the subjective feeling of the individual.

This relation between rational statement and affective response, reminiscent of the notion of respect for the law (*C2*, V:80-81/83-84) underlies the doctrine of the postulates in general, and in particular accounts for the precise position occupied in it by the concepts of *hope* and of *faith*. As is well known, each of these concepts was presented by Kant as the central theme of the doctrine of the postulates. On one occasion, he states that the doctrine is concerned with the question, "What may I hope for?" (*C1*, A 805/B 833). On another, he says that he has "to deny knowledge in order to make room for faith" (*C1*, B xxx). This may give the impression that the notions of hope and faith compete, whereas in fact they complement one another to constitute a single matter. The faith in question is a piece of knowledge of a special type, common (at least in principle) to all rational beings, while hope (as *grounded* hope) is the emotional response that faith arouses in each individual. Faith and hope are thus interrelated and may be regarded as two facets of the same awareness. At the same time it should be stressed that this is a one-way relation, faith being prior to hope both logically and temporally.

Wild Hope and Justified Hope

The concept of hope requires further elucidation. As a matter of fact, one hopes in *any* event, even without presupposing the existence of God. By his very nature, the man who does right also hopes for the success of his intentions as well as for personal happiness. But this hope may be wild or well-founded. One may have, besides the hope itself, a good reason for expecting its fulfilment; or conversely, one may be aware that one's hope is almost or altogether absurd, having slight or no chances of being fulfilled. The faith in "God's existence" precludes the latter possibility. By attributing to the world and to human history an implicit principle of moral teleology (this is the precise and the only objective significance of the postulate), it also makes the individual feel that he "may" hope for the historical ideal, and that the multiplicity of his isolated acts has a sense and a direction. The exact function of the postulate in respect to hope is therefore not to arouse it, but to furnish it with a rational ground and thus prevent its absurdity.

By thus relating conceptual ground and psychological response, Kant tries to keep the notion of hope within the limits of rationalism. But the notion in itself tends to transcend such limits, and suggests an unintentional link between Kant and the later romantic movement. For hope is, so to speak, a subjective shortcut to an objectively absent object; it links one to the final goal not through the latter's actuality but through the representation of its possibility. Moreover, the Kantian hope provides this contact only while projecting the goal to infinity, and thus it is tied up with the awareness—which a romantic might stress as crucial—that at every moment the goal lies beyond one's reach, and only the *way* to the goal and the hope itself remain as concrete in one's life. Again, although hope also affords a

108

particular kind of satisfaction, this satisfaction stems from
the abstract possibility rather than the actualization of the
desired object, and thus paradoxically depends on its absence and perpetual pursuit. The Kantian hope can therefore be viewed as mediated by constant frustration, and this
ambivalent and infinite structure may create an opening
for romantic views. (Among other things, it may be argued
that an abstract possibility is in fact an *impossibility*, or else
that if the goal were attained, there would remain nothing
but emptiness and despair). To avoid such conclusions,
Kant denies hope any immediate or primary status, making
it a psychological corollary of a conceptual argument. But
it is doubtful whether a philosophy that stresses the infinite
character of hope and extends its range beyond that of actualization can be completely free of semi-romantic undertones.

The double nature of the Kantian God has now become
clear. On the one hand, as has been shown before, He is a
systematic device, designed to round out the system and
solve the problem of practical schematization: a *deus ex
machina* who plays, in form and content alike, the classical
role of the "God of the philosophers." At the same time,
God has also been shown to have a bearing on the subjective consciousness and assurance; and the point is that both
functions are interconnected. God is *also* meant to be the
"God of the individual," not directly but through the mediation of a systematic argument. Yet such a conceptual
apparatus—even if it were not further qualified as a "postulate"—is incapable of becoming a source of *religious* assurance; and we may add that *concealed behind the conventional religious terminology are the secular ideas of historical progress and of a moral finality in nature.* But to
analyze and describe the Kantian theory of the Deity adequately, one must see the double nature of God and rational faith, and the systematic as well as the affective role
which they are intended to play.

God and Internal Morality

So far we have considered the relation between the concept of God and the external manifestation of morality in nature and in history. The complementary problem, that of internal moral perfection and the attainment of virtue, is generally held to be correlated with another Kantian postulate, the immortality of the soul. This view is certainly supported by many central passages, especially in the second *Critique*. Yet it should be noted that, in the *Religion*, Kant extends the divine assistance to the attainment of internal perfection as well—both in its individual form as virtue, and in its collective form as the ethical community.

The Ethical Community

The ethical community is an elaboration of the idea of the kingdom of ends known from the *Foundations*. It corresponds to the political commonwealth, but differs from it as morality differs from legality. Whereas the political commonwealth relates to the empirical existence and the judicial persona of the citizens, the ethical community relates to their trans-empirical, moral, personality. In his political thought Kant adopted the ideas of the social contract and the state of nature,[25] and these he now transfers to the sphere of internal morality as well, speaking of an *"ethical* state of nature" and of an *"ethical* community" (*Rel.*, VI: 95-96/87-88; italics added). An ethical state of nature is characterized by mutual ill-will among men and by the dominion of social passions, which is the ethical counterpart of Hobbes's war of all against all. But this is no real, empirical war, and the social passions in question have no ordinary utilitarian character. It is rather a conflict between pure subjective consciousness, each of which refuses to recognize the other and seeks to subordinate it and eliminate its status. (In this Kant anticipated the Hegelian dialectic

[25] As an explanatory principle, not as a historical fact.

of master and slave.) The ethical state of nature is overcome
by the foundation of an ethical community, whose operative principle is the mutual recognition of all conscious-
nesses and the constant decision of ˉeach to regard all the
others as equal in status and as ends in themselves. The
creation of such a rational system may be seen as a collective
conversion, corresponding to the conversion or "revolution"
that takes place in the individual personality when it overcomes the "original evil" that it had chosen and adopts a
moral disposition (Rel., VI:47,72-75/43,66-69). Kant stresses
that the departure from the ethical state of nature depends
on the existence of a political community (a state), since it
is only after the *external* relations between men have been
put to some rational order that one may expect the more
difficult and more important step, namely the conversion of
their personal attitudes (Rel., VI:94/86).

To understand the part Kant assigns to God in relation
to the ethical community, we should distinguish in it the
three stages of *foundation, propagation,* and *completion.*
The important and only actual stage is the propagation and
enlargement of the ethical community. This, according to
Kant, is the concrete historical state of mankind, and in it,
as we have seen, it is man himself who has the duty to act,
while God's existence only guarantees his capacity to do so.
Education, enlightenment, moral religion are modes by
which this process is promoted. By contrast, at the two extreme states of foundation and completion God is, as it
were, assigned a more active role. Man alone cannot bring
about either the absolute beginning or the absolute end of
the process, and it is only here, in these *merely abstract*
situations, that one must assume some kind of superhuman
intervention. But we have seen that for Kant such intervention is an insoluble problem, which he accordingly leaves as
a residuum of impenetrable mystery. What God does, or
whether He does anything at all, has no philosophical import and remains unknown, while the sole function of the

idea of this mystery is to encourage human action in the *intermediate* stage, which is the concrete situation.[26]

Virtue and the Immortality of the Soul

In relation to *virtue*, the idea of God fulfils a similar regulative function. Here, too, it is supposed to offer spiritual support but no theoretical explanation, forcing the idea of mystery to extreme uses.

To attain moral perfection or virtue, one must first adopt a good ultimate disposition and then express it in all one's acts. But since man is finite and subjects to natural limitations, there is always a gap between the ultimate resolution and its expression in particular decisions, as well as between any such decision and its empirical manifestation in an act. The act, says Kant, "is *always* . . . defective"; "we must . . . regard the good as it appears in us, that is, in the guise of *an act*, as being *always* inadequate to the holy law" (*Rel.*, VI:67/60; Kant's italics). The reason for this is the ontological assumption that phenomenal externalization of an intelligible content is only an "appearance" that falls short of that content, or that there is a dichotomy between purity of the heart and concrete realization. To overcome the effects of passivity and discouragement that are likely to follow the awareness of this gap, one must postulate an intellectual intuition that can grasp the intelligible essence of one's moral personality without depending on its phenomenal manifestations, or, in Biblical terms, a God who "looketh on the heart." The thought of such a divine insight should reassure the moral agent who lapses into petty sins, and who is inextricably enmeshed in his phenomenal being, that there is a deeper point of view from which he may still be considered morally good, "notwithstanding his permanent deficiency" and "at whatever instant his existence be terminated" (*Rel.*, VI:67/61). The significant disregard of

---

[26] The other two may be seen as analytical categories rather than as concrete historical situations (like the state of nature in Kant's political theory).

the length of existence suggests that Kant *here renounces the postulate of the immortality of the soul*, which, as is known, was supposed to make the progress toward virtue possible, and transfers its functions likewise to the postulate of God's existence.

To sum up the shift: in both the second *Critique* and the *Religion*, Kant maintains that virtue is *not* a holy will but the perfection of a *finite* rational being, or "a moral disposition *in conflict*" (*C2*, V:84/87, italics added; cf. V:128/133). But in the second *Critique* he speaks of a disposition to be attained only at the abstract "end" of an asymptotic progress, whereas in the *Religion* the disposition appears at the very beginning of the moral progress, being the product of a one-time revolution; and the concrete moral problem is to narrow the gap between the global resolution and its particular expressions. Accordingly, the second *Critique* needs to postulate indefinite existence—or the immortality of the soul—in order to guarantee the possibility of an infinitely remote virtue, while the *Religion* transfers this guarantee to the existence of God, since the question is no longer how to achieve the ultimate moral disposition but how to bridge between it and its phenomenal manifestations.

Let us add that the postulate of the immortality of the soul should be renounced by Kant in *any* case. For if virtue is not a holy will but a good disposition in conflict—and the adversary in this conflict is always the natural inclinations—then the attainment of virtue would also require the immortality of the *body*, a strange Schellingian notion that could never have entered Kant's mind.

Grace as the Eradication of the Past

The same divine point of view is supposed to solve another problem. Every man, Kant believes, begins his life with a free disposition that is evil: this is an empirical dogma by which he replaces the theological dogma of original sin (*Rel.*, VI:32,50-51/27-28,46). Since every act has its own

113

good or evil value, a man who attains a good disposition during his lifetime still carries over a surplus of evil from his past and thus may despair of attaining complete perfection. What reason is there to strive in each and every case, when in any event life will culminate in a mixed result owing to the balance of the past? While Kant does not do justice to the depth of this problem, neither can he accept the conventional answer that repentance atones for past sins. According to him, whatever has been done pertains to me as such and cannot be erased.[27] The moral biography of a man is a series of self-contained acts, each of which has its own moral value and is incapable either of corrupting any other act or of atoning for it. Thus, the eradication of the past can only be postulated as a mystery of divine grace. Here, Kant makes a rather far-fetched use of the principle the primacy of pure practical reason, which justifies belief in whatever is needed for purposes of moral action; and at this point he seems to come closest to philosophical self-deception.

Duty As Such and its Particularization

Another, perhaps more important problem is this. The categorical imperative demands the fulfilment of duty *as such*. But this can be done only by means of *specific* duties. The content of a specific duty, cannot, however, be deduced from the concept of duty in general: like human understanding, human will is not self-specifying. Here, once more, there arises a problem of bridging the form and the content of duty, which can be resolved only by postulating a divine understanding *(intellectus archetypus)*. Even as the regulative idea permits us to assume that the specific laws of nature cohere in a single system, so the postulate of God's existence (the archetypal origin and point of view) is supposed to make sure that all particular acts of duty, with

27 A modern variation on this motif may be found in Sartre's concept of *facticité*.

their empirical, contingent content, interlock in a coherent intelligible world. This is one (though not the main) meaning of the Kantian definition of religion as "regarding all our duties as divine commands": we assume a transcendent point of view, from which the relation between form and content in our deeds is no longer accidental, and accordingly affirm that the occasion-dependent concretions of our pure will approximate the coherent system of a self-specifying divine will.

All the points that have been discussed in this part of the present chapter are distinguished by their relation to the question of *subjective encouragement* of action on the one hand, and by the obscurity of their systematic explanation on the other. It is not clear how one can possibly erase the sins of the past, the lapses of the present, or the externality of duty-contents, all of which are irreducible factors. And indeed, in at least two of these problems, Kant renounces a rational explanation, openly representing the matter as a "mystery."[28]

God, Man, and Nature

What is the fundamental problem which the concept of God is designed to solve, and why does it arise? In one sentence we may say that God is called upon to solve the difficulties that stem from the fact that the free activity of man is limited by receptive elements. The same "critical" principle of strict separation between thinking and intuition and between finite and infinite intellect, that led Kant

---

[28] Kant would, then, have been more consistent had he repeated what he had said earlier in the first *Critique* in this context, namely, that in this case our reason would have only "obscure" grounds of explanation, "of which it does not have any knowledge, and which are incapable of proof" (A 626/B 654). What was said there with reference to natural teleology should also apply to the moral or historical teleology under consideration. In both cases Kant presents the notion of God as having merely subjective significance.

to reject the claim of God's existence in his theoretical philosophy, produces all the problems that lead him to reintroduce this claim in the form of a postulate in the practical philosophy. For, despite the so-called Copernican revolution, the world is not a free creation of man. Its factual courses are determined by given, contingent elements, which the critical philosophy declared to be alien (heterogeneous) to human freedom. This, among other things, removes the results of our action beyond our control, explains why our intentions may get lost in the world confronting us, and in general casts doubt on human capacity to propagate and embody the moral idea, namely, to realize the goal of history. Consequently, Kant needs a further assumption that would attribute to *nature itself* a principle that makes it susceptible of moral development and reshaping. Why he considered it necessary to make this purely teleological principle depend on the existence of a God is another question, which remains to be examined. The present point, however, is that the very need of the postulate, be it represented as God or as something else, would not have arisen had the Kantian system not taken its departure from the rigorist separation of spontaneous form and receptive content.

God Subservient to Man

Our analysis has also made it plain that the Kantian doctrine of the Deity is subservient to a strictly *human* interest. The ultimate object of the system is not God but the highest good, grasped as the ideal of historical realization; the existence of God is only an auxiliary thesis that derives its meaning and its justification from the double role that it plays, enabling the maintenance of the doctrine of the highest good and encouraging those who act upon it. To put it more figuratively, God has been explicitly transformed into the assistant of man.

But here we have to ask: does God really assist in anything? Can the possibility of the highest good be guaranteed or accounted for by that supreme understanding and will of which Kant speaks only by way of analogy? The answer seems to be negative; and if we do not assign to it a restricted meaning that is teleological and not theological, immanent and not transcendent, we shall have to conclude that the postulate is superfluous.

God and Freedom

This objection is based mainly on the two-stage analysis of Kant's postulation as presented above; but before returning to it, let us first compare his method of justifying the postulate of God with his method of justifying the postulate of *freedom*. It has been argued that since the categorical imperative is a practical datum or a fact of moral consciousness, and since the concept of duty implies capability, man is *able* to act out of pure respect to the law without being coerced by nature. Thus the consciousness of the law served in Kant's words as a *ratio cognoscendi* of freedom ($C2$, V:31-32/31-33; 4n./5n.).

With one characteristic difference, the same method recurs in the demonstration of God's existence. This time, indeed, we are concerned with a broadening of human powers: not only with man's negative capability to avoid external determination of his will, nor even only with his positive power to produce a *particular* action in nature, but also with his ability to contribute to the systematic and complete reshaping of the world. Freedom is a minimal condition for the possibility of moral action, whereas the power now in question is a condition for the total realization of morality within a historical project. But precisely this difference accentuates the analogy between the two cases. In the present phase, duty demands that we do not rest within the sphere of personal virtue but help to create the highest good, and accordingly Kant concludes that man is not only free from natural coercion but is also capable of imprinting his moral schemes on the world as a whole.

117

The Indefinite Reference of God: Objective and Subjective Parts of the Postulate

At this point the analogy ends. With regard to freedom Kant finds it sufficient to assert its mere existence without seeking any further theoretical explanations. On the contrary, he explicitly represents freedom as an "inscrutable," ultimate fact (*Rel.*, VI:21,24,43/17-18,20,38;*C*2, V:72/75). In the case of historical ability, however, he is not content with the conclusion at which he has arrived out of an independent moral consideration, but tries to supplement it with a semi-theoretical stage. From the fact of the historical ability of man he goes on to "infer" the existence of a semi-personal God, endowed with something analogous to our will and understanding, whose internal object is the "supersensible substrate of creation," and who is supposed to include the ground for the virtual unity of all heterogeneous principles. This complicated apparatus is surely intended to fill a gap, that is, to prevent the assertion "we can" from appearing obscure and dogmatic. But in fact it explains nothing, and, moreover, remains unproved even in terms of Kant's own primacy principle; for the argument that "we can since we ought" *does not necessarily lead to it.* All that has been proved in terms of that principle is that there is "*something*" that contains the ground of the possibility" of realizing the final end (*C*3, V:457/II:127; Kant's italics). But the *transition from this "something" to the complex speculative image of God and His faculties is according to Kant himself only a subjective addition.* As a matter of principle, one could have pictured that factor in some other way, for instance, as a principle of *internal finality* that rules the universe. The fact that we represent it as the product of a God and project upon the latter some semi-anthropological attributes is inessential and depends on our subjective limitations. For the same reason, the concept of God cannot *explain* the origin of ability. The ability in question is a real ontological power, whereas God and His

118

attributes are merely modes of representation by which we picture the source of this ability to ourselves. But can a mere representation, an *ens rationis*, originate a real power? Can a non-entity produce an entity or guarantee its possibility? The answer is obviously no, both in Kantian terms and in terms of any other rationalistic metaphysics. The speculative apparatus of the doctrine of the Deity thus furnishes no explanation but only a subjective *decor*, and the source of human historical ability remains no less inscrutable than that of freedom.

God and Teleology

Let us look at a passage from the second *Critique*:

> The command to further the highest good is itself objectively grounded . . . . *But as to the manner in which this possibility is to be thought, reason cannot objectively decide whether it is by universal laws of nature without a wise Author presiding over nature or whether only on the assumption of such an Author.* Now a subjective condition of reason enters which is the only way in which it is theoretically possible for it to conceive of the exact harmony of the realm of nature with the realm of morals . . . . (*C2*, V:145/151; italics added).

Only this "subjective condition" leads us to accept the idea of a wise author; and Kant goes on to stress that from a purely objective viewpoint, "the manner in which we are to think [of the highest good] as possible is subject to our own choice" and is therefore "a voluntary decision" (*C2*, 145-146/151). Only this choice exists in principle alone, for in Kant's belief the human mind cannot avoid the *psychological* passage from a teleological pattern to an external wisdom:

> *The nature of our faculty of reason is such,* that without an Author and Governor of the world, who is also

a moral Lawgiver, we are wholly unable to render intelligible to ourselves the possibility of a finality related
to the moral law and its object, such as exists in this
final end (*C3*, V:455/II:25; italics added).

And again:

> But suppose teleology brought to the highest pitch of
> perfection, what would it all prove in the end? *Does it
> prove for example that such an intelligent Being really
> exists?* No: *it proves no more than this, that by the con-
> stitution of our cognitive faculties* . . . *we are absolutely
> incapable of forming any conception of the possibility
> of such a world unless we imagine a highest cause oper-
> ating designedly.* We are unable, therefore, objectively
> to substantiate the proposition: there is an intelligent
> original Being. On the contrary, we can only do so
> subjectively for the employment of our power of judge-
> ment in its reflection on the ends in nature . . . . (*C3*,
> V:399/II:52; italics added).

What Kant says here with reference to natural teleology
in general would apply equally to the *moral* finality of
nature, with which we are concerned. That man is always
driven to make a transition from teleological phenomena
to an external intellect that is supposed to have designed
and created them is a subjective process that does not establish the existence of such a creator, and is unjustifiable *even
in a moral context*. In the first *Critique* (A 620-630/B 648-
658), Kant describes this procedure as logically defective,
attributing it to a "natural necessity" of our reason, which
cannot rid itself of the analogy with works of art. And although he praises it as a noble fallacy (*ibid.*), and although
he tries in subsequent works to find new ways of introducing teleological principles into the critical system (as "reflective concepts" or as postulates), he never allows any
passage systematically beyond the teleological principles
themselves. He rather maintains his view that if natural
necessity drives one to take such a step, then one should

treat it in the same critical way reserved for other transcendent ideas, namely to become aware of its logical fallacious-
ness while doing it as a matter of natural inevitability. And
this applies no less to the passage from the objective postulate of the moral teleology of nature to the purely subjective notion of God.

What, then, remains as the objective content of the
postulate of God's existence once it is stripped of its subjective accidents? In one sentence we might say: the assertion that the given world is the highest good *in potentia*,
and that human praxis can make it so actually. This is a
teleological principle that completes and enriches the concept of freedom. For it affirms that in the world itself, with
all its given and factual constituents, there is something
which makes it susceptible of moral transformation in response to the free and intentional action of man, and that
we are therefore able to act fruitfully upon it. It also implies that human freedom is not altogether alien to nature,
and that history and the universe should be regarded not
as opaque and meaningless scenes but as having a definite
moral meaning and direction. To be sure, all these convictions are founded solely on the primacy of moral consciousness and have no cognitive support. In this, Kant may have
been overcome by a certain moralistic optimism (the world
must be structured in a way that would make moral action
possible), and one may perhaps question a procedure that
on Kant's own admission "is the only case where my [moral]
interest inevitably determines my judgement" (C_2, V:143/
149).[29] But it is still crucial to see that all the convictions
mentioned have no theological import. The postulate of
the existence of God tells nothing of God, only of man and
the world, and the Kantian theory of the Deity remains
strictly humanistic.

[29] For a more detailed discussion of this issue see the Epilogue, pp.
294-298.

PART II

The Vehicles of Progress

CHAPTER III

TELEOLOGY AND
THE CUNNING OF NATURE

So far I have reconstructed Kant's concept of history from his critical theory of the highest good and God. The reconstruction was based on Kant's *systematic* works (notably the three *Critiques* and the *Religion*), revealing the elements of an implicit critical philosophy of history. Before I turn to Kant's more marginal essays—which are explicitly devoted to history, and on which most existing accounts of Kant's view of history are based—let me recapitulate.

Despite the many interpretations given by Kant to the highest good, the most comprehensive and *only coherent* way of construing this concept is to see it as the regulative idea of history.[1] No other view makes sense of the moral duty: "Act to promote the highest good." Furthermore, when he speaks of history, Kant does not mean an independent, natural process which takes place automatically, without the participation of human consciousness and the rational will. He is talking specifically about *rational* history, which grows out of men's conscious intentions to change and reshape the world in accordance with a moral ideal and to contribute to the realization of this ideal as a whole.

Analyzing Kant's concept of God and the method of practical postulation, which is supposed to justify its use, I claimed that, since the affirmation of the existence of God is made possible in the system only as a necessary presupposition for the possible realization of the highest good, the

---

[1] Using "idea" in the technical sense of a pure rational concept, serving as a principle of *totalization*.

concept of God depends for its significance on the theoretical context provided by the concept of the highest good. In other words, the essential meaning of the highest good determines the essential meaning or role of the concept of God. If the highest good means the ideal of conscious rational history, then the existence of God means that there is some ontological ground that guarantees man's capacity to produce rational history. It ensures that the activity of individuals will not necessarily be wasted in an indifferent and alien natural world, but that it can combine with other activities to constitute a meaningful process, advancing towards the *conscious* realization of the goal of history. Furthermore, I showed that this is all the objective significance which Kant gives the concept of God. As a postulate of practical philosophy, the statement, "God exists," is equivalent to the statement that "there must necessarily be *something* (in the structure of the world or of man) that makes the realization of the highest good through human activity possible." This is the *whole* objective significance of this postulate. To the additional question, "*What* is this something?", or "How are we to conceive of a teleological principle that makes the historical totalization of all our rational actions possible?", the philosopher can give no answer, even in the form of a postulate. This is where *the objective range of the method of postulates ends*. It is true that man, with his limited understanding, must take an additional step, and picture this teleological "something" as produced by a God who possesses infinite understanding and will. Yet this is merely an analogy possessing only subjective necessity and deriving from our psychological limitations. It has no objective philosophical justification *even in terms of the logic of the postulates*.

From my reconstruction three things follow. First, the goal of history is not merely political in Kant. Although it has a legal or institutional facet as well, its core is in the intersubjective moral system, which has to spread and embrace the whole human race. Second, transforming the world in light of the highest good is itself a moral duty and thus involves the conscious action of the rational will. Third, understood in terms of the highest good, the idea of history is not only compatible with the critical system but actually central to it as the supreme end of reason that gives it systematic or architectonic unity.[2]

However, Kant's more peripheral but more explicit essays on history seem to suggest a different picture. These essays— mainly the *Idea for a Universal History*, the *Conjectural Beginning of Human History*, and the second appendix to *Perpetual Peace*—tend to reduce history at large to *political* history. They also attribute historical progress to a hidden purposive scheme working *unconsciously* in nature through violence and strife; and by affirming the existence of such a natural teleology, they seem to transgress the boundaries of critical reason and commit a "dogmatic" fallacy.

Since these essays, if taken in isolation, seem to confront my thesis with counter-evidence, I shall have to re-examine them later in some detail. My interest will focus mainly on their *systematic status*, but for the sake of completeness, their basic content must also be expounded. To avoid misunderstanding I should point out at the outset that I do not at all discount the value of these peripheral essays, which Kant wrote at the same time as his systematic works; I cannot dismiss them (as Ruyssen and others did) as merely occasional reflections, simple adjuncts that lie completely beyond Kant's system. I think it is both necessary and possible to reintegrate Kant's philosophy of history into his critical system. But in order to do so, one must first reconstruct the foundations of Kant's philosophy of history from his *systematic* work (as Chapters One and Two attempted to do), and then appraise the lesser essays upon this background. In addition, before discussing these texts specifi-

2 See Chapter Six.

cally, I must consider the broader question of *teleology*, since it supplies the conceptual framework for Kant's historical essays as well.

The Problem of Teleology

 The concept of historical progress in Kant is an aspect of teleology, a problem occupying his thinking since his precritical days. He solved it only with the *Critique of Judgement* and the notion of a moral teleology of the universe, the highest good. Despite the systematic gap between Kant's philosophical periods (and the fact that he characterized his later system as a "revolution"), there are more fundamental continuities between them than is generally supposed. Perhaps the most important of these links is the theme of teleology. The young Kant was struck by the manifestations of teleology in the empirical world, a world he had learned to interpret in simple mechanistic terms, and this intuition was never to leave him. In his critical period it became a systematic challenge that, after several twists and partial solutions, gave birth to the *Critique of Judgement*. Kant was an astronomer and a geographer as well as a philosopher; his empirical investigations thus relate to the *extension* of the world, both of the earth and of the universe at large. What fascinated him as a geographer was the amazing way in which human beings spread to every corner of the earth, differentiating themselves into many peoples and languages, and miraculously adapting themselves to the most extraordinary ecological conditions —an adaptation that presupposes not only man's faculties but a certain responsiveness or even cooperation of nature itself. Almost every book by Kant refers to this phenomenon, either in passing or at length, sometimes with a plethora of examples. Kant considers this a sign of a hidden teleology governing man's life and his history upon the earth; and although he may seem to subscribe thereby to a medieval or Aristotelian tradition, in fact his teleological interests have completely modern sources, following the Renaissance and Enlightenment; for they no longer focus on the permanent structure of animal species or the cycles of the seasons, but on *the changing and developing character of man himself*, his daring conquests of nature and the revolutionary discoveries he makes throughout the world. The discovery of new continents and virgin lands, of new pathways on land and sea, of remote cultures and their relation to their natural environment—this is the main empirical source of Kant's teleological intuition. Kant contemplates the hidden purposiveness of the world no longer as a biologist, like Aristotle, but as a geographer and anthropologist; his teleological intuition is not expressed in terms of the circular repetition of the medieval world, but in terms of the leap forward, of development and change, that originated in the world of the Renaissance.

The Experience of Infinitude in the Cosmos

In Kant's astronomy, too, we see a thrust towards expansion, towards breaking the confines of the closed universe in favor of one open to infinity. This is the broader spiritual implication even of the famous astronomical theory, the Kant-Laplace hypothesis, that Kant had formulated early in his career in the *Universal Natural History*. The impetus toward an infinite universe was later held in check by critical reason, when the first antinomy denounced as meaningless ascribing to the cosmos either infinity or finitude in space and time. And yet, when Kant declares at the end of the second *Critique* that the starry heavens above him, and the moral law within, fill him with "ever new and increasing admiration and awe" it is again the open universe of his youth that speaks through these famous words. The admiration is for the *infinity* that seems to be implied in the cosmological object; it resembles the experience of the sublime that Kant was to analyze in the *Critique of Judgement*. Man is facing the open heavens, with their remote and immense galaxies, and is filled with awe in front of the infinitude he attributes to the object of his contemplation.[3] Kant's wonder is somewhat different in kind from that of Pascal, who exclaimed: "The eternal silence of these infinite spaces frightens me."[4] The mental effect of the infinite is described by Kant not as fright but as awe, admiration, and once even as esthetic pleasure. But fundamentally, both philosophers share a common characteristic, which may be called existential, even in Kant; for their experience is not merely related to theoretical questions in knowledge or esthetics, but involves the individual's *fundamental experience of existence* and the image it contains of his place in the universe and his relation to the infinite. By contemplating the infinity of the external object, Pascal apprehends his paltry position: and the discovery of his *finitude* becomes for him a source of anguish. Kant, too, begins by attributing infinity to the external object and finitude to the contemplating subject; but this is not his last word on the matter. On the contrary, further reflection reveals that the experience of the sublime is based on a *distorted* self-consciousness that must be corrected by a philosophical analysis of this experience, involving a Copernican reversal. We have here, indeed, a fundamental question that haunted Kant almost from the first, penetrating the very foundations of his system. Can man's apparent finitude, of which he becomes so dramatically aware when facing the infinite world of astronomy, be overcome? Is man condemned to being merely finite (as Pascal and Kierkegaard were to believe), or does he possess within him a principle of infinity greater than the cosmos itself? Having pondered on

---

[3] In his early essay on astronomy *Universal Natural History and the Theory of Heavens* (I:306/135), Kant writes: "The universe, by its immeasurable greatness and the infinite variety and beauty that shines from it on all sides, fills us with silent wonder." He later distinguishes between the wonder of imagination and the "rapture" of understanding when confronting the order of law that prevails in this immense cosmos.

[4] Pascal, *Meditations*, Par. 206 (see also Pars. 72, 205, 207).

this question at great length, Kant finally gave it a systematic answer in the third *Critique*, in the doctrine of moral-historical purposiveness and in the analysis of the sublime.

This analysis reveals that the experience of sublimity involves a form of false self-consciousness. The infinity belonging to me, as a being endowed with moral capacity and destiny, I project upon the external object, and then I belittle myself in awe before this object. The experience of the sublime—as its analysis discloses—should have led to the opposite self-image, for it is based upon man's own moral infinity, which rebounds and is reflected in the object before him. "The starry heavens above me and the moral law within me" fill me with awe, not each independently of the other but *each by virtue of the other*. Our sense of sublimity when facing the cosmos, with its alleged infinity of power and magnitude, is in fact mediated by a latent consciousness of man's own infinite destiny in the cosmos, realizing the highest good; but we tend to miss the true object of this experience, and instead of identifying it with the moral-historical ideal that lies within our power, and by virtue of which we are superior to nature with all its infinitude, we imagine it as an alien physical object that opposes us.[5]

From this point of view, Kant's analysis of the sublime represents in microcosm his whole Copernican revolution, which also is an attempt to reverse man's false self-image and set it aright. People assume that objectivity belongs to things in themselves; but the Copernican revolution shows it is their own subjectivity that constitutes objects as such. People assume that norms and moral commands are given to them from without, independently of their will; but Kant's analysis shows that all value-status derives from man's own legislation as a rational will. The Copernican

[5] Indeed, oppresses us. Kant's analysis of the sublime contains the basic elements of the notions of false self-consciousness and alienation, as developed later in Hegel, Feuerbach, and Marx.

revolution in all fields of philosophy may thus be seen as extending the basic model implicit in the analysis of the sublime.

This is also a link between the cosmological problem and the problem of teleology. By the Copernican revolution, Kant restores man to a central position in the universe, not in a physical sense, but by virtue of his transcendental or constitutive function. I am not just a finite and bewildered part of a strange cosmos, because the objects of the cosmos itself are determined in accordance with the laws of my consciousness. If the original Copernican revolution relegated man to the fringes of the universe, making such experiences as Pascal's possible, Kant's new revolution restores man's central status by making the objective world itself depend upon the universal forms of his thought.

But this in itself is not sufficient, for the problem of man's position in the universe is not only theoretical. Man's preeminence is based not just on his constitutive powers but primarily on his role as the *generator of morality*; and this raises the question of man's *moral* position in the universe. When observing the world around him, can he identify the marks of his moral decrees in the objective world, the way he can identify the structure of his cognitive reason embodied in objects? This link between morality and man's cosmic position occurs even as early as the *Universal Natural History,* where he discusses the respective moral position of man in relation to other "rational creatures" in the universe. But Kant's more systematic problem is the one we indicated above. The cosmos is a purely mechanistic system, subject to universal causality.[6] But man discovers in himself another rational system—moral intentions and goals— to him more essential, although he cannot recognize its imprints in the mechanical environment around him; and

[6] *UNH* is specifically devoted to showing this point, using Newtonian mechanics as the sufficient and unique explanation of the most remote cosmic phenomena.

from this additional perspective as well he may feel estranged within the universe.

Overcoming the Alienness of the Cosmos: Kant and Leibniz

Kant thus faces the problem of the alienness of nature.[7] The conquest of nature by man—a modern slogan that originated in the spirit of the Renaissance—has not merely a technological or ecological meaning for Kant, but a metaphysical one. How can we overcome the *metaphysical* strangeness of the cosmos, so that we may eventually discover the imprints of our moral reason and human ends within the cosmic order? Prior to Kant, Leibniz was concerned with a similar problem. He tried to establish a reciprocal relation between the "kingdom of nature" and "the kingdom of grace," so that the mechanistic explanation of the world and its moral-teleological explanation would complement one another. It should be recognized that Leibniz' reversion to the old concept of teleology was not a reaction against the modern world-picture nor an anachronistic attempt to abolish it. On the contrary, it was deeply rooted within the modern world-picture itself. Having accepted without qualification the validity of the mechanistic explanation of the new science, Leibniz was faced with the modern experience, well described by Whitehead, that threatens to turn the cosmos into a place of exile for man, an alien system in which he cannot recognize himself. Leibniz tried to overcome this typically modern problem by reverting to the classical world-picture which was essentially static. Arguing that a complete explanation of the cosmos requires using final causes no less than mechanical laws, Leibniz tried to make it possible for man to rediscover himself and his ends in a universe that the natural sciences had made to appear alien. However—and this is an essential dif-

7 See Chapter One, note 66.

ference between Leibniz and Kant—Leibniz does this ahistorically, by relying on the idea of a *preestablished* harmony. The causal and the teleological systems complement each other eternally, by virtue of the original constitution of the universe. The only task left to man is to discover this preordained harmony and contemplate it. It is not by his praxis that the harmony will be produced, and in this respect he has no role as a historical agent, only as an admiring observer. The world with both its systems is eternal, finished, and closed upon itself.[8]

It might be said, then, that Leibniz tried to solve a modern problem with classical means. After natural science had discovered the mechanical structure of the world, and after the danger of estrangement had appeared, Leibniz showed that the ends of reason also belonged to the structure and explanation of the world, by virtue of the preestablished harmony of the two systems. Kant, however, takes a different line. *Man's task is not to disclose a harmony which is preestablished but to produce it.* Man is the being who must *impose* the system of rational ends upon the causal system of nature. His metaphysical problem thus becomes a problem of praxis.[9]

[8] Cf. his dictum: "If we could sufficiently understand the order of the universe, we should find that it is impossible to make it better than it is" (*The Monadology*, tr. by R. Latta (Oxford, 1898), Par. 90; italics added). It is true that Leibniz introduced a perspective of "perpetual progress to new perfections" (*Principles of Nature and of Grace*, the concluding sentence): but this applies only to personal biography, not to the universe in general. On the other hand, Leibniz also supplied Kant with some of the key notions of the theory of the highest good, as when he spoke of a "moral world within the natural world" (*Monadology*, Par. 86) or of the harmony "between the physical realm of nature and the moral realm of grace" (*ibid.*, Par. 87). But this conceptual apparatus is *historicized* in Kant.

[9] This change appears with the critical conception of man. In his early book on astronomy, Kant is still enmeshed in the Leibnizian conception: "Thus everything is co-dependent on the whole extension of nature, in a continuous series of degrees, according to eternal harmony." (*UNH*, I:365). These degrees apply to all rational beings populating the planets in the cosmos and to their degree of morality. Are the inhabitants of other planets more moral than we, asks Kant, by

History and the Copernican Revol

In Kant's critical period, this task becomes
cal project. But the seeds of this view of hist
present in his earlier Leibnizian position.
with its infinite number of worlds, is actually finite anu
limited. But man, who is a limited rational being, is infinite
by virtue of his moral destiny. He has a power that transcends nature itself and may subject it to his will. Kant
makes this idea of subduing nature and reshaping it in
accordance with human reason the principle of critical history.

The natural, cosmological world follows pure mechanistic
laws and has, as such, no teleological significance. Only human reason and praxis can endow it with ends. Man discovers in himself not only an understanding that can know
nature, but also a moral reason that demands that its aims
be realized in nature and the world be reshaped according
to its laws. Moral or teleological reason thus is now understood as the principle of *will*. The end of the world lies in
something beyond itself, in something it has yet to become,
and the power which has to transform it is the human will,
functioning as practical reason.

Clearly this turning point would have been impossible
without the Copernican revolution. Kant's critical system
introduces two novel ideas that seem at first to work in
opposite directions. The first is that we may not use teleological categories when explaining natural phenomena.
The world should not be understood, by an analogy to human creativity, as the product of a transcendent author

---

their basic disposition? Is their rung on the ladder of virtue above or
below ours? Kant says that this question borders on far-fetched imagination; but the need to raise it testifies to a permanent philosophical
interest in Kant, which later finds expression in the theory of the
highest good and history. Man's destiny in the cosmos and his preeminence over the natural systems which confront him in all their
power and infinitude, lies in his ability to produce something which
transcends itself.

THE VEHICLES OF PROGRESS

who has planted his purposes in it. The critique of reason requires that we avoid transcendent explanations, making do with the immanent categories of the world of experience; and these permit only mechanical laws and causal explanations, and exclude teleological principles in physics, psychology, and anthropology alike.

But the Copernican revolution also brings about another change, which we have already intimated. Indirectly *it creates a radically new picture of man's place and role in the universe.* Man is no longer a member among other members in nature. Rather, by virtue of his rational consciousness, he now becomes the focal point of nature itself. As an active being, endowed with *constitutive* reason, man's activity is not only physical, embodied in a chain of events within nature, but also metaphysical; for it makes nature itself possible by imparting a logical structure to it. Human reason thus becomes a world-shaping power.

But here a distinction must be made between constitution and agency. The determinative spontaneity of human reason is expressed primarily by Kant's theory of objectivity, i.e., in terms of his cognitive philosophy. Instead of merely copying a given world order, human reason now constitutes it. But this theoretical constitution does not yet involve an actual transformation of the world. The activity of theoretical reason does not change a given world into another world, because there is no objective world given as yet. It is therefore *spontaneity without praxis.* Man is, indeed, playing an active rather than a passive role with respect to the natural objects; but his activity is that of constituting, not of changing and reshaping.

Had the Copernican revolution been confined to the theoretical sphere, there would have been no place in it for history. One would then be right to take it only as a reinterpretation of such ontological terms as objectivity, empirical existence, and the like. But Kant extends the fundamental principles of the Copernican revolution to the sphere of rational action as well; and what is more, he does so *as an*

136

inner development of his philosophical program, arising from the limitations of theoretical reason. Those fundamental interests of transcendent metaphysics that cannot be satisfied validly by means of knowledge, yet are to Kant essentially rational, can find a legitimate mode of expression in the field of praxis.

As a principle of action, reason again faces nature as something externally given, upon which it must now impose new types of order, reflecting man's moral goals and interests. At this stage, the question is no longer whether things exist in themselves, but whether, in their *constituted* mode of being, they also embody the ends of practical reason and can reflect man's rational image. Is nature *initially* shaped in a way that manifests the ends, values, and interests of man so that he can fully realize himself as a rational being in and through nature?

The Historical Imperative

Kant's negative answer opens up the way for a critical philosophy of history. Because our reason is finite, the object—nature—is alien to us even after the work of theoretical reason has been completed. Objective nature, as constituted by the transcendental ego, does not and cannot embody any goals. It has neither an immanent nor a transcendent end; it merely confronts us as something factual, obeying its own mechanical laws. Moreover, we see that the ethical ends of reason, which alone can provide the universe with a rational goal and justification, are not initially manifest in the objective world and do not even receive from nature sufficient support for their realization. In Kant's words, "there is a great gulf fixed . . . between the realm of the natural concept and the realm of freedom" (*C3*, V: 175-176/I:14). Yet it is an "essential end of reason" to bridge this gap and to imprint its own ends upon the natural world. Thus, *what is not given initially has to be created by rational praxis*. It is not an ontological fact, but a historical *task*, in which human spontaneity finds a more elaborate field for its world-shaping function. Envisaging the systems of nature and morality as moments of an ideal totality, human action, taken collectively or historically, is now to reshape the actual world in light of the ethical idea and thus gradually to bridge the "great gulf" between the two realms.

As Chapter One has shown, this interest of reason assumes the form of a specific imperative, to promote the highest good in the world, that may therefore be called "the historical imperative." As a rational task, history cannot be left to automatic natural processes. It is basically a moral affair, not only in its ideal outcome, but equally in *its mode of progress*. The historical imperative prescribes a *totalizing* mode of moral action, one which sets the moral progress of the world, not just of the particular individual, as its objective. It requires the gradual transformation of nature into a system that embodies the practical ends of reason and assists in their further realization.

This signifies that empirical nature and its objective laws should be used as the material ground or substratum for creating a new world within the given world. Needless to say, by the realm of nature Kant means only those natural factors that are relevant to human life and action. These include, in the first place, social and anthropological structures, psychological dispositions, and given political institutions; but, through them, Kant also has in mind the physical world upon which all human life is based. History in the proper sense is the moral reshaping of nature; but the basic historical activity lies in culture, or what we would call today civilization, which is the shaping of nature in view of human goals and interests *in general*. This includes the development of natural substances, the use of tools, cultivation of land, adaptation to climate, and transformation of ecological conditions. In addition, physical nature is morally shaped in the form of *property*, whereby natural objects enter the context of social relations and juridical institutions.

138

In these and similar ways, physical nature is made a moment in a higher synthesis, a "new world," that is in fact the world of culture and history, produced by the human will in its confrontation with raw nature. At the same time, the will is equally confronted with its own inner nature—man's feelings, instincts, habituations, dispositions toward other men, etc.—and also with the social institutions and norms it produced in the past. All these empirical factors play their role in producing the historical world, which as such has still to be *moralized*. The overall task set by Kant's practical philosophy is to remold historical nature in the light of the moral idea, so that it will become a copy or an embodiment of this idea. And this, as we saw, is at once the regulative idea of history and the "final end of creation itself."

How should we describe more closely the nature of this end?

The complete goal of history consists in Kant of a *dual* system; it has an internal (moral) and an external (legal) side that complement each other. The first is an intersubjective system of *attiudes* that embraces, ideally, the whole human race. Each member in this "invisible" system[10] recognizes the equal status of all other members as free subjects or ends in themselves and is constantly disposed to act from this recognition. The external system objectifies the pattern of morality within the empirical world. It includes a free civil constitution, rational jurisprudence, and a world confederation that ensures permanent peace; and it presupposes the right and use of property and a developed technological civilization. (As such it is also supposed to contribute to universal happiness or welfare). Although the external system is desirable in itself as the embodiment of morality in objective institutions, it is only secondary to the moral system, from which its value derives. In addition, progress in the field of politics and civilization is a precondition for the growth and propagation of the ethical com-

[10] Also referred to as "the ethical community," "the kingdom of ends," the "invisible Church," and "kingdom of God on earth."

munity, which is the crux of the whole development and the true meaning of "moral history."

The Cunning of Nature as a Rival Principle of Progress

These two complementary facets of the final end are mirrored in Kant's two seemingly rival answers to the question, *What guarantees the possibility of historical progress?* Their difference lies mainly in whether or not historical progress is conceived of as an object of *duty*. In the previous chapter we analyzed Kant's postulate of "God's existence" as his major answer to this question. By analysis it is obvious that this answer can apply only to conscious rational acts that are performed as explicit moral duties. Yet Kant's works also provide a rival answer based upon the dialectic of blind natural forces. It is that man's instincts, his antisocial inclinations, and especially his disposition to violence and to war ultimately cancel themselves and lead to the actualization of a rational political system. The character of this thesis has rightly earned it the title "the cunning of nature," and I, too, will adopt it.[11]

The dogmatic[12] sound of this thesis has led many critics to dismiss Kant's total philosophy of history as incompatible with his system. I have already argued that Kant's "official" essays on history are less important for understanding his view on history than his systematic works. Now, with particular reference to the cunning of nature, I intend to argue

[11] The expression "the cunning of nature," is intentionally reminiscent of Hegel's "cunning of reason" (*List der Vernunft*), but for Hegel reason is immersed in the empirical world and in human instincts and representations, so that it is an active dialectical factor working towards its own self-realization by means of its opposite. But for Kant there is a radical division between reason and nature; dialectical "cunning" must therefore be attributed to nature itself. The term "the cunning of nature" is used by Eric Weil in *Problèmes kantiens* (Paris, 1963).

[12] I use "dogmatic" in the Kantian sense, as the opposite of "critical."

that it *complements* rather than excludes the other principle, which puts forth history as a conscious rational project.
More specifically (a) the cunning of nature is only a vehicle of *political* progress and of the rise of external "civilization," not of history in the moral sense; (b) ever since the
Enlightenment—with philosophers (i.e., Kant) deciphering a "hidden plan of nature" corresponding to the ideal
of practical reason, the cunning of nature is no longer an
exclusive vehicle of progress even in politics, but makes way
to the complementary principle of conscious praxis; and (c)
as for the dogmatic character of the thesis, it obtains only in
the context of the *Idea*; but ever since its reappearance in
the *Critique of Judgement* (Par. 83), the thesis acquires the
status of a *reflective judgement*, and is thus re-integrated
into the critical system. Moreover, in the *Critique of Judgement* the cunning of nature is no longer applied to history
at large, as in the *Idea*, but only to "culture," now recognized as the external facet of history. Thus, although the
content of the thesis remains basically the same throughout
its variations, its systematic status changes radically.

History as a Totality

The title of the essay *Idea for a Universal History From a
Cosmopolitan Point of View* already hints at its intention.
The term "universal history" indicates that the subject-mat-
ter is not the history of some particular field or people, but
what was later to be called *Weltgeschichte*, i.e., the totality
of human actions and products, taken as a whole.[13] In order
to totalize the object of inquiry, we must look for the dynamic structure or pattern that underlies it and makes it
intelligible *as* a totality. This search is certainly carried out
from a certain perspective, but as the term "cosmopolitan
point of view" and the context of the essay make clear, the

[13] This is also indicated by the term "idea," which in Kant's systematic works indicates a rational concept that functions as a *principle
of totalization*.

perspective for totalizing history is taken from the immanent goal of the process itself, not from an extraneous or
arbitrary interest of the particular observer.
As for the term "history" (Geschichte), it has two alternat-
ing meanings in this text. On the one hand, Kant defines it
as the story (Erzählung) of empirical phenomena born of
man's will and actions but interconnected in accordance
with the laws of nature. On the other hand, he treats history as the process of what is told in the story, the process in
which the human species actualizes its hidden potential and
develops its reason and its freedom. The relationship between both meanings of the term "history" is such that if
we discover the teleological structure that governs the process, it becomes possible to recount the events of history and
perhaps even predict them and control them in advance
from the inherent standpoint of the process itself. Doing
this will yield *philosophical* and not empirical history, because selection and arrangement of the events will be governed by a principle that is not accidental but belongs to
the nature of reason itself, and whose traces can actually be
detected in the empirical matter. (In this sense Kant anticipates Hegel's idea of a philosophical world history, just as
at the end of the first *Critique* he anticipates Hegel's program of writing a philosophical history of philosophy.)[14]

Chaos, Freedom, and Unconscious Plan

Observing history, the philosopher is struck by a dual
characteristic. As *limited* rational beings, men do not act
from mere instinct like animals, nor do they follow a common rational plan. Human history cannot be represented
in the manner of a society of ants or bees. But the chaos
that seems at first to prevail in history is a sign of men's
peculiar advantage, his being endowed with freedom and
reason. This distinctly human feature expresses itself, however, primarily in wickedness, egoism and antisocial behav-

[14] See Chapter Six.

ior. Kant surveys the scene of history and utters the traditional complaint:

> One cannot suppress a certain indignation when one sees men's actions on the great world-stage and finds, beside the wisdom that appears here and there among individuals, everything in the large woven together from folly, childish vanity, even from childish malice and destructiveness (*Idea*, VIII:17-18/12).

The semblance of chaos and the reality of wickedness present the philosopher with a problem. How can we totalize history significantly if no common rational intention can be ascribed to its agents? Kant answers by relegating the totalizing principle from reason back to nature, i.e., from men's conscious design to a blind natural teleology:

> Since the philosopher cannot presuppose any [conscious] individual purpose among men in their great drama, there is no other expedient for him except to try to see if he can discover a *natural* purpose in this idiotic course of things human. In keeping with this purpose, it might be possible to have a history with a definite natural plan for creatures who have no plan of their own (*ibid.*).

On his admission, Kant resorts to this "expedient" because he has no alternative. Reviewing the past history of mankind, there seems to be a rational pattern without a rational intention, and so this pattern must be ascribed to the blind work of nature alone. But it may be noticed that this expedient forces itself only with respect to *past* history, the only one we can review. There is nothing in Kant's words to exclude the possibility that at a certain point in history, a *conscious a priori* plan of reason would emerge. As we shall see, this turning point occurs with the Enlightenment and with the full explication of reason's inherent designs in Kant's own *Critiques*. Henceforth, men would be able to promote history, even political history, from a common rational goal;[15] but since not all of them will choose to share it, the cunning of nature will keep its role as a vehicle of progress, although no longer the sole vehicle.

Man's Finitude and Historicality

Before turning to the exact mechanism of the cunning of nature, attention should be paid to the basic terms of human historicality, as laid down by theses 2 and 3. Having stated in thesis 2 that the actual subject of the history of reason is not the individual but the human race collectively, Kant adds:

> Nature has willed that man shall, by himself, produce everything that goes beyond the mechanical ordering of his animal existence, and that he should partake of no other happiness or perfection than that which he himself, independently of instinct, has created by his own reason (VII:8/13).

Theses 2 and 3 combined define man's historicality as a sign of his finitude. Although history is marked by progress, the very need for progress indicates that history represents man's limitations no less than his capacities. Essentially, *man is condemned to be a historical being.* There is no shortcut to a full rational life, neither for the individual nor for the species as a whole. The individual depends upon the species and cannot leap like the ancient sage to rational perfection by himself;[16] and the species cannot arrive directly at the perfect social order that is the precondition for a full maturation of its faculties. As a *limited* rational being, man must rather develop his faculties step by step out of himself, through the trial, error, and suffering of generations, expecting no *deus ex machina* miracles or divine redemption; and whatever welfare or social improvement

15 This is partly hinted in the *Idea* itself (Thesis 9).
16 See also *Education*, IX:445/9-10.

the human race may attain, must be the product of its own creative exertion in an arduous historical course.

If history appears to man as a fate, this is because it is part of his *ontological* condition. Man is not an infinite but a finite rational being; he is not an *intellectus archetypus*, in which no gap exists between possibilty and actuality; and therefore he must suffer a long historical process before his freedom can fully realize itself and overcome the opposition of nature. At the same time history also presents man with the perspective of self-transcendence, in which the natural forces themselves are directed to their dialectical self-overcoming.

This conception imputes a certain injustice to history; for only subsequent generations will profit from the "toilsome labor" of their predecessors (*ibid.*, 20/14). If the ancient prophets complained of the injustice in "fathers have eaten sour grapes and the children's teeth are set at edge,"[17] Kant faces in "puzzlement" the reverse injustice implied in man's historicality. But he has no systematic means for solving this puzzle (which must remain another facet of human finitude).

It is true that Kant conceives of history in terms of the species as if it were an organic individuum, developing itself and enjoying its own products. Yet there is no legitimate way for Kant to *personify* the historical human collectivity and assign to it a single consciousness and responsibility. This is why unlike Hegel, who has the concept of Spirit as a historical individual, Kant cannot present the deciphering of the meaning of history as a form of rational theodicy.[18]

---

[17] Ez. 18:2; Jer. 31:29.

[18] At the end of *Conj. Beg.* he seems to do so, declaring that knowledge of the secret plan of history will lead to "contentment . . . with the course of human affairs, taken as a whole" (VIII:123/68). This is, however, a purely contemplative solution: although I do not share the rational system myself, I am content with knowing it is about to come. But Kant offers in the same essay another, more interesting answer: justification of the individual's existence lies not in knowledge of the course of history, but in *action*, by which man "*gives* value to life"

From the viewpoint of the actual individual, thrust into history at an age that limits his powers, history must appear a contingent fate even if he discovers its hidden rational pattern. For him, living only once, it is purely fortuitous that he happens to be bound by an inferior culture; and the fact that he may contribute to the advance of future generations, although supplying him with an ideal, cannot fully justify history for him, since existentially he remains severed from the outcome and thus from the actual totality.

Conflict As the Motivating Power in History

The work of the cunning of nature is first described in the fourth thesis, whose text is fairly self-explanatory and may be quoted at some length:

> The means employed by nature to bring about the development of all the capacities of men is their *antagonism* in society, so far as this is, in the end, the cause of a lawful order among men (VIII:20/15).

Having stressed "antagonism" in the original, Kant explains:

> By "antagonism" I mean the unsocial sociability [*ungesellige Geselligkeit*] of men, i.e., their propensity to enter into society, bound together with a mutual opposition which constantly threatens to break up the society. Man has an inclination to associate with others [*Vergesellschaften*], because in society he feels himself to be more than a man, i.e. [he feels] as more than the developed form of his natural capacities.[19] But he also has a

---

(*ibid.*, 122/68); it is not the contemplation of history but its actual *creation in praxis* where finite rational beings should look for their metaphysical satisfaction.

[19] "Weil er in einem solchen Zustande sich mehr als Mensch d.i. die Entwicklung seiner Naturanlagen, fühlt." Kant is not saying that man becomes more than man through society (by itself), but rather that

strong propensity to isolate himself from others, because he finds in himself at the same time the social characteristics of wishing to have everything according to his own wish. Thus he expects opposition on all sides because, in knowing himself, he knows that he on his part is inclined to oppose others. This opposition it is which awakens all his powers, brings him to conquer his inclination to laziness and, propelled by vainglory, lust for power, and avarice, to achieve a rank among his fellows whom he cannot *tolerate* but from whom he cannot *withdraw*. Thus are taken the first true steps from barbarism to culture, which consists in the social worth of man; thence gradually develop all talents, and taste is refined; through continued *enlightenment* the beginnings are laid for a (new) way of thought [*Verwandeln*], which can in time convert the coarse, natural disposition for moral discrimination into definite practical principles, and thereby change a society of men driven together by their natural feelings into a moral whole (italics added).

Kant adds:

Without those in themselves unamiable characteristics of unsociability from whence opposition springs—characteristics each man must find in his own selfish pretensions—all talents would remain hidden. . . . Men, good-natured as the sheep they herd, would hardly reach a higher worth than their beasts. . . . Thanks be to Nature, then, for the incompatibility [*Unvertragsamkeit*], for heartless competitive vanity, for the insatiable desire to possess and to rule! Without them, all the excellent natural capacities of humanity would forever sleep, undeveloped (VIII: 20-21 / 15-16).

---

within society he feels more than an ordinary, given man, that is, he can feel the *development* of the talents nature has given him.

These passages speak for themselves in a clear and strong language. But some comment is needed with respect to the foundations of Kant's social philosophy, as they emerge here.

The Conflict of Wills Is Not Merely Utilitarian

What invites attention is Kant's attitude to the social contract theory. Kant uses, indeed, the language of a "state of law" established by "contract." He has read Hobbes, and Locke, and has been influenced by Rousseau. But Kant does not see the foundation of political life in the wish to regulate physical needs or promote utilitarian interests. Men do not live in states in order to protect their lives, divide labor, ensure property, or pursue happiness. The foundation of the state lies in man's "unsociable sociability," that is, in a certain propensity toward others that inheres in his very nature as a rational being. Man senses that only in relating to others within a state will he be able to assert his free subjectivity and realize in himself something that transcends raw nature; he is attracted to social life not to ensure his *natural* survival but to satisfy his *consciousness* or ego. As a free subject man needs the confrontation with another free subjectivity, from which he will secure recognition and esteem, whom he will rival, and whom he might also recognize eventually as his equal. Similarly, the hostility he feels initially to his fellow men and his inability to "tolerate" them arise not from any threat to his life but from the danger they pose to his *will*. As an ego-centered principle of will, I, like every other man, want everything to be run according to my subjective wishes; but the other denies the centrality of my will and tries to force his will on me. As long as each will operates in a merely *particular* mode, unmediated by a universal principle, a general conflict of wills is inevitable. This conflict is not utilitarian. It does not occur because men have conflicting material interests (although it may assume this shape), but fundamentally be-

148

cause they are subjects endowed with consciousness and will, each trying to subject the other to his own will. This *pure assertion of self* is the actual meaning of the concept of "selfishness";[20] and it is characteristic that Kant presents the pursuit of fame, prestige and power as more powerful agents in the creation of social life than the sheer impulse for survival or for "lazy" material satisfaction.[21] Rather than the *natural* inclination to survive and promote happiness, we have here an inclination that *surpasses* nature, the inclination to power and to impose one's personal will and consciousness upon the social system.[22]

This conception recurs in Kant's essay on "Radical Evil,"[23] which further elaborates the concept of unsocial sociability without naming it as such. Anticipating Hegel's master-slave dialectic, Kant connects the very "predisposition to humanity" in man with his inclination "to acquire worth in the opinion of others," itself the expression of his desire for recognized equality. From here the various "vices of culture" arise—vanity, rivalry, jealousy, spitefulness, etc. —which are distinctly *human* and differ radically from our "beastly" vices. Inasmuch as human beings possess consciousness, they have genuine social dispositions, irreducible

[20] See also the discussion of egoism in *Anthropologie in pragmatischer Hinsicht* (Bk. I, Pars. 1 and 2; VII:127-128). Selfishness stems from man's advantage over things and beasts, his having self-consciousness or ego. "From the day man began to speak by way of I, he produced his beloved Self wherever he only could and egoism stepped forth unhindered: if not overtly (for here it was opposed by the egoism of the other) then disguised, assuming the appearance of self-denial and modesty, *in order to gain even more securely superior worth in the judgement of the other"* (italics added). Here the idea is the same, but the conflict of wills takes a more sophisticated shape, anticipating Nietzsche's analysis of self-denial as disguised will to power.

[21] Even in avarice we should not understand the love for material goods per se, but the assertion of the particular will, in the mode of "mine," in their possession.

[22] In Hegel this was expressly brought out as a will to endanger one's life for the sake of satisfying one's will for recognition and power; but the same idea is already inherent in Kant, including his theory of war.

[23] Later included in the *Religion* (Book One).

to natural desires. Man is jealous of others or wishes them evil because on the one hand he needs their presence on the horizon of his world, yet on the other hand he needs them as partners in conflict, over whom he must prevail and against whom he must assert his ego and will. I perceive the other as a subject, not as a mere object in the world; and it is precisely because he is subject and *as a subject* that I want to subdue him to my will, treating him as a mere instrument for the accomplishment of my aspiration. This aspect of radical evil, also called the *ethical* state of nature,[24] is among other things constitutive of communal life and the political state itself; and as such it is genuinely human, irreducible to the natural interests of survival and happiness. And similarly, when Kant says in the *Idea* that man can neither *tolerate* the other nor *withdraw* from him, he is referring to the threat proceeding from the other, not to my existence but to my ego.

We should add that Kant's use of the social contract language is analytical, not historical. The transition from the state of nature to the state of law is, systematically speaking, a kind of pre-history.[25] It is not an event that occurred in time but a fundamental condition of humanity, explaining the grounds of social life along all recorded history, including the present.[26] History proper begins with man as a social being, already within a political context, and its goal is to transform political life from inside. Since all individuals want to impose their particular will on the others, they stand in conflict even within the state of law; the outcome of this conflict is the victory of the strong, institutionalized in the legal framework of the state. All historical constitutions were to some extent despotic, since they were based

24 A term paraphrasing but opposing Hobbes's *material* conflict in his state of nature.

25 In this respect it resembles in status the analysis in *Conj. Beg.* (see end of Chapter Four: "The Pre-History of Reason").

26 In *TP* Kant says the original contract need not be taken as "a fact" but "merely an idea of reason" with normative implications (VIII:297/79).

on the principle of the particular will, which must produce antagonism and its (tentative) resolution in a *particularist* regime: excessive power and privileges on the one hand, and excessive obligations and repression on the other hand. The goal of progress *within* the state (motivated by conflict itself and its fundamental instability) is to produce a constitution of civil society, transforming the ground-principle of the state from mutual conflict to mutual acknowledgement by all citizens of each others' equality in freedom, and thus objectifying the pure pattern of morality in the field of legal institutions.

But this objectification is only an external copy *(simulacrum)* of morality. It secures external freedom but does not abolish the *subjective* antagonism of wills. Even within the perfect constitution men may remain in the *ethical* state of conflict, using their political freedom immorally, conflicting within the law while each is trying to use the other only as a means, with no regard to his inherent worth as end in himself. The goal of political history thus leaves the horizon of moral history wide open. There still is a historical perspective of progress: toward the ideal *moral* world community, where conflict will make place for solidarity, and mutual freedom will be realized in the *intersubjective dispositions* of all members.

The Role of War

As there is conflict within a society, so there is conflict among societies, expressed in the state of war. War is the international parallel to domestic antagonism. But there is a difference: a political state is already beyond the brute state of nature. Even the least rational and most despotic state had already given a legal framework to the antagonism among its members, monopolizing violence and transforming its raw expressions into new modes of social conduct, such as competition, struggle of interests, and repression and exploitation *within the law*. In international relations, however, the state of nature still prevails. Knowing from its own experience that it wishes to harm the other, each state suspects the other of the same and expects to be suspected in return: and in order to forestall being the victim, it is tempted to become the aggressor. This introduces a fundamental instability to the international scene. Although this model resembles the conduct of individuals *within* a society, there is a crucial difference; for on the international level there is no central government and no enforceable law. Hence the *bellum omnium contra omnes* that prevails in principle between all sovereign states, even when actual hostilities are absent; and from this philosophical viewpoint, all so-called treaties of peace are simple cease-fires.

As long as the international state of war has not been overcome in a cosmopolitan confederation, Kant believes that single states cannot be expected to become *fully* free, either (seventh thesis). The existence of war is therefore a sufficient indication that the goal of political history has not been attained.[27] At the same time, war is also the power that drives historical progress forward, leading eventually to its self-cancellation. Hence the central position of war as a mode of the cunning of nature:

> Through war, through the taxing and never-ending accumulation of armaments, through the want which any state even in peacetime must suffer internally, nature forces them [human beings] to make at first inadequate and tentative attempts; after devastations, revolutions, and even complete exhaustion, she brings them to that which reason could have told them at the beginning, and with far less sad experience, to wit, to step from the lawless condition of savages into a league of nations (VIII: 24/18-19).

For conflict and war to overcome themselves in accordance with the cunning of nature, a revolution must take

[27] It does not follow from this that the suppression of wars is a sufficient sign that the final end of history has been achieved.

place both internationally and within the state, for by definition the grounding principle of political life must be converted from mutual antagonism to its opposite, mutual recognition. But Kant does not conceive of this revolution as involving necessarily rebellion.[28] It can also be brought about by peaceful means within the law, as a result of the growing spirit of Enlightenment. On the other hand, *the emergence of the Enlightenment as a vehicle of progress represents a true revolution in itself.* It is a *conversion (Verwandeln)* of the mode of consciousness, whereby reason frees itself from dependence on the blind natural dialectic and, becoming aware of its own structure and precepts, it projects them as a conscious historical plan and makes this awareness an actual agent of change. (Here as in *Theory and Practice* and *What Is Enlightenment,* Kant sees the Enlightenment, like reason itself, as a genuine incentive [*Triebfeder*] for action.) The Enlightenment is thus a turning point in history. No longer a form of the cunning of nature, it represents the arising of a new, opposite principle that henceforth endows history with a *conscious* rational direction.

The Enlightenment As a Dialectical Turning Point in History

This indeed is the outcome of Kant's early essay on history. Once the philosopher has succeeded in grasping the immanent plan of nature, it ceases to be hidden; and its coming to philosophical consciousness creates a new historical situation. As long as the meaning of empirical history has not been deciphered, no other principle is available for transcending nature than the blind dialectic of nature itself. But after the work of the cunning of nature has made the Enlightenment itself possible, there is a new departure

---

[28] Not necessarily, but possibly. Rebellion, like the French Revolution, may prove *ex post facto* a sign of progress, even if it cannot be condoned *a priori.* But it is not a *necessary* condition for progress.

in history. From here on we must no longer rely on the cunning of nature alone to teach us through many trials what reason could have told us from the first. Now that rational consciousness, too, has broken forth, it can already plot out a conscious historical plan and move us *intentionally* toward its realization.

In this spirit Kant's other historical works, especially *Religion, What is Enlightenment*, and *Theory and Practice*, should be read. Although they emphasize the role of conscious rational intention as an agent of progress, they do not declare the cunning of nature obsolete. Enlightenment has a limited power and cannot affect everyone, only those who both understand the precepts of reason and choose to *adopt* them. And yet the advent of this new rational era, despite its debt to the cunning of nature that preceded it, cancels the latter's *exclusive* status as a vehicle of progress, and places itself alongside the cunning of nature as a *complementary principle.*[29]

From Dogmatic to Critical Teleology

From expounding the cunning of nature as it appears in the *Idea*, let us return to its systematic status. The *Idea* seems to commit a major dogmatic error. It ascribes to nature as such a hidden teleological plan, by which the totality of empirical history is to be explained and predicted; but this stands in open conflict with the *Critique of Pure*

[29] The complementary effect in history of conscious and unconscious action, moral freedom and natural compulsion, as two different forces of progress, is stated clearly by Pierre Hassner ("Les Concepts de guerre et de paix chez Kant," *Revue française de science politique*, XI (1961), 661-663). Hassner's analysis tends, however, to shift the emphasis towards natural compulsion (the cunning of nature), while Kant's position—more utopian, perhaps, than Hassner's interpretation suggests—ascribes to moral action proper a growing and significant role in the era after the Enlightenment. (See also Hassner, "Situation de la philosophie politique chez Kant," *La philosophie politique de Kant* [Paris, 1962].)

Reason, which admits only of mechanistic principles in nature. According to the *Critique,* our synthetic logic, which constitutes the ontological structure of natural entities, includes only the category of causality, excluding the category of purpose. Using this category in cognitive explanations transgresses the boundaries of critical reason and lapses into transcendent speculation. It seems, therefore, that the *Idea* commits precisely the error that the *Critique* forbids.[30]

Can this difficulty be resolved? Within the context of the *Idea* itself, the answer, I think, must be No. All we can do is call attention to the fact that, in content if not in time, this essay still belongs to Kant's pre-critical thinking, summarizing the views he held on history even before he applied the principles of his new criticism to the fields of action and teleology.[31] According to the logical order of things one would expect him to do the reverse: first develop the *a priori* foundations of ethics and teleology, and only then apply them to history as well. But Kant had written the *Idea* (in the conclusive style of "theses") even before the second and the third *Critiques;* which indicates that the *Idea* is indeed a vestige of his "dogmatic" thinking, chronologically but not systematically simultaneous with the beginning of the Critical period.[32]

---

[30] In addition the *Dialectic* of the first *Critique* forbids treating the universe as one totality, to which various predicates are attached as such. One can speak meaningfully of distances and time-lapses within the physical world, but one cannot ask about the spatio-temporal features of the world as one whole. Should not this ban extend to the world of empirical history as well, which may not be treated as a totality, or be ascribed global patterns that, presumably, apply to it as one whole?

[31] A summary of Kant's various positions on history, in his explicit statements before and after the *Idea,* is given in Klaus Weyand, *Kants Geschichtsphilosophie* (Cologne, 1964).

[32] It is true that a discussion of the highest good occurs already in the first *Critique,* but the notion appears there in a transcendent, unhistorical sense, as a revised or critical version of the idea of the world to come. As Chapter One has shown, the conversion of this theological notion into a historical one, the practical ideal of *this* world, begins

And yet, how should we explain that Kant so bluntly adhered to a dogmatic principle of purpose three years after the publication of the first *Critique*? Although I cannot give a full answer to this query, I have no doubt it should be sought in Kant's philosophical temperament and biography. Although he rejects teleology in the first *Critique*, he does not see its problem as satisfactorily solved. The teleological intuition, later called "reflection," is too direct and genuine to be completely disposed of. Renouncing it is actually harder for Kant than renouncing other dogmatic beliefs that the *Critique* had banned, such as the existence of God or immortality. Even with regard to God, Kant regarded the proof from design, based upon teleology, as the most respectable and persuasive of all, adding that it is the hardest to dispense with (*C1*, I:A 623/B 651). It always seemed to Kant that by completely abandoning the notion of purpose, the razor of his critique had cut too deep. How can teleology be omitted when the very structure of reason —the power determining the world—is teleological or "architectonic," that is, related to "essential ends?" We might safely say that the teleology was *the major problem of dogmatic philosophy that Kant was not completely successful in solving even after the first Critique*, and in fact, when he finally found a "critical" solution for it (in the *Critique of Judgement*), he considered it a feat almost as new and revolutionary as the original Copernican revolution.

With the *Critique of Judgement*, the systematic status of the cunning of nature changes radically. First, reappearing in Par. 83 of this work as a special area for a reflective teleological judgment, *it is now restored to a legitimate critical context*. And secondly, it is no longer identified with "history" at large as in the *Idea*, but only with "culture," which now is recognized to be only the external facet of the histori-

only with the second and third *Critiques*; so that Kant, when writing the *Idea*, possessed only the ahistorical conception of the highest good and had no conceptual basis for dealing with moral history, as distinguished from the "natural" progress in politics.

cal goal. This recognition presupposes the critical theory of the highest good and appears in the third *Critique* in conjunction with a crucial distinction Kant draws between the ultimate end of *nature* and the final end of *creation* as a whole. Let us now review these systematic shifts (and their corollaries) in more detail.

CHAPTER IV

RATIONAL HISTORY
VERSUS NATURAL DIALECTIC

With the *Critique of Judgement* (1790), two novel elements are introduced with respect to the cunning of nature. First, this teleological idea is restored to a legitimate critical context. And second, a crucial distinction is made between the *final end of creation* and the *ultimate end of nature*.

The First Innovation: The Reflective Concept of End

Even after the first *Critique* had rejected the concept of end from the categories of synthetic logic—by which the *ontological* structure of objects is determined—the problem of teleology was not yet settled. Quite the contrary, it was still so pressing that Kant finally devoted a whole new critique to its solution. For indeed, the third *Critique* should be seen as a Critique of Teleological Reason. Here Kant tries to rehabilitate the concept of end and assign a critical use to its major varieties. We have seen that Kant's system does not grow simultaneously in all its parts; signs of his exertions are visible even in works that seem to impart final results. But even without considering Kant's personal evolution, it is an inner characteristic of his system that concepts and principles declared invalid in one usage are not necessarily rejected in every respect or deprived of all philosophical significance. On the contrary, it is typical of the critical mode of thinking to change the function of many dogmatic concepts, transferring them from a context in which they have no validity to a context in which they gain a legitimate if limited use. Such are the dynamics of Kant's critique in general, that the claims of transcendent metaphysics (totality, God, supersensible matters) are translated from their spurious cognitive expression into genuine expressions in the spheres of morality, aesthetics, and history. And this is the source in Kant's system of such typically critical concepts as regulative idea, practical postulate, rational faith, and *reflective judgement*.

Reflective judgement is known as the basis of Kant's critical solution to the problem of teleology. The question: What are the legitimate functions of the concept of end? stands at the origin of the whole third *Critique* and so provides a unity that runs throughout its parts. Kant discusses partial aspects of this subject even earlier, but only in the third *Critique* does he think he has succeeded in answering all of them in terms of one fundamental principle. Kant considers this success a new philosophical achievement, second only to that inherent in the Copernican revolution itself.

How is the concept of purpose reintroduced into a critical framework? Kant realizes that certain fields of phenomena disclose the following characteristic. Once their objects have been constituted and we review them or their constituents by *ex post facto* reflection, grasping in a more synoptic way their mutual relations and correspondences, we are bound to discover in them in retrospect an *additional* kind of unity and organization that cannot be reduced to mechanical laws alone, and yet makes up the peculiar character of this type of phenomena. The reflection in question is at first pre-philosophical; it occurs of itself without explicit intention, as if the new pattern is read off the subject matter itself rather than being imposed on it from without. But this is sufficient to invoke a new intellectual need, introducing a sense of lack or privation into our comprehension and prescribing new conditions for the intelligibility of the subject matter at hand. We feel that without using the concept of purpose, we cannot approach this kind of phenomena in a fully rational manner and must fail to comprehend them in what makes up their most unique character. Thus the initial reflection, although occurring *ex post facto*, seems to lay down further *a priori* conditions for our comprehension of certain classes of phenomena.

Is this demand justified? Can the pre-philosophical reflection from which it stems be brought to a philosophical level by discovering in it an *a priori* structure of its own? Or is it just a caprice of the mind, a mere delusion that must rather be *suppressed* as a condition for rationality? This question occupies the critical aspect of the third *Critique*; and Kant's answer may be summarized as follows. The demand is justified in so far as it concerns the structure of our intersubjective response to certain classes of phenomena; but it is delusory when it pretends to partake thereby of the Copernican principle, that is, determine the actual being of the object itself. The teleological form is thus an *a priori* condition for the *intelligibility* of these phenomena but not for their *ontological possibility* as real entities in nature.

Although the teleological reflection takes place *a posteriori*, the *Critique of Judgement* brings out the *a priori* elements that operate in it, together with the critical restriction on their use. This kind of reflection is found in four areas: esthetics, the organic world, the methodology of science, and empirical history ("culture"). Despite their material differences, all four areas are united by the principle of the reflective judgement of purpose; for in all of them it is necessary to use a teleological explanation, with the qualification that its use is only "reflective" and not "determinative" ("constitutive"). This means that although the teleological form of judgement is necessary *a priori* to make a given discipline possible and to understand the phenomena in it, its validity does not apply to the structure of the object itself, only to the observer's subjective ways of relating and responding to it. It therefore provides a set of universal and necessary forms of judgement which, like the categories of the understanding, determine our intersubjective ways of relating to objects *a priori*; but unlike the categories, the teleological forms do not thereby determine the ontology of their objects and do not inform or commit us at all concerning these objects as actual entities.

What follows is a fundamental change in the status of the idea of the cunning of nature. Reappearing in Paragraph 83 of the third *Critique*, this idea now becomes an integral part of the critique of teleological reason, subject to the reflective restriction introduced by it, and thus it loses its dogmatic character and becomes a critical concept. This is stated expressly by Kant at the beginning of Paragraph 83. He says that now we have a "sufficient reason" for accepting this teleological concept critically, "according to principles of reason," on condition that its validity is "for the *reflective*, though not of course for the *determinant*, judgement" (V:429/II:92; italics added). From now on, when attributing to nature a semi–moral pattern of development, we no longer commit ourselves as to its ontology; using the teleological model is necessary only for us, all rational subjects, when reflecting back on history and trying to make it intelligible for ourselves, i.e., to overcome its apparent contingency and chaos, and grasp history as a meaningful whole, as this reflection suggests it should be grasped. But when we do so, even using a metaphor like providence or saying that "nature has intended," we do not (and may not) mean that the purposive principle inheres in the object of our investigation; and we certainly are not committed to see nature as a quasi-person, nor to assume a supreme rational being who organized nature in accordance with this hidden intention.

The Systematic Context

My claim is, then, that the topic of the cunning of nature recurs in the third *Critique* not accidentally, but as part of its systematic context. This will become more manifest if we survey succinctly the work of the reflective judgement in the other areas of teleology, showing that the *same* principle that makes a critique of teleological reason possible and endows systematic unity to all its parts is also at work in the field of empirical history or culture.

Esthetics and Beauty

Abstention from ontological commitment is most clearly manifest in the esthetic judgement. When judging an object as beautiful, I discover that its being beautiful depends upon a purposeful correspondence between the components of the object and the free play of mental faculties it is likely to arouse in me, in a way that produces disinterested pleasure. When such a purposive relation obtains with regard to a given singular object, there is sufficient ground for a universal and necessary judgement, valid for all esthetic observers. But this does not mean that we regard the property "beautiful" or "purposive" as one of the properties that constitute this object as an actual entity, as we do regard its spatio-temporality or causal dependence; similarly we completely ignore the question of whether there actually was someone—the artist, nature, or God—who intentionally arranged the object in this way. The esthetic judgement is based upon a subjective norm of *impression*, not upon an objective norm of constitution. Hence it tells us nothing about the metaphysical origin of the object or its structure as a natural entity.

The Biological End

In the life sciences we are already investigating a real entity in nature to which we may attribute, as such, only mechanical processes. But these processes cannot provide a complete explanation of organic phenomena. In order to make intelligible—that is, to overcome the seeming fortuity of—the mutual cooperation of natural laws in producing this particular system, and even to be able to discover the causal factors themselves, we must postulate a holistic, functional pattern at their basis, as if all were working *"according to an intention,"* even if not *because* of an intention.

In other words, we must assume the concept of an end, by which the various natural processes are integrated within the living organism, and which alone can explain their mutual relevance and even lead us to the discovery of further causal connections as yet hidden from our sight.[1]

However, using the notion of a mechanism working "according to an intention" has a fundamentally heuristic function. We are not projecting the teleological model in conjunction with any metaphysical interpretation; and certainly we do not postulate any real *intender* behind this intention. Thus, even though the two explanatory systems, the causal and the teleological, complement each other in the process of inquiry, their roles are asymmetrical; for the former determines the ontological structure of the creature under inquiry, whereas the latter only prescribes a methodological rule for the inquirer.

The Correspondence of the Elements of Knowledge

The problem of purpose appears not just in the life sciences but also in the methodology of knowledge in general. Here it takes two aspects. First, scientific knowledge is the synthesis of two heterogeneous elements: the receptivity of the senses and the spontaneity of the understanding. For this synthesis to take place, the two dissimilar elements must be brought into correspondence with one another. But we cannot account for this correspondence without assuming, at least reflectively, that they share a common substrate beyond the realm of experience in the realm of the supersensible. Yet we do not postulate this substrate as an actual metaphysical being, only as a necessary presupposition for reflecting on the phenomenon of knowledge, without which it would not be intelligible to us.

The second aspect concerns the specific laws and species

---

[1] Kant emphasizes that the issue is not external purposiveness, making a certain creature exist for the sake of another, but internal purpose, i.e., relating the various parts of a creature to the whole as their goal and making each part both an end and a means relative to the others.

of nature. The special content of every law and of every individual species in nature is contingent, since it derives from empirical observation and not from *a priori* deduction; how, then, can we expect them to form a coherent and continuous system in terms of their *material* aspect? At first Kant sought the answer in the notion of a regulative idea (*C1*: A 653-662/B 681-690, A 671/B 699, A 686-687/B 714-715); but in the third *Critique* he replaced it, too, with the reflective judgement. When investigating nature in physics as well as in biology, we must conceive of all the particular laws and species as if they were connected in accordance with a teleological scheme of totality. This idea would direct us to look for new laws and for more species of nature in such a way as to make the content of the different branches of science, and of the particular ingredients of each branch of science, as continuous as possible. But here again the idea is only a heuristic norm, necessary to systematize science, but totally uninformative with regard to the metaphysical structure of the universe or what lies "beyond" it.

Empirical History: The Cunning of Nature as a Reflective Principle

In line with the former instance, the fourth area of teleology in which the reflective principle comes to bear is empirical history, the self-overcoming of nature in the products of culture. It should be noted that the issue at hand is not the capacity of nature to respond to intentional moral reshaping from without; for this Kant has a different guarantee, based upon a practical postulate, that makes a stronger claim and enjoys a higher methodological status than a reflective judgement.[2] The issue at hand is nature's capacity

---

[2] A practical postulate should make an ontological statement about the world. For example, it claims that metaphysical freedom actually exists, or that there is "something" in the nature of the universe which makes its responsiveness to formative activity possible (see Chapter Two). The postulate is nevertheless accompanied by its own critical

to produce semi-moral (legal and political) systems from within itself, i.e., it is the "cunning of nature."

In all previous instances we saw that they cannot be made intelligible, and the seeming arbitrariness of the singular correspondence they imply cannot be overcome, unless we suppose that the laws of nature are united by some individual plan, *as if* they were put in the service of an intention. Yet we abstain from reifying this intention or attributing it to some real intender. We only use the pure *form* of purposiveness without assuming a real purpose (*zwecklose Zweckmässigkeit*);[3] and while this procedure is necessary for our comprehension, it does not entail a metaphysical interpretation of the actual working of the universe or of the ontic structure of its entities. The need for a quasi-intentional form expresses the properties of man, not the hidden interiority of the world.

In a similar way, the reflective restriction now applies to the study of empirical history. When speaking of a hidden plan that nature itself follows in history, we commit ourselves only to the presence of a quasi-intentional *structure* in historical phenomena, not to the existence or the identity of any intender. Our language is metaphorical, based upon an analogy with human works; but the use of this analogy is indispensable, since we could not otherwise grasp the phenomenon of history as a sphere with its own distinctive characteristics.

What is the major finding that, by reflection, makes a teleological judgement necessary in history? Kant does not spell this out sufficiently, and his hints add up to a much weaker argument than in the case of biology or even of beauty. Still, we must reconstruct his reasoning from the context and see what is supposed to make it plausible.

---

limitation, namely, that it is only rational to believe in the truth of its claim in the context of actual *praxis* and when this claim is regarded as undecidable in pure cognitive terms.

[3] This is one of the basic connotations of this well-known expression.

History is conceptually distinct from mere chronology or a chaotic aggregate of facts. Its concept presupposes a pattern of unity or totalization: in this Kant agrees with a number of his contemporaries.[4] But why must we suppose that this pattern is teleological? And how can we know that the concept of history is not empty, but actually exhibited *in concreto*?

Kant's answer relies on the theory of reflection as put forth in the third *Critique* in general. Reflecting in retrospect upon the sum of human deeds and products as already given, an interesting second-degree unity is bound to strike the observer. Throughout the chaotic multiplicity of events, man is seen to realize his faculties and civilize himself, following a line of progress that is parallel to, although not caused by, what reason itself would have recommended *a priori*. This striking correspondence forces itself on the observer, and the problem is not so much identifying it as subjecting it to criticism, that is, determining its methodological status by discovering an *a priori* structure in it. This again is done in terms of the "*a priori* of the *a posteriori*," i.e., the reflective judgement. The philosopher of history cannot construct his theories prior to all experience. He must reflect back on the actual course of human affairs. But this reflection, although occurring *ex post facto*, is not itself empirical. It is focused not on sensual objects but on *relations*—analogies, correspondences, etc.—that manifest themselves between empirical objects that have already been or are still being constituted; and its find is not taken from any science of nature, although it is supposed to direct the study of a specific realm in nature. Thus we have the same methodological pattern as in esthetics and natural science: the *Critique* explicates the *a priori* ground of a certain field of objects on the basis of a nonempirical reflection that grasps the relations between these objects as they formed themselves *ex post facto*. The philosopher reflects back up-

[4] This concept is modern in its secular form, but it is a venerable idea in the history of religion.

on a phenomenal field already given; and when he discovers in it a new pattern of unity, he regresses to the *a priori* level in which this unity is grounded, using the form of purpose as a necessary yet only reflective norm.

What is, more specifically, the finding supplied by the initial reflection? Observing past human history from the standpoint of the Enlightenment, the observer is bound to trace the marks of *two* kinds of unexplained correspondence: first, among the empirical deeds and events themselves, and secondly—this is the main point—between the actual course of history and what practical reason lays down as an ought. These signs are still fragmentary, and the correspondence they indicate is only external, as between morality and legality. But they are genuine enough to provoke an irreducible impression of purposiveness and call for its conceptualization.

First, even without considering the demands of practical reason, we discover that there is a significant line of development evolving in the midst of the confusion, madness, and retrogressions of empirical history, although no one in particular intended it: man is gradually realizing his capacities, expressing them in ever higher degrees of civilization and of personal achievement. Thereby he is also progressively *emancipating* himself, first from the arbitrary rule of the powers of nature, and more recently from the despotic rule of political and judicial institutions.[5] We have therefore a pattern in the organization of historical events that cannot be explained exclusively in mechanistic terms,

[5] Kant views history from the point of view of the Enlightenment, the new science, enlightened despotism, and even the French Revolution. The third *Critique* was, by the way, published a year after the beginning of the Revolution, that is, before the beginning of the Terror but after the *Declaration of the Rights of Man and of Citizen* and after the abolition of the privileges of the nobility. Liberty, equality, and fraternity became *political* values that could be institutionalized in the *government itself* instead of being just an abstract ideal. This reinforced Kant's faith that consciousness of rational imperatives (the Enlightenment) ultimately leads to their becoming a real political force.

since it presupposes even if only reflectively the concept of intent or purpose, while the laws of nature are indifferent to any purpose. But that is not all. In the second place, and here is the crux of the argument, we discover a *surprising analogy between the line of development evolving on its own in the natural course of history, and the plan which practical reason, too, prescribes as a moral ought.* It is as if empirical history realized of itself an intention determined *a priori* by reason. As far as we know, however, this has not occurred as a result of the intentions of actual men. It is doubtful that they would have been capable of acting, at least before the Enlightenment, out of a common moral program. In fact, their actions flow from selfish motives, violent competition, and unsocial sociability. Yet without anyone intending it, a semi-intentional, even a semirational, system is evolved and produced in history. We must therefore attribute this intent "to nature itself," although only metaphorically or by analogy, and turn to look for the details of the dialectical mechanism (conflict, war, inequality, economic self-interest, etc.) by which nature itself produces a system that overcomes nature.

The cunning of nature thus becomes an *a priori* principle in the explanation of history, founded by pure reflection on empirical history and on its relation to reason. Having presupposed the cunning of nature, we must go back to experience in order to discover the empirical laws by which this model is realized. (Here we study the role of wars, social stratification, international trade, economic relations, etc.) Equipped with these laws, we can understand history as one global system, as a *Weltgeschichte,* arrange the material of past events *in accordance with principles,* and even guide our anticipation for the future. Among other things, we will have the rules for selecting relevant topics for historical research, for sifting out contingent and incidental particulars, and no less important, for discovering additional *causal* factors by which to supply the missing links in the chain.

The Existential Dimension of the
Interpretation of History

So far we have discussed the methodological aspect of using teleological judgement in history. But there is, I think, another. When Kant says that this judgement is "subjectively necessary" for us, he may have in mind a *second* meaning of subjective necessity, which does not apply in the case of biology or beauty. The need for an interpretive stance towards history is a matter not just for professional investigators whose job is interpretation, but for every man in so far as he is a rational being with intentions and interests. History is not an external object, given to us in completed form, but is continuously being produced through men's actions and intentions. Hence man does not only *confront* history, he also stands *within* it. This is the field in which his moral ends and practical interests are supposed to be realized, so it is *relevant* for him to ask about the meaning of history in terms of these ends and interests[6] and to try to make it intelligible *in their terms*. We can therefore say that history confronts man not only as an intellectual but also as an existential problem.[7] His need to give it a meaningful interpretation flows from the very actuality of his life, not just from the needs of antiquarian research.

The Historization of the Earth,
Evolution, and Genius

Before dealing with the second systematic innovation introduced by the third *Critique,* let me call the reader's attention to three additional topics in this *Critique* that have a bearing on our theme. First, Kant introduces historicity

[6] As it is irrelevant to ask a question like this about the phenomenon of beauty or the laws of physics.

[7] Historical interpretation would belong, accordingly, to the question "What may I hope for?" and not only to the purely cognitive question "What can I know?" History is supposed to actualize my moral interests and to advance the development of my freedom; my perceptual relationship to it derives *from these interests*.

into the subhuman world itself, anticipating the historicity of the humanized world. This applies both to the inorganic sphere of geology—the evolution of the earth (V:427-8/11: 89-91)—and, more importantly, to the organic sphere of biology (Par. 80). Anticipating Darwin's theory of evolution in a teleological way, Kant argues that without regarding the world of living organisms as one totality, whose varieties had evolved from an original mother species by way of mutations and adaptation for survival, we shall not be able to make intelligible to ourselves the amazing affinities and analogies between the existing species, discovered by an *ex post facto* reflection.

Finally, in his theory of artistic genius, Kant ascribes to nature an unconscious activity whereby, through the artist, it transcends itself and produces "something that surpasses nature" (Par. 49) or constitutes "a new nature, as it were" (*ibid.*). This theory of the hidden *esthetic* teleology of nature serves as a prototype for the hidden *practical* teleology (the cunning of nature) discussed in Par. 83.[8]

The Second Innovation: The Final End of History Is Not Merely Political

I now pass to the second new principle introduced by the third *Critique*. Not only is the idea of the cunning of nature now restricted to the realm of reflection; it is also only given a secondary function in the framework of historical progress. This change derives from the fact that history occupies a more central position and has a broader significance within the critical system than it had before. It is not just empirical history but above all moral history;[9] and the ideal toward which history is to progress is not only political but first and foremost it is the attempt to found a system of

---

[8] In fact, Kant combines the two in *Perpetual Peace*, speaking of political progress as the work of "that great artist nature" (see p. 186 below).

[9] See Pars. 84-91, parallel to the Dialectic in *C2* and to the idea of the kingdom of God on earth in *Religion*.

intersubjective attitudes based on the mutual recognition of the principle of morality.[10] This system is "invisible" in the sense that it is not observable like political or cultural institutions but consists of inner attitudes and dispositions originating in the noumenal realm of freedom rather than in nature. This system is given different names. In the *Religion* Kant calls it an "ethical community" as opposed to "civil society," which is a *political* community; and sometimes he calls it an "invisible church,"[11] and even "the kingdom of God on earth"; but basically, it is supposed to develop the idea of "the kingdom of ends" known from the *Foundations.* In terms of the theory of the highest good we may say that it is that moment of the highest good that represents the totalization of morality in the genuine sense, that is, in the sense of subjective intentions and attitudes.

The Ethical Community

The members of this ethical community are united by the constant disposition to recognize each other's freedom and equality and to actually act out of this recognition. They arrived at this state of affairs not by obeying the will of a divine legislator, but by exercising the autonomy of their own reason. The members of the ethical community have emancipated themselves from transcendent fears and from all dependence on an external basis for morality, and they have in principle overcome natural inclinations, ego-

---

[10] This is recognized by Keith Ward in *The Development of Kant's View of Ethics* (Oxford, 1972), who states that "the purpose of nature alone, in developing a world-federation and a civilized, cultured human nature, must always fall short of the final end which alone gives the process meaning, the realisation of the *summum bonum*" (p. 139). And yet a little later he reverts to the thesis that "Kant . . . sees history as progressing toward the establishment of a universal federation of states" (p. 142). These two statements are incompatible unless we understand the second, as we should, as expressing only *one facet* of history.

[11] *Die unsichtbare Kirche* (*Rel.*, VI:152/140); and *das ethische gemeine Wesen* (*ibid.*, VI:94/86) or *die moralische Gemeinschaft* (*Ibid.*, VI:199/188) as distinguished from *die bürgerliche Gesellschaft* (*ibid.*, VI:94/86).

ism, and the conflict of particular wills in their interrelationships. Thus, instead of everyone seeing everyone else's will as an obstacle that contradicts his own particular will, their wills now are, and are seen as, compatible with each other in accordance with a *universal* principle, so that each treats the other as an end in himself, not only as an instrument for the fulfillment of his desires.[12]

Moral history proper involves the propagation of the ethical community. This invisible system is supposed to expand until ideally it encompasses all of mankind. It is to be realized through moral education, enlightenment, and chiefly by the religion of reason, which is to replace all traditional religions. Indeed, the ethical community translates the religious ideal of the kingdom of God on earth into its secular analogue, established by man's autonomous reason. The history of religion thus assumes a central role as a major aspect of historical progress. Hence, the philosopher has to employ religious metaphors while transforming and reinterpreting their meaning, and hence also he needs to give a purely philosophical explication to the concepts of traditional religion, since on the grand historical scale the religion of reason cannot be expected to become prevalent unless the principle of enlightenment is brought to consciousness and thus becomes an active and catalytic historical force. In these two complementary ways, the philosopher is personally supposed to take an active part in promoting the historical process which he recommends.[13]

It is true, however, that the ethical community is not the sole moment of the highest good as the end of rational history. The moment that completes it is institutional—legal and political. Spreading the rule of the moral principle over the inner lives of individuals is not enough. This principle must also be embodied in the external world, that is, in the institutional system that determines the empirical relations

---

[12] In the ethical community all the elements of ethics (universality, man as an end in himself, etc.) are synthesized.

[13] This will be dealt with in Chapter Five.

between these individuals. This system—law, jurisprudence, political constitution, international relations, or in a word, the political community—must assume a quasi-moral form. It certainly cannot be moral in the strict sense, for it lacks personality and has but an external mode of existence. At most it can function in accordance with duty, but not out of duty; and so it falls under the concept of legality. But this is the indispensable loss of content, involved wherever an idea is embodied empirically. The moral idea cannot, by definition, find an empirical setup that perfectly expresses its content, and all institutional arrangements can only be analogous to it, as a mere simulacrum. Yet there is a *moral duty* to produce such analogues and reshape existing political institutions in their light. This duty is part, but only part, of the meaning of the imperative to promote the highest good; since the point of the imperative is to make the world and not only the individual good, it relates, among other things, to embodying moral laws in the organization of the empirical world itself.[14]

Systematic Consequences: Shrinking the Role of the Cunning of Nature

Three consequences follow immediately. First, since the political organization is the embodiment of morality in legality, there may be a considerable overlap between the political institutions advocated by the utilitarian approach that Kant rejects, and those required by purely rational motives. Indeed, the highest practical principle states that reason must always also be an end in itself and not just an instrument for increasing utility; but this does not exclude the possibility that these two approaches will produce partly similar results on the level of empirical institutions.[15]

---

[14] For a more complete discussion of this problem, see Chapter One.

[15] But not all of them. In the realm of law important differences are possible, e.g. over the question of justifying punishment; on the constitutional level, universalized institutions that do not serve merely to advance particular interests are conceivable in the Kantian system.

Similarly, an action that is in accordance with duty may be done by the individual either out of duty or from selfish interest, even though it will manifest itself in identical behavior. In itself, the political community is a system of empirical laws and institutions that mediate the behavior of its members toward each other without determining their good or evil will. A reformed political regime, as Kant later points out, can exist even in a society of intelligent devils who have succeeded in solving utilitarian problems which affects them in common.[16]

Second, since the institutional system is only an analogy to morality in the realm of legality, *its place within the historical ideal is subordinate and secondary*.[17] True, both systems—the internal and the external, the moral and the political—are necessary for the realization of the ideal. Moreover, they require one another. The political system is *in principle* or *a priori* dependent on morality, being its embodiment, while the moral system is *pragmatically* or empirically dependent on the political order; for even if outstanding moral persons can emerge singly in almost any kind of society, the totalization of morality and its extension to the masses cannot be expected in practice, unless some rational social order already prevails and anarchy is overcome.[18] Yet within their complementary relationship, the ethical community clearly has precedence over the political, for it has self-sufficient value, whereas the other's value is derived from it. The moral aspect of the ideal is its core, conferring meaning and status on its political complement as well.

Finally, and this is the main point, by the very definition of morality, the moral system cannot be founded except by

16 See, VIII:366/112.
17 This is hinted even in the *Idea*, when Kant characterizes the perfect political union as "the halfway mark in the development of mankind," (VIII:26/21).
18 This means that even inner morality requires empirical preparation: the improvement of political institutions and the refinement of inner desires.

the conscious intentions of individuals; therefore, *the principle of the cunning of nature is irrelevant to it and cannot serve to guarantee it.* Saying that the cunning of nature is responsible for moral progress of history is clearly a contradiction in terms. And since precisely this moral moment is the essence of the historical goal, the cunning of nature is restricted to a limited role. It can contribute to progress only in the external sphere of legality; it can also remove external obstacles to the spread of morality; but it cannot contribute anything to the creation of the moral-historical end itself.

But this is not all. *Even in furthering political progress, the cunning of nature is no longer the sole principle.* According to Kant, as soon as practical reason is explicated and becomes conscious, a new principle emerges that competes with the cunning of nature even on the institutional level. Kant always emphasizes that the Enlightenment is not just a form of consciousness but a real historical force that can be institutionalized through praxis and become embodied in historical reality. This view is consonant not only with the general optimism of Kant's period but especially with his own theory of rationality, which views reason as an actual, self-sufficient, practical motive.[19] In this way the cunning of nature is first excluded completely from the most important facet of historical progress (morality), and in addition loses its exclusive role even in the secondary field of politics and law.

The Ultimate End *versus* the Final End

This change in the status of the cunning of nature receives systematic expression in the crucial distinction Kant makes (in Pars. 82-84, see also 87) between *the ultimate end (der letzte Zweck) of nature* and *the final end (der Endzweck) of creation* (with the cunning of nature applying

---

[19] See the chapter on "The Incentives of Pure Practical Reason" in *C2*. This is also one of the central meanings of the Kantian postulate of *freedom* and of the claim that pure reason is capable of being practical.

only to the former). The context of the discussion is clearly historical: it is the moral-teleological significance of the world that Kant approaches here from two different angles. First, he asks what nature by itself (including human nature: man's inclinations to violence and egoism) can do to prepare the ground for the rule of morality, and to produce a *quasi*-moral external system within itself. Second, he asks what man as a free (noumenal) being unbound by nature can and ought to do in order to reshape the world as a moral system. The first factor is culture, the second is the highest good. Culture (or man as a natural being through which the process of culture takes place) is made the ultimate end of nature. But he can be so considered only on the condition that he "wills to give nature an end which suffices to itself and can, therefore, be a final end" (Par. 83). The latter is the highest good, or man as a rational being who brings himself "under [the rule of] moral laws" (V: 448/II:116). Kant's text wavers between saying that man *is* the final end and that man *gives* the final end to creation; but there is no contradiction. Man is the final end not as he is, but by virtue of what he has to *become and bring about*; and this is the ideal of the highest good, which human reason projects as an ought for itself and as a final end for creation as a whole.[20] Only in light of this final end can we

[20] The final end of creation is also defined as "man, and every other rational creature, under moral laws" (*C3*, V:448/II:116). As Kant's long footnote makes clear, he means thereby not man as given, but as he still ought to make himself; and by the term "under moral laws" he means both aspects of the highest good, the internal and the external. The final end is a system in which empirical consequences no less than the free act are "derived according to moral laws." such that when we "reflect upon the course of the world from a moral viewpoint," we can identify the rules of morality embodied in the external organization of the world no less than in the pure motivation of agents. In other words, the final end is the highest good with both its facets. (See also Chapter One, pp. 69-70.

Incidentally, when Kant speaks of "man and every other rational being" he must be referring to other creatures that in his belief inhabit the universe, sharing man's reason and moral ideals even if not his

look back upon nature, assigning a teleological significance to it, too, and identifying culture as the last link in its chain.

Despite the verbal similarity between the ultimate end of nature and the final end of creation, they are conceptually distinct. A final end (*Endzweck*) is "an end that does not require any other end as a condition of its possibility" (V:434/II:98). This means it is absolute and does not derive its teleological status from a higher goal that it might serve. Its end is within itself, and it cannot be considered a means for any other purpose.[21] This kind of end, according to Kant, cannot inhere in any *natural* thing. It can be found only in something higher than nature, to which nature itself must be subordinate. But this does not preclude that at a second stage, when reflecting back on nature from the viewpoint of the final end, we might discover some empirical system that, although produced by nature, seems to support the supernatural ideal or to prepare the ground for its realization. Such a system could then be identified as the ultimate end of *nature* without being thereby the absolutely highest end; for like nature itself it is subordinate to something that transcends nature. Furthermore, had we not found that this natural system contributed to the realization of the final end, we would not be permitted to attribute *any* teleological significance to it; and so it is clear that the concept of end we are using, even with regard to nature itself, is a practical and hence critical concept, not a theoretical and dogmatic one.

---

physical constitution. Kant's vision of the final end of creation thus seems to go beyond the moral evolution of mankind and take up cosmic dimensions. In comparison, Hegel's identification of human history with the genesis of the Absolute itself appears as a kind of cosmic provincialism!

[21] In this respect the individual as an end in himself in the *Found.* is not a final end, because he may also be a means for others as long as he is *also* an end. A final end, on the other hand, can never be a means in any sense. This goal is absolute also in so far as it is *total.*

Moral History and the Place of Man in the Universe

Before turning to the details of the concept of culture, let us examine the systematic context of the discussion as a whole. At the background there is the attempt to *totalize* the concept of end, that is, to use it to review the totality of the universe and to determine man's place within it. In so doing, Kant changes the concept of end he is using, by passing from structural teleology to that of existence;[22] and he thus faces the metaphysical question of what the universe at large exists for. Although this question is legitimate and even necessary for critical reason, the answer is to be sought on the level not of existence but of the moral ought. For questions about the world as a whole have no critical answers in cognitive terms, only in terms of the metaphysics of praxis; and by the hierarchy of the interests of reason, empirical existence is subordinate to the moral idea, in which alone it can find a justification or an end. Furthermore, *when speaking of the moral idea, we are not dealing with a Platonic idea in itself, but with an end projected by man's rational will.* Kant's Copernican revolution also manifests itself in the supreme metaphysical sphere of the final end. The final end of the world can be critically discussed only from the point of view of the intentional subject. Since the concept of divine will must be removed from metaphysics, the only subject whose will can assign the very existence of the universe a final end is man himself—when he is acting by his universalized practical reason and not by his particular interests.

22 Kant calls the end of existence "extrinsic" to differentiate it from the "intrinsic" character of structural teleology; but it seems to me that there is no exact overlap between the two, since extrinsic teleology is defined as "the finality that exists where one thing *in nature* subserves another as a means to an end" (*C3*, V:425/II:86). Hence, only the ultimate end of nature is extrinsic. The final end is already immanent, even though it too is discussed as an end of existence. (See the title of Par. 84: "The final end of the existence of a world, that is, of creation itself"; "Vom dem Endzweck das Daseins einer Welt, d.i. der Schöpfung selbst.")

Here we have an excellent example of the dynamics of the critical system, translating the ultimate metaphysical questions from their delusory, cognitive form into their proper expression in the field of praxis. Already the first *Critique* has found it necessary for reason to seek the final ground for the existence of the world as a totality. This question, which pervades the whole history of religion and philosophy, expresses a genuine interest of reason. But in the first *Critique*, the question is put in terms of the first and absolute *cause* for the existence of the world, to which no critical answer is possible. In the third *Critique*, however, the question is put in terms of the final *end* for the existence of the world; and this, Kant argues, can be given a critical answer, though only in moral and not in cognitive terms, and as a projection of *man's own* reason. Existence as such is contingent; there is nothing in it that can give it teleological justification. Only man's moral consciousness can assign the world a final end that justifies the very existence of the universe. This end, the highest good, represents the future moral totality that man and the world must still *become*; thus *moral history is made into the factor justifying the very being of the world*. As for man, he retains his unique place in creation, neither as a given natural being nor even as a *knowing* rational being, but as a practical, historic being who assigns the universe its final end and is himself supposed to actualize it.

This is what Kant calls (here and elsewhere) "man's destiny." And this is also the meaning of his equivocal saying that "without man . . . the whole of creation would be a mere wilderness, a thing in vain, and have no final end" (*C3*, V:442/II:108).[23] This dictum does not mean that the appearance of man as a *natural* being supplies the rest of nature with a teleological center to which all others are subservient. On the contrary, if man were just another link in nature, creation would still be "a thing in vain and have no

---

[23] This passage should be read along with the ones discussed above. Our analysis is based on these paragraphs read together.

final end." The universe needs man so that he, as a free and conscious creature, can *confer* its final end on the world and change himself and nature in such a way as to realize it. Kant uses the language of traditional teleology to express a new and revolutionary conception that transcends it, leading to the historization of man's position in the universe and of his relations with himself and with nature. Nominally Kant belongs with those for whom man is the center of creation. Yet for Kant man's preeminence is not given and automatically guaranteed; it is something intended and destined. In other words, man enjoys a central position not by virtue of what he is, but by virtue of what he *ought* to do and to become. He must *make* himself the center of creation by using his practical reason to determine its end and by consciously acting to realize it. It follows that history in the conscious, rational sense is not just an accidental human activity, but *the realization of man's essential position in the universe.*

This also provides an answer for Kant the astronomer, who looks at the infinity of the universe in wonder and awe. From a physical standpoint, as a being in space and time, man is nothing compared to the vastness of creation. But by virtue of his moral destiny man becomes higher than the whole creation, for he alone can endow it with value through his action. This reversal of man's self-image is existentially at the heart of the results of the Copernican revolution and obtains its clearest and perhaps its most paradigmatic expression in the analysis of the sublime, as I have already suggested.

To complete the systematic context, I shall finally examine the place which the present discussion holds in the third *Critique.* From what we have said it is clear that the final end of creation is not discovered by a reflective judgement but is imposed on reality by practical reason in a completely *a priori* manner. In this sense it is a break in the continuity of the third *Critique,* but at the same time it is the *link between it and the Second Critique,* and in fact the link

connecting all three *Critiques*. The first *Critique* had asked
what is the ultimate ground for the universe. The third tries
to answer teleologically, taking the ideal of the highest good
—identified independently by the second as the supreme
goal of praxis—and adding a further dimension to it:
the highest good is not only the supreme end of man but
also the only teleological justification that the world itself
can be given. Finally, after the final end has been determined *a priori*, we can reexamine the empirical world by
reflective judgement to see whether we can detect within it
some natural process or system that can be said to assist the
final end or pave the way for it. Discovering the cultural
process as such a factor, the faculty of judgement declares
culture, or man as the producer of culture, to be the highest
teleological phase within nature itself. But it is clear that
the discussion is now subject to the concept of practical reason and thus to the criteria of the critical outlook.

The Concept of Culture

Although methodologically Par. 83 places the cunning of
nature in a critical context, in content it reiterates most of
the points made in the *Idea* and expands them somewhat.
What the *Idea* presents as history at large is now subsumed
under the narrower concept of culture. Culture is "what
nature can supply for the purpose of preparing him [man]
for what he himself must do in order to be a final end" (V:
431/II:94).[24] As the dialectical self-overcoming of nature,
culture takes up two different forms, depending on whether
it is man's inner nature (his crude passions) or outer nature
(his social and physical environment) that is being re-

[24] Sometimes Kant says that man as a moral being who has to create
the highest good is the final end, and that man as a natural being who
creates culture is the ultimate end. But this formulation is not completely accurate, because as we shall see, man is worthy of being an end
not because he exists but because of what he has yet to do and to become. It is therefore better to use the formulation that identifies the
end with the product and not with the producer. (This is another
example of Kant struggling with traditional terminology to express a
conception that transcends it.)

molded. These two branches of culture are teleologically asymmetrical, for the latter is considered higher than the former.[25]

The Culture of Skill

Through the culture of skill (*Geschicklichkeit*) man reforms his outer environment, developing a technology for the supply of his needs[26] and advancing toward freer political institutions. This includes virtually the whole scope of the *Idea*, with a significant addition: progress is achieved not only through war and competition but also through exploitation and social stratification.[27] These give rise to a leisure-time elite that creates knowledge, education, enlightened ideas, and refined luxuries, thus contributing to the self-abolition of exploitation; for the new ideas spread out to the oppressed classes, making them discover their own humanity and equal status with their oppressors; while the

[25] "But not every form of culture can fill the office of this ultimate end of nature . . ." (*C3*, V:431/II:95), because only a culture of discipline is capable of functioning, as a negative condition, for the improvement of moral will; the culture of skill only produces external orders, technological and legal. But Kant quite rightly does not return to this side issue, for according to his system, a technical and political civilization is also a negative condition for the possibility of a moral community!

[26] The term *culture* should also be understood in the sense of physical production, as in agriculture, and not just as a spiritual and intellectual remolding.

[27] "Skill can hardly be developed in the human race otherwise than by means of inequality among men. For the majority, in a mechanical kind of way that calls for no special art, provide the necessaries of life for the ease and convenience of others who apply themselves to the less necessary branches of culture in science and art. These keep the masses in a state of oppression with hard work and little enjoyment, though in the course of time much of the culture of the higher classes spreads to them also. But with the advance of culture—the culminating point of which is called luxury—misfortunes increase equally on both sides: with the lower classes they arise by force of domination from without, with the upper from seeds of discontent within. Yet this splendid misery is connected with the development of natural tendencies in the human race, and the end pursued by nature itself . . . is thereby attained" (*C3*, V:432/II:95-96).

exploiting classes degenerate by their luxuries into bore-
dom, anxiety, and decadence, such that "misfortunes increase
equally on both sides."[28] The solution for both parties lies
in transforming the social order. Instead of the present regime, in which the freedom of each is considered as exclusive of that of the others and stabilization is possible only
by institutionalizing the victory of the strong (inequality),
a civil society will rise, embodying in its constitution the
principle of mutual recognition by all parties of each other's
equality in freedom.[29] This political totality rises from intentions that are contrary to morality, and yet it creates an
analogue to morality in the sphere of legality.[30]

However, the solution attained so far is not yet sufficiently
stable; for in the absence of external security, there is no
guarantee for internal freedom within the state. The state
of war that prevails in principle in international relations
serves as a spur for the development of culture "to the highest pitch" (V:433/11:96);[31] but at the same time, the hor-

[28] Kant writes this at the height of the French Revolution, and the
example of the old regime and the Enlightenment that preceded it
must be in his mind. Nevertheless, he presents this as a model for the
interpretation of empirical history in general. It is interesting to compare it with Hegel's master-and-slave model. Unlike Hegel, Kant sees
the higher classes as the motivating force in history, but he agrees with
Hegel in that misery belongs to the ruling class as well, which is cut
off from reality and its needs, so that the transition to the rule of
freedom is a solution for exploiters as well.

[29] For Kant, the concept of civil society does not express economic
particularism as it does for Hegel, but directly expresses a political
totality.

[30] These are the philosophical principles on which the regime we
are considering is based. The details of this constitution are dealt with
at length in various works, especially in *MM*, *TP*, and *PP*.

[31] These are clearly historical observations, not recommendations.
The force of the observation is even greater in our own day when the
interest in armaments has led to unprecedented advances in knowledge
and technology. Moreover, the dialectic of the "catastrophe of war"
indicated by Kant is not irrelevant to an explanation of today's international relations, and to the relaxation achieved by the balance of
terror, even though this relaxation is, of course, not peace on the
Kantian model. Let us add that Kant witnessed the French Revolution
just as he had the wars of Frederick the Great, in which tens of thou-

rors and waste of war and of preparing for war will grow to a point where fear and utility, guided by the calculating understanding (to be distinguished from reason proper), are liable to abolish all wars by way of a world confederation.

Filling this picture with Kant's other writings, we can describe the external aspect of the historical idea as composed of a number of strata. At its basis we have labor, technical skill, the reworking of physical nature ("culture" in the basic sense), and its appropriation as "mine," giving rise to the legal principal of *property*.[32] On this basis other legal institutions develop, first marked by conflict and inequality, then producing (a) a government of civil society within the state; (b) enlightened criminal and civil law; and (c) a world confederation, establishing a state of peace internationally and reinforcing freedom within each state. In addition, freedom, equality, peace, and enlightened jurisprudence are likely to raise the level of individual happiness or welfare, a result which is also included in the "highest political good" even if it does not constitute its *raison d'être*.

The Culture of Discipline

The second mode, the culture of discipline (*Zucht*), does not embody a quasi-moral system in the outer world but is supposed to work on man's *inner will* and prepare it for the rule of morality.[33] By refining the crude passions and cutting

---

sands of men were killed in one day's battle and the land was laid waste. Frederick the Great's battles were among the bloodiest of all times. There is no doubt that the enormous effort that Frederick exacted from his always outnumbered armies and his country was part of the experience to which Kant was constantly exposed.

[32] Property is "the juridical postulate of practical reason" (*MM*, VI:246/52). It is an external concept of will, which loses the arbitrary and provisional character it has in the state of nature by entering a legal state in which it is guaranteed by a civil constitution (see *ibid.*, Pars. 1-17). The principle of property forms the basis of Kant's civil society and even serves as a necessary condition for the political right to vote.

[33] This form of culture was not discussed in the *Idea* but was later elaborated with some variations in Kant's lectures on *Education* (IX:449-450; 469-470/1-2; 66-67).

man off his immediate, instinctive desires, it cultivates his freedom of choice and creates the type of the "civilized" man, who not only masters his brutish instincts but at the same time develops a new kind of passions and needs, determined by culture itself. This, Kant recognizes, is still a far cry from morality proper. A civilized man may exercise his self-control and power of choice in the service of the most extravagant schemes; his greater education may lead to arrogance; his refined tastes can produce capricious tendencies; and his newly acquired cultural interests are likely to lead to the "vices of culture"[34] like envy, intrigue and resentful competition. Yet exposure to culture, even with its luxuries and "artificial needs" indicates "the liberation of the will from the despotism of [instinctive] desires, whereby, in our attachment to certain *natural* things, we are rendered incapable of exercising a choice of our own" (V:432/II:95; italics added). In other words, from the viewpoint of the development of the inner will, culture stands between the brutish natural will and the purely moral will, preparing the latter for the eventual dominion of the former.[35]

Perpetual Peace: Systematic Considerations

Five years after the third *Critique* Kant reiterated the role of the cunning of nature as a vehicle of progress in the first supplement to *Perpetual Peace*. Since this essay was written when Kant already possessed a critical theory of teleology and had applied it to empirical history as well, we may assign to *Perpetual Peace* the same systematic place, and read it in the same critical context, as that of culture in the third *Critique*. In other words, we may now understand the cun-

[34] *Rel.*, VI:27/22 and p. 149 above.

[35] The natural will, as Kant had recognized in *Religion* (although not clearly in the *Foundations*) is itself "innocent" or amoral. Even the vices of culture are higher than man's animality, which lies altogether outside the sphere of morality. A civilized man has already developed the human *potential* for morality and free choice, although he may exercise it in the wrong direction.

ning of nature as a *reflective* principle of purpose, serving as a non-exclusive guarantee for political progress, which is but a partial aspect of the historical ideal.

I should make clear that my argument is mainly systematic, not historical. I claim that from the third *Critique*, the Kantian system has within it a ground for giving the cunning of nature a critical reinterpretation. Whether Kant in his later essays exploits this principle consciously or fails to use its systematic potential fully is a different question, less important for the purpose of our reconstruction. The crucial point is that *the system itself* now allows a legitimate if restricted place for the cunning of nature, and we may therefore read the text of *Perpetual Peace* as falling within this systematic place.[36]

Kant himself seems to indicate this at the beginning of our text. When reviewing the mechanical course of nature, we discern in it a tendency to produce harmony among men "against their will and, indeed, through their discord" (VIII: 360/106). This result is surprisingly akin to the *objective* final end *(endzweck)* of reason, and a theological mind would have seen here the marks of providence. Kant, however, prefers a less transcendent-sounding idiom, speaking of nature itself as the "great artist" that produces this effect through its "cunning contrivances" (VIII: 362/107).[37] Yet

---

[36] Needless to say, this systematic situation has a history of its own. It was still absent when Kant wrote the *Idea*, and appeared only with the *Critique of Judgement*. The latter work marks, therefore, a crucial change in Kant's philosophical development, dividing the critical period in two parts: before and after a critical theory of teleology was available. In consequence, when Kant wrote the *Idea*, his doctrine is still marked by antithetical tendencies: while the *Critique of Pure Reason* abolishes natural teleology, the *Idea* reinstates it. But unlike other conflicting tendencies, which persisted throughout the whole critical period, this one was *resolved* in the *Critique of Judgement* when it put forth the theory of reflective judgement and applied it to culture as well. Henceforth we need no longer admit a systematic antithesis, for the logic of Kant's system can now allow for the cunning of nature as a legitimate if restricted principle.

[37] *Kunstanstalten* can also be rendered as "artistic designs" or "artistic arrangements."

Kant takes care to explain that in using this metaphor he does not attribute the artistic feature to nature substantively as an objective determination,

> but, as in questions of the relation of the form of things to ends in general, we can and must supply it *from our own minds*, in order to conceive of its possibility by *analogy* to actions of human art. (*ibid.*; italics added)

This warning is made in the language of "reflective" teleology and seems clearly to invoke it.

The Highest Political Good

Having determined the systematic status of *Perpetual Peace*, we need not discuss its content in detail. It differs from the earlier essays mainly in making war the most important, all-inclusive factor that develops culture in *all* its branches.[38] The essay on perpetual peace is thus, in fact, a treatise on the role of *war* in history, including the history of its own abolition. Of all the forms of human conflict serving the cunning of nature, war is the most formidable, the most enduring, and the most effective in spurring societies and individuals to the utmost exertion of their talents and natural faculties. But at a certain point it is likely to turn dialectically against itself, when the particular nations, driven by fear, suffering, greed, and intelligent self-interest, will unite to create a world confederation and abolish war.

The term "perpetual peace" has for Kant a qualitative rather than a temporal meaning. It indicates the state of "true" or "actual" peace that will replace the international state of nature that makes war the fundamental relation among states even in the absence of actual hostilities. As the apex of political progress in history, perpetual peace is duly called "the highest political good"; but as such it should be distinguished from the broader concept of the highest good

[38] It seems that Kant saw a necessary function for wars in the international arena for the long-range goal of realizing peace, for a considerable time after the Enlightenment.

simpliciter, which includes the political ideal as a secondary facet of itself, the external completion and external representation of the ethical community.

Political Technology and the Kingdom of Devils

Since many have read *Perpetual Peace* as if it identified the goal of history with that of politics, it is worthwhile to note that even in *Perpetual Peace* Kant takes care to distinguish between moral and political progress, emphasizing that the latter has nothing to do with morality, only with a certain pragmatic proficiency. It represents no more than intelligent self-interest and the growth of political *skill,* that is, the instrumental capacity to solve an organizational problem that could be equally solved by "a race of devils if only they are intelligent" (VIII:366/112). The problem is:

> Given a multitude of rational beings requiring universal laws for their preservation, but each of whom is secretly inclined to exempt himself from them—to establish a constitution in such a way that, although their *private intentions* conflict, they check each other, with the result that their *public conduct is the same as if they had no such intentions (ibid.).*

Kant clearly speaks of an external imitation of rationality, which has nothing to do with morality and may represent and even perpetuate its opposite. Based upon heteronomy and the coercive power of the state, the model described above is in fact, the very opposite of the ethical community. By a skillful organization of laws, the immoral intentions of the citizens are mutually neutralized, to produce the same external behavior that would also have resulted from morality. This is all that can be expected from politics; and organizing the state on these lines, hard as it may be, is merely a problem in *political technology:*

> It is only a question of a good organization of the state . . . whereby the powers of each selfish inclination are

so arranged in opposition that one moderates or destroys the ruinous effect of the other . . . *and man is forced to be a good citizen, if not a morally good person (ibid.;* italics added).

Good citizenship is possible even in a kingdom of devils. It requires no ethical community (kingdom of ends) and presupposes none. It is something that can be imposed by coercion, while morality can be rooted only in the free or spontaneous will of individuals. Therefore, *even to the best of states cannot be attributed a moral value per se, and it is not in any political organization that the end of history is to be placed.*[39]

[39] The same is stated in the *Contest of the Faculties* (the other later text mentioning the cunning of nature). The supreme political goal may be attained "without the moral foundation in mankind having to be enlarged in the least"; it secures "an increase in the products of legality," but not yet "an ever-growing quantity of morality with regard to intention" (VII:92/151). For these reasons, I cannot agree with Gerhard Krüger when he ascribes to Kant the notion that "Ihrer Materie nach sind alle Rechtspflichten zugleich moralische Pflichten" (*Philosophie und Moral in der kantischen Kritik* [Tübingen, 1967], 107). If indeed materially, all legal duties were moral duties, then no rationally ordered state could at the same time be a kingdom of devils. The resemblance between morality and state laws lies only in their form, a resemblance—as Krüger himself points out—in the nature of *Darstellung,* or one between an Idea and its *Typus* (which amounts to the same). On the whole, Krüger's interpretation vacillates between recognizing the inferior place of the state and ascribing to it, nevertheless, some moral worth in itself. On the one hand he retains the strong distinction between morality and legality, between the politics of a civil society, regulated by mutually limiting interests, and the system of a moral spontaneity or a kingdom of ends. Yet on the other hand he sees the state as offering the medium of publicity to moral attitudes, and thereby the "juridic horizon" in which morality is, so it seems, to come to a fuller expression. Krüger in fact approves of Schleiermacher's erroneous observation that the "inner spirit" of Kant's moral system was "throughout more juridical than ethical"—a statement which Schleiermacher made in complaint, while Krüger accepts it with sympathy (106), but which misses, on our interpretation, the issue. Krüger's inclination towards a "politicized" reading of Kant's ethics leads him to place at the center the dubious (in fact, incoherent) concept of the "ethical state" (*ethischer Staat,* 105-106, 98). Kant recognizes either an Ethical Community (*ethisches gemeines Wesen*), which is not and can-

In addition to emphasizing the secondary place of politics and the cunning of nature in historical progress, our text also focalizes the difference between practical reason proper and mere intelligence. Intelligence belongs to the understanding, not to reason as such; it is the instrumental capacity of solving problems, maximizing utilities and adjusting means to ends that are already given, dictated by desires or other external sources. This instrumental capacity may be shared by men, devils, and perhaps also the higher animals. But the uniqueness of man—what makes him an end in himself and the subject of morality, assigning to him a *historical* role in the universe—lies not in his intelligence but in his reason. Reason is not merely an instrumental calculus but a self-sufficient *interest*. It does not have to derive its ends from elsewhere, but projects or determines of itself the end for which it adjusts means and summons up resources. And this end is none other than reason itself, i.e., realizing rationality in human life in a *conscious* way and for its *own* sake.

The Pre-History of Reason

We cannot conclude this chapter on history and natural dialectic without considering another text as well. The idea of a self-overcoming of nature, whereby a rational principle emerges, applies in Kant not only within history but also as a precondition for it. This is discussed in his somewhat unusual essay, *Conjectural Beginning of Human History* (1786). Written as a philosophical interpretation of *Genesis* 2-6, this essay deals with man's very humanization—his pas-

---

not be a state, and which is no other than the inner system of the "kingdom of ends" (the same, and not its external *Typus*, as Krüger suggests on 104), or the political state, which as such has no moral status per se, although it may externalize and manifest (*darstellen*) the form of morality in the matter and field of legality. There is no conceptual place, therefore, for the hybrid ethical state. Even when state laws are rational, they are not thereby ethical in the strict Kantian sense.

sage from an animal condition to the "state of humanity" (VIII:115/60).[40] The central topic of the essay is therefore not the history of reason proper but what may be called its *pre*-history; for it does not discuss the progress of reason toward maturation, but goes back to explore the more primordial and obscure stage, at which human reason had first broken away from "the womb of nature" and established itself as an independent principle, higher than nature and opposing it.[41]

The prehistory of reason begins in paradise, where man is still a child of nature, guided by mere instinct. "But soon reason begins to stir," producing *comparisons* between different sources of nourishment, some of which are not advised by instinct, or are even contrary to it. This gives rise to "artificial desires" (luxuries), which Kant considers as genuine humanizing factors.[42] With man deserting the immediate instinct and "doing violence to the voice of nature," his reason asserts itself as a power of *free choice*; and thereby, on the basis of the actual practice of choice, he also becomes *aware* of his freedom, that he is not "bound without alternative by a single way, like animals" (VIII:112/56). The discovery of freedom, however, is inescapably attended by *anxiety* and *alarm*, destroying the bliss of paradise.[43]

The next stage in the prehistory of reason, the fig leaf

[40] Kant's use of a semi-historical account of the emergence of rationality, based upon a Biblical story, is not dissimilar in function to Plato's use of myth where an issue cannot be made fully intelligible in terms of pure *logos*.

[41] Kant says that his topic is not the "progression" of freedom but its "first development" (VIII:109/53). He also defines his subject as an "original" human history (*ibid.*, 115/59) or its "most ancient part" *ibid.*, 123/68).

[42] Contrary to Rousseau (and partly also to Marx), who sees such artificial needs as signs of derangement or alienation. Kant, however, does not condone luxuries morally; he only views them as necessary shapers of culture, like wars and exploitation. (cf. above, pp. 182-183).

[43] It is noteworthy that most of the basic "existentials" that Heidegger ascribes to the being of man—anxiety, care, future-directedness (temporality), and the consciousness of death—can be found in Kant's account of "the state of humanity."

story, brings the sublimation of the sexual instinct. By internalizing the inclination and removing the object of desire from the senses, man is led from direct animal attractions to more ideal ones, giving rise to love and to a taste for beauty. This stage also marks the first appearance of man as a *moral* creature, since the power of choice is no longer used in subservience to impulse, but reason is dimly recognized as inherently higher than the impulse. Moreover, the appearance of shame discloses a deep human feature, the attempt of man to secure the esteem and respect of others, that is the basis of all human sociability (*Geselligkeit*).[44]

An even more essential moment of humanity was attained when "reason took its third step": *the conscious expectation of the future.* Man is no longer totally immersed in the present, as animals are but "he faces up in the present to the often distant future" (VIII:113/58).[45] This enables him to make designs and prepare himself for distant aims "according to his role as a human being." But again, it also shreds him with uncertainty, care, and fear of the one certain prospect: death. Kant declares both aspects to be "the most decisive mark of the human's advantage" (*ibid*), indicating that by "man's role" he means the projection of moral aims as well, not only eudaemonistic designs.

Man's actual humanization is, however, achieved only in the next stage. Having separated himself from the rest of the animals, he becomes aware that he is the "true end of nature," not because he is intelligent but because his rationality is *more* than simple intelligence; i.e., it is an end in itself, not a mere instrument for furthering external ends (like desires). This recognition is tied up with another: that by virtue of sharing the same rationality, man enters a

[44] Again we see that the origin of society is not utilitarian but stems from the wish for *recognition* inherent in a rational being as such. (Cf. pp. 148-149 above, and also Hegel's similar doctrine.)

[45] Cf. *inter alia* Nietzsche's conception of man's capacity to tear himself from the immediate presence, as the source of his historicality (*The Use and Abuse of History*, §1).

relation of equality with all other rational beings[46] with respect to the claim of being an end in himself. The rise of this *new form of rationality*, and the moral consciousness implied in it, finally marks man's "release from the womb of nature" and constitutes the "state of humanity" or "the state of freedom" (VIII:115/60).

At this point a far-reaching "destiny" opens up for man, consisting of "nothing less than progress toward perfection" (*ibid.*). Expelled from paradise, man is now endowed with a genuine rational potential; but this must still develop in accordance with its inherent structure and assert itself in the world. In other words, with the end of the pre-history of reason, its history proper only *begins*.

It should be added that Kant conceives of this history as a reconciliation between nature and culture. With reason having broken away from nature and created culture as a principle that opposes nature, man is caught up in a conflict that must give rise to vices and to "various kinds of human misery." This picture of history will prevail throughout "the space of time during which there is conflict," namely, throughout the span of political history (VIII: 116n./61n.). Yet the opposition between nature and culture is to be finally overcome in the creation of "the perfect civil constitution" that would mark the end of political history,[47] creating a new harmony between reason and nature by reshaping the latter in view of the former. Kant's philosophy of history is thus, as Goldmann has rightly observed,[48] to-

---

[46] Kant says "whatever their rank" meaning not only God (as Galston rightly observes in *Kant and the Problem of History* [Chicago, 1975] 81), but in all probability also *other* species of "rational beings" with which the universe is populated, some of them higher than man. (Kant's belief in this hypothesis starts with *UNH* and even in the first *Critique* he is ready to "bet" with the reader the hypothesis is sound.)

[47] Or "termination" (*Beschluss*). Here Kant's text anticipates the Hegelian idea of the "end of history." It also indicates that the goal of political history is *attainable*, whereas the goal of *moral* history is but a regulative idea.

[48] *La Communauté humaine et l'univers chez Kant* (Paris, (1948), 246-248.

,y *future*-oriented; it seeks the remedy and even the justification for the ills of the present in the historical world *to come*, not in a romantic and impossible return to a "golden" past; and it has no sentiment to spare in the longing (with some readers of Rousseau) for a lost paradise, the ideal state of nature that to Kant is the state of sheer *animality*. In other words, it is not by renouncing reason but by the power of reason itself that its ills and conflicts with nature are to be finally resolved.[49]

Conclusion

The diagram on p. 195 presents schematically the relationship between the various factors of historical progress. The origin of historical progress is seen to reside in the action of man, both as a natural being and as a free agent transcending nature. As a natural being he is subject to the unconscious cunning of nature; as a free being he advances, at least ever since the Enlightenment, to realize his internal and external freedom through conscious intention. The goal of historical progress is the highest good, built as a synthesis of two systems, internal and external. The former, the ethical community, totalizes the relations of morality proper, as subjective interpersonal dispositions; as such it is also called an invisible church and the kingdom of ends. The latter, the political community, is an analogue of the moral totality in the world of external institution; it includes a world confederation of states, each having a constitution of civil

---

[49] Apart from the notion of the end of history, this essay contains various other affinities with Hegel's philosophy, including the account of the rise of rationality as "violence" to immediate instinct; the alienating effects of culture, which however are necessary; history as a kind of "theodicy"; and, especially, the reconciliation of the opposition between reason and nature by the power of reason itself, which transforms nature into a humanized world (anticipating Hegel's Spirit). The basic differences, however, remain: reason is external to nature, not an intrinsic moment of it; history can end only politically; and the more important facet of historical purpose (which does not come to an end) is itself practical (moral), and not speculative, as in Hegel.

HISTORICAL PROGRESS AND THE PRIORITY OF ENDS

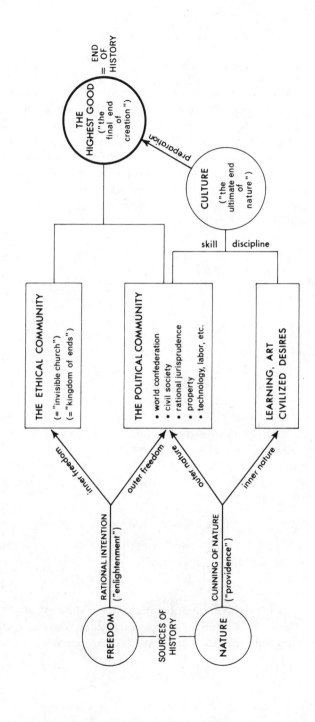

society; and it is based upon labor, technology (the manipulation of nature), property, and rational jurisprudence.

As the diagram shows, the cunning of nature cannot produce the goal of history. It reaches only as far as the stage of culture. As such it can produce the political facet of the highest good, but even here it is only a sufficient, not a necessary condition. As for the ethical community, the core of the historical ideal, the cunning of nature can only prepare the external ground for it by ensuring a political order, guaranteeing life and property, refining the brutish instincts. But it cannot bring about the system of ethical dispositions itself. On the contrary, for this system to arise, the cunning of nature, representing the opposite dispositions, must rather be *destroyed*.

Realizing the highest good with both its facets is supposed to promote empirical welfare (happiness) as well; but this is only a corollary of the rational system and not an end in itself. By abolishing the waste and suffering of wars; cancelling oppression and economic exploitation; ensuring equal opportunities to all; allocating the natural resources to peaceful uses and to the real needs of man; developing international trade; and on the moral plane, by reinforcing mutual good will—man is likely to expand his empirical welfare as well. But Kant must and does see this only as an appended result that may certainly be hoped for and even expected but that cannot constitute the goal of history per se. This goal is the realization of freedom and rationality *for its own sake*.

Moral History and the Moral Law

Throughout this chapter we have stressed the difference between political and moral history; but what precisely does this concept signify for Kant? Can there be a moral history at all?

Kant holds that moral consciousness inheres, as a "fact of reason" in all human beings, even those who act against it. Moreover, the moral law itself is *a priori* and has as such no history at all. On the other hand, moral history is possible, and for a finite being inevitable, in the sense of *closing the gap between the ought*—the abstract recognition of the moral law implicit in all rational beings—*and its actual manifestations in the life of the human race.* For Kant this involves the propagation of the ethical community, incorporating an ever-increasing number of individuals into its framework, and ideally, spreading its rule over the whole human race.

The concept of moral history finds its parallel in the moral biography of the individual. When discussing the concept of personal *virtue*,[50] we saw that although each act is either moral or not, with no gradation or compromise, there still is a problem of moral personality and way of life, stretching beyond the limits of the single act. Kant resolves this problem by postulating a global disposition, the decision to act morally throughout a lifetime, that must, however, be implemented and reenacted in all particular acts; and moral progress for the individual consists in closing the gap between the two and reducing to zero the cases of deviation. Moral progress on the historical scale is likewise a *totalizing* concept, stretching beyond the boundaries of the single person to incorporate all rational beings in all their acts and decisions.

In addition, moral history signifies the gradual awakening of man's moral consciousness, its breaking out from the dim, distorted, and sensuously embedded forms it takes at first, towards its full and self-conscious *explication.* In this respect, the growth of rationality has a qualitative rather than a quantitative significance; it represents a passage from dim to clear, from dormant to awakened, from covert to overt, from intuitive to self-conscious. In the language of the history of reason in general, it is the process whereby the latent paradigm of rationality explicates itself and attains consciousness in its *pure* form.

This is again manifest in the education of the individual,

50 Chapter 1, pp. 52-53.

where the moral consciousness implicit in the pupil is gradually awakened by practice, example, and identification.[51] A similar idea comes to the fore even methodologically, when Kant in the *Foundations* explicates the pure form of morality out of its embedded form in popular consciousness. But perhaps the most important expression of this idea is given in the history and critique of religion, presented as the awakening of moral consciousness and its purification from the "sensuous" form it takes in the successive historical churches; and also in the history of philosophy itself, which progresses along similar lines. These two avenues of the history of reason will be our next topic of discussion.

[51] See *Education*, IX:488-491/100-106 and the "Methodology" of C2 (V:151-161/155-165).

PART III

The History of Reason Manifested

CHAPTER V

CRITIQUE· AND
HISTORY OF RELIGION

Kant's view of the history of reason is manifested specifically in two domains where the growth of rationality is the central issue: the *critique of religion* and the *history of philosophy*. Religion is a most powerful historical force, dominating people's ethical attitudes throughout the ages; but although historically it has irrational and heteronomous features, in essence there is only one religion, the religion of reason, identical with rational ethics; and the first role of the critique of religion is to reveal this rational essence of religion beneath the "sensuous" cover it assumed in history.

This theoretical explication cannot remain on the level of pure philosophy alone. One must explicate the moral essence of religion through the actual beliefs and practices it assumes in the history of religion; and this requires a special technique, for which Kant turns to Biblical hermeneutics. In using its rhetorical potential for moral-educational purposes, the philosophical critic of religion can find his own proper mode of praxis, enhancing the historical growth of rationality that his own theory advocates.

As the history of religion is a latent totality, governed by the implied religion of reason, so the history of philosophy is a latent totality, governed by the pure architectonic or system of reason, of which it is the distorted manifestation. I shall deal with religion in the present chapter and with the history of philosophy in the next.

The Religion of Reason and Historical Faiths

The first point to note about Kant's philosophy of religion is its negative character. It is a *critique* of religion and not a positive religious doctrine. Almost every positive idea that Kant has to express under the title of rational religion has already been expressed in his ethics, while what is new in the *Religion within the Limits of Reason Alone* (1793) is mainly an uncompromising attack upon the existing religions and an attempt to eliminate them from the historical scene. It may thus be said that Kant does not have a philosophy of religion in the same positive sense that he has a philosophy of knowledge, of morals, of art, and of politics. In all these fields, philosophy has a constructive function, to establish the *a priori* grounds of a genuine and relatively autonomous field; whereas the role of the philosophy of religion is to *abolish* religion as an independent sphere and to reduce it to rational morality alone. Its character is therefore critical in the destructive sense—destructive, that is, to anything in the religious phenomenon that cannot be approved by practical reason. But at the same time, as we shall later see, the commands of practical reason are now elaborated into the realm of the *sacred*; i.e., the typical religious properties and accompanying states of mind are not lost in the process but are rather transferred into the domain of humanistic morality.

In the *Religion* Kant no longer considers morality from a pure or transcendental point of view but within a *historical* context. He is interested in the historical totalization of morality, i.e., in the actual creation and propagation of a kingdom of ends or an ethical community. In this context he also puts forth a historical doctrine, stating that rational morality is the latest essence of all forms of religion and is present, if in a distorted fashion, even in the crudest historical faith. This makes it possible to purify the historical religions and gradually bring them to their rational essence, that is, to reduce religion to morality not only in theory, in the works of enlightened philosophers and their followers, but also in historical reality.[1] Moreover, the *Religion* is de-

---

[1] He calls this process allegorically "the Founding of a Kingdom of God on Earth" (*Rel.*, VI:91, 122, 115/87, 113, 105).

signed not only as a theoretical treatise but as a practical tool in furthering the ends that it recommends. Using suggestion and persuasive techniques, it discusses specific strategies and suggests immediate applications. And the main strategic device that Kant has in mind in furthering the historical propagation of morality through a purification of traditional religion is a tendentious moral interpretation of the Holy Scriptures and of theological dogma.

In religion one can usually distinguish a body of theoretical assertions and a system of moral and ritual commands. In Kant's critical conception of reason, as expressed in the Dialectic of the first *Critique*, reason is denied theoretical access to the transcendent and the infinite and thus all theological *knowledge* becomes impossible. This eliminates the immense theoretical part of religion and leaves us with its practical side alone. Dogmas and miraculous stories can have no claim for truth and may serve at best only as moral symbols. Morality itself can also no longer be based on the will of a problematical God, who cannot be even known to exist. If morality is possible at all, it must be grounded independently of the idea of God, namely on the autonomy of human reason. This, in fact, is what is said in the opening passages of the *Religion*. And since religion can have only a moral sense, it follows that *religion itself has to be grounded independently of the idea God.*

The Dual Condition of Rationality

These results of the first *Critique* are further developed in Kant's ethical writings. If morality can be based only on humanistic grounds, it remains to be seen of what precisely it does consist. And in developing the principles of ethics— or for that matter, of religion—Kant's special conception of reason played a decisive part. For Kant, reason is not just a set of given objective principles but also the free activity of the ego who constitutes these principles and recognizes them as *his own*. In other words, rationality is an attitude in which a free individual adopts and thus reconstitutes a universal point of view.[2] This conception of reason applies to knowledge as well as to ethics, but in the case of ethics it becomes more explicit. By definition a rational action cannot be imposed from without but must always stem from a person's own decision and recognition. What can be imposed is a universal pattern, but it would thereby cease to be rational. A universal law that cannot be approved by a thinking subject is no less irrational than a person who prefers a particular point of view. In the first case we shall have totalitarianism (or what Kant calls, paradoxically, "the despotism of reason"), in the second egoism and mutual contradiction. In order to achieve rationality the universal pattern must be capable of recognition by the subjective conscience, and on the other hand, the individual must be capable of adopting, by his own activity or choice, a universal point of view. In a word, rationality implies freedom.

The only conception of duty which respects this principle is the so-called concept of autonomy, which regards duty as emanating from the free decision of an individual who abides by a law he has himself legislated. But this is precisely what the religious conception, which Kant calls statutory and analyzes as heteronomous, contradicts. According to it, the individual's duty is imposed upon him by a foreign will, into whose reasons he may not inquire and to whom he must sacrifice his judgement; and this makes man, who is basically free, the slave of a transcendent despot.

A further charge against historical religion concerns the nature of religious practice and institutions. If religion is morality, then the only valid religious practice, in Kant's metaphorical language the only "way to please God," is to act from the categorical imperative and be disposed to recognize in action all other men's freedom and rationality. But in the historical religions the wish to please God has become a sort of interested flattery, and developed into ar-

[2] This is also Kant's definition of the *Aufklärung* in the *Critique of Judgement*, Par. 40 (V:294-295/I:152-153); and in fact he identifies *Aufklärung* with rationality.

bitrary customs. Men think they will please God by bizarre cults, by mere praise and prayer, or by fanatical enterprises. Kant rejects these means as "religious delusion" and as "pseudo-service" (*Afterdienst: Rel.*, VI:170/158), and reserves a further reproach for clericalism and "papacy." What Kant rejects in *Pfaffentum*[3] is the idea that man has to be ruled and guided not only by a Supreme Being but also by a host of secondary masters—popes, priests, ministers, rabbis, illuminati, and various interpreters of the Scriptures. As Kant puts it, this is a kind of "spiritual despotism, to be found in all forms of ecclesiasticism, however unpretentious and popular they may declare themselves" (*ibid.*, 175n./163n.).

The Definition of Rational Religion

In light of these criticisms and after what had been said against statutory laws, it might seem puzzling that rational religion is defined by Kant as "the recognition of all our duties as divine commands" (*Rel.*, VI:153/142). Having excluded the concept of God's commands from moral religion, how can Kant make this concept reappear in its very definition?

To answer this question, we must examine the crucial phrase "*as* divine commands" (*als göttliche Gebote*). Kant avoids the the noun *God* in all versions of the definition (in the *Religion* as well as in other works) but always uses the adjective *divine*. This precaution is most significant; for Kant takes an adjective traditionally associated with God and ascribes it to human duties. The correct reading of his definition is therefore that rational religion is the attitude in which the duties of reason are taken to be as holy and divine, as one would usually regard the commands of God.[4]

[3] The German term *Pfaffentum*, which has derogatory connotations, is used not only in reference to Catholicism but to all forms of priesthood and institutional religion.

[4] Kant expressly talks of "the performance of all *human* duties as divine commands" (VI:110/100). The definition mentioned in VI:84/79 likewise relates to "human duties," while the definition mentioned

The only thing that we retain from traditional religion is the attribute of divinity, now ascribed to the ethics of reason alone.

But if this is the case, why is this equivocal definition suggested at all? The main reason is, I think, that since Kant asserts that both rational and historical religion have a common ground, he has to find a formula applicable to both. In fact, when he presents his definition in the *Religion*, he affirms its equivocal nature and goes on to divide it into two subcategories. Of revealed or statutory religion he says: "I must know in advance that something is a divine command in order to recognize it as my duty"; of rational religion: "I must first know that something is my duty before I can accept it as a divine injunction" (VI:154/142-143). This supports our interpretation. At the same time it is apparent that what the definition expresses is not the "essence" of all religion—which Kant claims is rational religion—but a general phenomenological feature, of which rational religion is only one of two possible and mutually exclusive instantiations.[5]

One Religion in Many Faiths

Let us now consider more closely the historical relation between the different religions. A central passage in the *Religion* states:

---

above in VI:153/142 is imperfectly translated, since in German it is "das Erkenntnis aller unserer Pflichten als göttlicher Gebote," which should be rendered as "the recognition of all *our* duties as divine commands" (italics added): the translators, it seems, overlooked the importance of the possessive "our."

It is noteworthy that the word *as* ("*as* divine commands") occurs in all versions of the definition and is underlined in most of them. In one place (*Reflexionen*, No. 8104) Kant adds the Latin equivalent "tanquam" to the underlined "als" in a way which suggests that the duties of reason must be regarded *as if they were* divine commands; and Kant goes on to assert that this does not at all imply that one has to believe in the existence of God.

5 It seems that Kant is mixing two meanings of *essence* here, a descriptive and a normative, and his descriptive definition also seems partial and implausible.

There is only *one* (true) religion; but there can be *faiths* of several kinds. We can say further that even in the various churches, severed from one another by reason of the diversity of their modes of belief, one and the same true religion can yet be found (VI:107/98).

This idea is closely analogous to Kant's account of the history of philosophy as underlain by the single *system* of philosophy. The diversity of religious opinion is not completely arbitrary but gives a "sensuous" form to one and the same moral consciousness, the religion of reason. In the language of the architectonic we may say that a single interest of reason underlies the history of religion, pushing through it toward pure explication. Kant even ranges the various historical religions on a progressive scale, thus giving, as the title indicates, a "historical account of the gradual establishment of . . . the good principle on earth." In particular, the progress from Judaism to Christianity, from Catholicism to Lutheranism, and finally from sensuous religion to philosophical religion, represents not only a succession in time, but equally the ascent of the rational principle toward full self-consciousness. Judaism is most inferior, having been "in its original form, a collection of mere statutory laws" (VI:125/116), and being based, as Kant believes, on the principle of theocracy. Kant even places early Judaism outside the moral scale, calling it a mere political religion.[6] When Judaism, however, came into contact with Greek influence, it lost its purely "patriarchial" nature, and assuming moral doctrines, it became interfused with a genuine "religious faith" (VI:128/118). This gave rise to Christianity, which "arose suddenly, though not unprepared for, from Judaism. . . . The Teacher of the Gospel . . . declared that servile belief . . . [was] essentially vain and that moral faith . . . is the only saving faith" (VI:128-129/118-119); but his

[6] See J. Guttmann, "Kant und das Judentum," *Schriften* (Leipzig, 1908), 42-62; N. Rotenstreich, *The Recurring Pattern* (London, 1963), 23:47; J. Katz, "Kant and Judaism," *Tarbiz*, XLI (1971-1972), 220-237 (Hebrew).

teaching was distorted in the long history of Christianity. The mystical fanaticism of the hermits and monks joined forces with the oppression of hierarchy and orthodoxy; and the Byzantine meddling of politics with religious statutes in the East came alongside the spiritual dictatorship of a "self-styled viceroy of God" in the West, suppressing the sciences and dominating "kings like children by the magic wand of . . . excommunication" (VI:130-131/121). Then came Crusades and religious wars within Christendom, also stemming from "a despotically commanding ecclesiastical faith"—and all exemplify the truth of Lucretius's complaint *tantum religio potuit suadere malorum* (VI: 131 / 122).[7] The reason for these aberrations was that at first Christianity had to introduce itself in forms acceptable to the pagan world, and *these* forms have become the basis for the universal world religion.

Without mentioning the Reformation Kant makes it clear that it represents a higher stage than Catholicism; but here his language becomes more prudent. Praising the present time as the best in the entire known history of the church (VI:131/122), he still leaves no doubt about the equivocal nature of this statement. It not only praises Lutheranism as a more rational faith than Catholicism, but equally criticizes Lutheranism with respect to a higher and radically new phase, the pure philosophical religion. The reason for the superiority of the present period "up to now" is that within Protestantism there are a few[8] who represent the spirit of religion in a way that eventually may lead to an approximation to the supreme visible form of church that represents the idea of pure rational religion.

To conclude, the history of reason is manifested in the

[7] "Such evil deeds could religion prompt" (*De rerum natura* I, 101) Kant's invocation of Lucretius, the exponent of the Epicurean critique of religion, whom Kant already worshipped during his "youthful slavery" in the Pietistic *Collegium Fridericianum* in Königsberg, indicates his being influenced by the same tradition.

[8] It has been suggested that Kant may have in mind the Pietists; but this is doubtful. At this point he does not advocate a specific *sect* within Protestantism but a specific mental attitude, regardless of sect.

empirical history of religion, where it is marked by three major revolutions: Christ emerging from Judaism, the Reformation emerging from the aberrations of Christianity; and finally, the rational church eventually emerging from a more purified Protestantism. Throughout the process a single interest of reason expounds and develops itself, and when it is fully explicated, we find that this interest is no other than the pure moral interest of reason, now taken as a *totality* of free rational wills.

Why Write a Book about Religion?

At this point a query must arise. If true religion is nothing but morality, what is left of religion as such? And why write a book about religion at all? The answer, I think, lies in the fact that in dealing with religion Kant is no longer analyzing moral concepts but trying to convert a state of mind. Religion adds nothing new to the *principles* of morality.[9] But the philosophy of religion promotes the *spirit* in which the moral principles are to be taken. Its aim is to prevent these principles from deteriorating into banality (not an improbable fate for rationalistic maxims) and to invest them with life and the sublimity of religious values. Morality for Kant is no ordinary matter, exhausted by telling the truth and returning deposits. It has something to do with "the sublimity of our destiny" (*Rel.*, VI:23n./19n.) and with the "final end of creation" (*C3*, V:434/II:98) itself; it has a "majesty" that evokes "awe" and "admiration" and

[9] The work *Religion*, however, does introduce some new elements. In the first two books Kant develops and amends a few elements of his ethics. For instance, he affirms that evil, too, originated in freedom and not in the determinism of natural inclinations; he introduces the idea of a global intention that totalizes the discrete series of free acts and makes a concept of moral gradation and progress possible; and he possibly also takes the first steps toward a distinction between the will as an arbitrary power of choice (*Willkür*) and the rational will as the consciousness of the law (*Wille*), anticipating the explicit distinction in the second part of *MM*, the *Doctrine of Virtue* (Cf. J. Silber's introduction to the English edition of the *Religion*). All these topics belong thematically to Kant's *moral* system proper, even though they are elaborated in a book that purports to be dealing with religion.

can elevate the spirit to the point of "exaltation." But these wider meanings may pass unnoticed in daily moral affairs. It is only too easy for the categorical imperative to be taken as a mere index of universalization. It is not improbable for the concept of human duties to be grasped in the spirit of petit-bourgeois obligations or of meticulous pedantry. And on the whole, one can be misled into thinking that to replace the commands of God by the duties of man is to deteriorate to banality, that to have to dispense with the idea of God is to lose all contact with the sublime. It is just such a devaluation that Kant's philosophy of religion attempts to avoid. In "reducing" religion to morality, it at the same time attributes the supreme features of religion to morality. The main idea of this philosophy is not only to reject the historical faiths but also to preserve their revered attributes and the sublime states of mind that they can offer—and to transport these into the morality of reason. This is also manifest in Kant's language when he compares the awe which morality instills to that of "the law of Sinai" and when he talks of it in such religious terms as "holiness," "divinity," "reverence," "admiration," "respect," "sublimity," "wonder," and "exaltation." These terms are not meant as metaphors. They are used literally, with the plenitude of their original content, only now they are applied to what Kant considers the appropriate object. The underlying assumption is that man has a certain mental constant that may be described as a religious consciousness or a religious disposition in some general sense. This religious disposition is not committed to any particular form of faith and can be converted from the wrong to the right objects without losing its fundamental qualities. It is the task of the philosophy of religion to do this, and in so doing it does not eliminate religion altogether but rather preserves its basic features in a new form. (This same model underlies, to a great extent, many actual processes of *secularization* and *sacralization* in modern history.)

At this point a word of criticism may be inserted. It is perfectly conceivable that such experiences as religious awe, dread, and reverence, and the sense of *tremendum* or the *nouminose* in general (in Rudolf Otto's phrase), should be found inseparable from the image of a transcendent Master whose power and authority *overwhelm* our own—and thus tied up with what, on Kant's program, cannot survive. It is equally conceivable that such experience presupposes a sense of the inexplicability, the mystery, or the helplessness of our existence in the world and thus cannot be divorced from the *theoretical* impact of religion. Furthermore, a radical critic of religion may conceivably charge that in his alleged conservation of the sublime religious states, Kant is engaging in self-deceit, since authentic enlightenment must contend with their inevitable loss. It may well be the price of emancipation from "statutory" religion that all claim to divinity be excluded from human affairs. Therefore, by setting out to reinstate the sacred within the secular Kant's theory is liable to defeat its purpose, even ending up with the grotesque or the profane. Moreover, while starting from a principle of autonomy or enlightenment it will frustrate its own principle when unwilling to face its less than sublime consequences.

A further critical comment may help to bring out Kant's dependence on the notion of history of reason. His book on religion describes the conflict between reason and revelation as a confrontation between the morality of human autonomy and that of the will of God. Can this confrontation be construed as a rational argument? In a sense we can do so, that is, if we have already accepted the superior authority of rational argumentation; but this is precisely what is at stake. Reason can refute the believer's position only if it had already done so implicitly; but in the case of a genuine believer, this is excluded by a definition. For the latter, reason cannot invalidate the commands of God since it has no authority over them. Indicating the dogmatism of such a position would afford little theoretical assistance, since for dogmatism to be an intellectual vice and for open-mindedness to be a virtue one must have already rejected the supremacy of revelation and opted for rationality. The believer who at least agrees to open his mind to the results of rational argument has ceased to be a believer even before the argument began. What we praise as open-mindedness is itself a specific option and a prior commitment exclusive of others. And so, in the last analysis, reason does not prove itself but asserts itself; it is *affirmatio sui* and not *ratio sui*.

It is at this point that Kant's idea of a history of reason becomes important. Since Kant is unable to prove the superiority of his position theoretically, all he may expect is that the rising self-consciousness of the audience and the effects of moral education and persuasion would suggest to their minds the desired conversion. Moreover, Kant is even more circumscribed in arguing with the believer in revelation than other rationalists, since for him part of the meaning of rationality is its subjective acceptance by whoever is supposed to be bound by its rules. The same conception of rationality that served Kant to reject statutory religion, makes it self-contradictory for him to impose rationality on a person from without. And so he cannot ascribe to a person a violation of rationality unless that person has already accepted, at least in some latent form, the authority-in-principle of what he is alleged to violate.

Although Kant recognizes that from a purely theoretical, a-historical viewpoint, his own position may be as dogmatic as that of his opponent, he places the conflict within the historical context in which the confrontation of reason and revelation both arises and is to be eventually resolved. But *Kant does not admit that opting for rationality is itself an arbitrary and irrational act. To him there can be a meta-philosophical theory, accounting to a significant if not a full extent for the rise of rationality in rational terms, although this theory must be historical, and cannot be based upon a formal argument or a transcendental deduction.*

The rise of rationality is not completely arbitrary, since

on the one hand it is the adequate expression of ourselves, and on the other hand it occurs within a structured process of enlightenment, a history of reason, in which we gradually come to realize it as such. But the self-assertive feature of reason is also preserved in the process in that every major stage is supposed to involve a new spontaneous act of the mind, a newly emerging self-awareness or mental awakening, that presupposes a whole set of previous theories and attitudes but cannot be simply reduced to them or deduced from them.

It is no accident, therefore, that in the *Religion* Kant is largely preoccupied with a philosophy of history,[10] as it is understandable why he also conceives of the book as a practical means of persuasion apart from its theoretical task. In both ways Kant admits that all he can expect is a rise in the self-consciousness of the audience, and that all he can do to encourage this process, insofar as religious believers are concerned, is to use suggestive educational means rather than formal logical arguments.

For this purpose, Kant is in need of a "sensuous" auxiliary. Statutory religion is already there as the dominant spiritual force in history. It must surely be eliminated if morality is to prevail; but on the large historical scale this cannot be done only by confronting it with an alternative. One must also proceed from within, addressing one's audience in its own terms, stressing real and alleged common features and trying to reinterpret, and where necessary misinterpret, the sacred themes in the proper direction. The idea, on the whole, is to convert revealed religion from an opponent into an aid. This explains the variety of dogmas, mysteries and Biblical sayings that Kant seems to reinterpret positively in the *Religion*: his brand of Bible hermeneutics is to serve as a moral-educational tool in the historical arena.

[10] As Despland rightly argues in *Kant on History and Religion* (Montreal and London, 1974).

Bible Hermeneutics as an Agent of Moral History

Bible hermeneutics does not aim merely at understanding religion; it intends understanding as an agent of change. The philosophical critic is not content with knowing for himself the delusory features of revealed religion and their corrupt effects; he wants to have this awareness shared by the multitude, thus purging their lives and institutions of the dominion of irrational powers, and opening their way to a freer and more enlightened existence.

Major obstacles in this way are the beliefs in the Bible's super-rational authority, in the literal truth of its stories, and in the sacred validity of the immense dogmatic, ritual, and institutional apparatus that have grown out of it in the course of generations. To be effective the critique must have an affinity with the mind of its audience; or without taking the public's point of departure into account, no dialogue, much less a change in its attitude, is possible. At this point Biblical exegesis becomes instrumental as a fictitious common ground between the critic and his audience. Since the believer in revealed religion cannot share the philosopher's first principles, the philosopher must pose as sharing the believer's first principles by appealing to the Bible, then turn the former against themselves.

On this point Kant subscribes to a program initiated by Spinoza,[11] but he gives it a different emphasis. Spinoza is more attached to a dialectical technique that accepts the Bible as a major premise in an argument, hoping to extract from the Scripture proofs against its believers. Kant, on the other hand, wishes to exploit his audience's deep-rooted respect for the Bible and divert it to serve his own philosophical interests; but he never seeks proofs of any kind in the Bible, nor does he claim that adherence to original spirit of

11 In his *Tractatus Theologico-Politicus.* For a full discussion of this issue, see my article "Bible Interpretation as Philosophical Praxis: A Study of Spinoza and Kant," *Journal of the History of Philosophy,* XI (1973), 189-212, from which this part of the present chapter is adapted.

the Scripture will of itself liberate people from superstition. For him the Bible is only a psychological and educational auxiliary, theoretically to be discarded at the end of the process.

This is not to deny that there are also other reasons for the appeal to the Bible, such as the need for prudence and personal security. Spinoza's works and letters provide ample proof of his mastery of what Leo Strauss called "the art of writing within persecution."[12] And the language of Kant's *Religion* must be read like Spinoza's.[13] His conflict with official and social censorship is reflected in his prudent discussions of political authority;[14] in his apparent ambivalence concerning revolution in general and the French Revolution in particular;[15] and more clearly, in the careful and convoluted argument that he had with the censorship of Friedrich Wilhelm II[16] in the Preface to the *Religion*, and in his attempt in this book to find a place, even if far-fetched, for counter-rational principles of theology.[17] It is

[12] *Persecution and the Art of Writing* (Glencoe, Ill., 1952).

[13] At this point I disagree completely with Despland's approach, who reads Kant's *Religion* as a *bona fide* religious document, disregarding its "cover" techniques.

[14] See *TP* and *MM*, Part I.

[15] Compare, for instance, the concluding chapter of *TP* to Par. 6 in *The Contest of Faculties*. In the former he states that revolution is absolutely forbidden and that any resistance to the supreme legislator or incitation to rebellion is the worst offense in a political community and the most deserving of punishment, since it undermines its foundation. In the second work he says the French Revolution not only calls for sympathy and enthusiasm, but also that suggests that the human race has an inclination toward the good and reasonable evidence of moral progress in history. Kant's final position is that one cannot justify any revolution *a priori*, but that there are revolutions that are beneficial *a posteriori*, that is, once they have occurred. He consequently leaves the matter in the hands of "Providence" (*Rel.*, VI:122/112-113).

[16] See Emil Fromm, *Kant und die Preussische Censur, nach den Akten im Königl. Geheimen Staatsarchiv* (Hamburg and Leipzig, 1894).

[17] Sometimes Kant's attempts become absurd, especially in the chapters of "general observations" supplementing each of the four books of *Religion*, where he treats counter-rational subjects like the belief in the Trinity (VI:140-142, 145-147/131-133, 136-138), the concept of grace (VI:174, 194-200/162, 182-188), and that of mystery in general (VI:142-

clear, then, that both authors use Biblical exegesis *also* to ensure their personal security: the nominal usage of sacred texts can help the philosopher tread the narrow common ground between faithfulness to his own ideas and apparent faithfulness to the ruling tradition.[18] Yet this is not the sole, or (I think) the main reason for using the Bible. Even unworried about his safety, Kant like Spinoza would have used the Bible to reach out to the masses and subvert their long-standing attitudes. In fact, reference to the Bible is often made where no security problem occurs and even where prudence would have advised that mention of a verse be avoided altogether, since the way in which it is used is clearly outrageous from a religious viewpoint. Moerover, prudence does not require and would perhaps even discourage the formation of *generalized* hermeneutic methods; Kant's is an overt challenge to the pious mind. It is crucial for our purpose to see that even when intended to avoid unnecessary risks, preoccupation with the Bible reflects a fundamental determination to take necessary ones. Its defensive value is a strategic corollary to the other and derives from the same feature that initially recommended it as an offensive weapon. In this sense Biblical exegesis is an aggressive activity, offering the philosopher a mode of *engagement* in the social and cultural processes of his time.

What does this concern with practical involvement stem from? Is it rooted in the philosopher's doctrinal statements or should we explain it, as today in the case of Sartre, in

---

147/133-138). It is hardly credible that Kant took his own interpretations seriously; he himself presents them as "*parerga* to religion within the limits of reason; they do not belong within it but border upon it" (*ibid.*, VI:52/47); and it is clear that he deals with these subjects only to avoid an open fissure with the religious public that would undermine his educational tactics.

18 Both Spinoza and Kant use the device of declaring the compatibility of reason with the Scripture or with theology. (See *Tractatus Theologico-Politicus*, Chapter Fifteen; *Rel.*, VI:13/11). However, this is mere lip service to an idea both philosophers actually refute in the contents of their books.

terms of personal formation, temperament, and pre-doctrinal insights and commitments? A complete answer would draw up into a vast issue in the history and perhaps the phenomenology of philosophy that I cannot claim to resolve. But restricting ourselves only to *systematic* grounds we may say that Kant must have considered practical involvement to be his moral duty. The categorical imperative ("Act so that . . .") commands action, not intention; and although it places the moral value of the act in its subjective ground, it does not exempt the agent from doing it.[19] In addition, Kant complements the formal categorical imperative with the command to promote the highest good in the world; and this, as Chapter One has shown, requires that the individual be concerned *not only with his private virtue but with the moral state of the world as a whole.* There are various avenues to this ideal, one of which is *moral education*: and this is based upon the rational Church and the critique of revealed religion. Its task is to propagate the ethical community which, as we know, is a purely secular system composed of morally free individuals who recognize each other's freedom and humanity and are disposed to act out of this recognition. It follows that Kant's involvement in the critique of religion can be explained, in the terms of his system, by the duty he thinks every man has: "the promotion of the highest good as a social good" (VI: 97/89).

Given the vast perspectives and also the political dimensions of the changes advocated by Kant, Bible hermeneutics may appear to have minor importance. But Kant considers rational education and the free dissemination of ideas to be the genuine *action* of the philosopher, which can transform social and political reality no less than the personalities of his audience. He considers that the process of liberating

19 It exempts him from being judged unfavorably only if the action turns out to be futile or unexpectedly counterproductive or, less significantly, if the agent who resolved and set out to perform the deed is prevented from doing so by uncontrollable circumstances.

thought, with its social and political results, cannot be historically effective unless it passes through a critique of revealed religion and finds support in the reinterpretation of its sacred documents. Seen from this angle, Bible interpretation, both in its detail and in the formation of its generalized principles, is not an incidental activity among many others, but a *major mode for the philosopher's social and practical involvement.*

In summary, to eliminate the effects of revealed religion, Kant has to consider its historical grip on the masses and attack it on its own ground. This appears to be a paradoxical concession that the critic makes to his opponent, since he accepts the authority he is seeking to destroy. But the concession is merely rhetorical, as can be seen by comparison with a genuine religious reformer. The latter will appeal to the Holy Book (or to its "true spirit") because he himself believes in its authority and wishes to rescue it from distortions, whereas the philosophical critic appeals to the Bible only because *others*—his audience—believe in its authority, while he wishes to rescue them from the distortion implied in this very belief.

Kant's Hermeneutic Method as an Extension of His Theory of Postulates

Kant's hermeneutic principle is not elaborated as a doctrine in itself, but the *Religion* supplies sufficient grounds for its reconstruction. Denying Spinoza's ideal of investigating the text as a pure scientific object, Kant declares that "Scriptural exegesis lies beyond the limits of the domain of reason" (VI:43n./39n.). By this equivocal statement he means that even assuming, as we should, that the Bible was written by men alone, not by the word of a transcendent God, we are unable to decipher its literal meaning and gain an objective, scientific knowledge of the authors' original intention. On the other hand,

> it is possible to explain how an historical account is to be put to a *moral* use without deciding whether this is

the intention of the author or merely our interpretation, provided this meaning is true in itself, apart from all historical proof, and is, moreover, the only one whereby we can derive something conducive to our betterment from a passage, which otherwise would be only an unfruitful addition to our knowledge (VI:43n./ 39n.; italics added).

Kant clearly recognizes the implications of his suggestion:

> This interpretation may, in the light of the text . . . appear forced—*it may often really be forced*; and yet if the text can possibly support it, it must be preferred to a literal interpretation, which either contains nothing at all [helpful] to morality, or else actually works counter to moral incentives (VI:110/101; italics added).

In other words, even if there is no cognitive decision about the literal meaning of texts, still there are certain constraints built into them; some can support a tendentious reading and some cannot. But these constraints are determined from a rhetorical rather than a scientific point of view: a text can support an interpretation if and only if it will sound *psychologically* plausible and will have the desired effect on the audience. Kant thus subordinates both the goals and the means of Biblical scholarship to the extrinsic interest of moral education. The study of the Bible is devoid of value unless it serves moral ends and reinforces the will to pursue them. The Bible is dead as a pure scientific object; its importance lies only in its power to influence. But taken literally, the Bible's influence is predominantly perverse, both morally and cognitively. In most cases, therefore, an allegorical interpretation is to be preferred, even at the expense of consciously distorting its author's original intent (which, Kant holds, cannot be fully grasped and cognitively is an unsolved problem). Allegorical interpretation is, however, not a rigid rule. The only constant criterion is the extrinsic or moral interest, which

THE HISTORY OF REASON MANIFESTED

should determine the proper mode of interpretation in each case.

This principle is further discussed in a section entitled "Ecclesiastical Faith Has Pure Religious Faith as Its Highest Interpreter," and is exemplified in Kant's polemics with the Biblical scholar Johann David Michaelis.[20] In Psalm 59: 11-16 the poet prays for a most cruel revenge on his enemies. Michaelis approved of this prayer in its literal sense, claiming that "the Psalms are inspired; if in them punishment is prayed for, it cannot be wrong, and we must have no morality higher than the Bible." Kant retorts by raising the question, *"whether morality should be expounded according to the Bible or whether the Bible should be expounded according to morality"* (VI:110n./101n.). Kant evidently accepts the second way; and his rhetorical question sums up both his method of Bible hermeneutics and the principle of the autonomy of ethics.

Because of its predominantly allegorical nature, Kant's method is not spelled out in a set of rules, but is mainly left to that talent of application—the power of Judgement "which can be practiced only."[21] Once we know the goals of Bible hermeneutics as defined in moral philosophy, all that remains is to improve our techniques, for which we need *examples* rather than rules. And indeed, Kant's *Religion* abounds in allegorical manipulations of verses and misquotations, religious symbols, and ecclesiastical dogma, to a point that determines its distinctive style within the whole Kantian *opus.*

Here one might wonder what could justify, in Kantian terms, the departure from historical truth implied in a ten-

---

20 Kant contends with his posthumous essay, published in 1792, a year after Michaelis's death and a year before publication of *Religion*.

21 See especially *C1*: A 133-134/B 172-173, where Kant says that the faculty of judgement has no rules, only examples, since rules would require rules of their own, and so *ad infinitum*; therefore it "can be practiced only, and cannot be taught." I am suggesting that this view accounts for the scarcity of the theoretical rules and for the large number of particular examples in Kant's method of Biblical interpretation as expressed in the *Religion*.

dentious moral interpretation. Kant could rely on his claim that a latent rational essence lies beyond the accidental aspects of revealed religions, and so an interpretation that would bring this essence to light would not be basically unfaithful to its subject matter. But this explanation can hardly do, since Kant is far from the simple-minded belief that the rational meaning inheres in each and every particular expression of a given historical faith. If Kant's *Religion* were isolated from the rest of his system, the question of justifying his hermeneutical principle would remain unsolved. But the Kantian system recognizes a special mode of justification, the primacy of pure practical reason, that yields the moral postulates; and his method of Bible interpretation may be roughly construed as an extension of the system of postulates. A postulate is a statement of a cognitive type that lacks a cognitive basis but derives its whole justification from moral-practical considerations. Moreover, such a statement must be cognitively undecidable, and this is indeed what Kant holds about the original sense of the Biblical verses, and the intentions of its ancient authors, which "lie beyond the domain of [cognitive] reason." Kant's willingness to give up the scientific aspect of Biblical studies is much too hasty, as he himself would at times admit, but it is necessary for his position.

Characteristic of Kant's hesitation and of the conflict between his scientific temperament and his moral-practical interests is the fact that he does make some room for a special type of Biblical study, although not as a science but as a kind of erudition (*Schriftgelehrsamkeit*) (VI:112/103). Kant does not develop this vague point sufficiently. But his basic idea seems to be the following: the Biblical savant, guided by philosophy, is the one who should mediate between the truths of rational religion and the masses who are unable to reach these truths without the help of a historical faith. To do this he must have a threefold gift: a vast inventory of facts, of the kind already demanded by Spinoza; correct moral insight (*Einsicht*); and judgement, understood as a natural gift for application. Wherever possible, he shows that the literal sense has a moral meaning; and where this is impossible, he mobilizes his gifts and encyclopedic knowledge to offer an adequate allegory. In this way the Biblical savant, guided by the philosopher, usurps the traditional role of the priest or theologian by becoming the direct authority for the masses. Kant admits that such a use of authority "does not pay proper respect to human nature," but comforts himself with the (utopian) belief that this is only a passing historical stage and that the general public will be eventually brought by moral education and enlightenment to the position where no historical religion and appeal to authority will be needed.

Conclusion

In conclusion we may say that Kant's concern with Bible hermeneutics is indicative of a *historical* world outlook and stems from it. With all his social utopianism Kant realizes the importance of history as the framework and medium of social change. He is well aware that a process means a sequence of intermediary states and thus, in a certain sense, a compromise. The concept of compromise contradicts the rigor of Kantian ethics only with respect to the character of a person or a deed. Kant does not impose on the sphere of history and social change a complete dichotomy between the rational and the empirical, but rather makes history their common ground. History is the process whereby reason explicates its latent potential, freeing it gradually from its sensuous cover and shaping the objective world in accordance with it.[22] This view of history is not merely evolutionary, but teleological. History is not just a change from one state to another but the realization of an original potential, namely reason or autonomy, that had already revealed itself in ancient times, even though under the sen-

[22] This process is not continuous and homogeneous; it has its digressions and inner dialectics, but for our purposes these may be overlooked.

suous cover of ritualistic and mythological religions. This explains Kant's special attitude toward these religions. Instead of negating them altogether, as Spinoza wishes to do, he regards them as stages in a process, and uses them only as a means or a *Leitmittel* to encourage its progress. This means that one should start from the Bible and the historical religions but abstract them from their sensuousness—namely, from their *literal form*. Kant's exegetical method thus reflects his historical outlook in two complementary ways. On the one hand the Bible is an example of the rational essence which became embodied empirically; on the other hand it serves as a means for gradually uncovering and developing that essence; and these two aspects of the Bible can be illuminated (the first aspect) or activated (the second aspect) only by a method which imposes external meaning.

The major difficulty in Kant's method arises from the possible conflict between the interest of truth and the interest of moral education. An exegetical method that is ready to overlook historical truth is incompatible with the spirit of enlightenment and the autonomy of objective knowledge of which Kant is a major representative. His vacillation over the issue of the Biblical savant and his refusal to dispose of historical studies altogether, testify to the fact that he is well aware of the theoretical difficulty and the practical dangers involved in augmenting the number of cases where "my interest determines my judgement" (C_2, V:143/149).[23] But, notwithstanding this difficulty, Kant's theory of the history of religion and the gradual explication of rationality within it is perhaps his clearest statement about a major area in which the history of reason comes to bear. Not so elaborately, but still in a genuine fashion, Kant presents the history of *philosophy*, too, as a historical self-explication of reason. To this topic we shall turn now.

[23] Here the concept of postulate is also explained.

CHAPTER VI

THE HISTORY OF PHILOSOPHY
AND ITS ARCHITECTONIC

Kant's diversified scholarship did not extend to a thorough and detailed knowledge of the history of philosophy. He was certainly acquainted with ancient and modern classics; he worked his way through recent British philosophy; and he was, in particular, deeply immersed in the German *Schulphilosophie* of his age, which incorporated a great deal of historical material.[1] On the whole, however, Kant's relation to the history of philosophy is not scholarly but philosophical. In the history of philosophy he sees a vast and indispensable inventory of concepts, methods, and typical arguments, which he was at liberty to regroup and classify from the point of view of his own philosophical interests, which he takes to be the "interests of reason" in general. For this it is worth his neglecting the detailed points and the fine systematic nuances that the scholar would rightly insist upon.

At the same time Kant is acutely aware of the *historicality of philosophy in general* and of the special place that his own system is to occupy within it. The nature of this place is twofold. On the one hand Kant sees his system as a continuation no less than as a radical change. His revolution relies on the previous history of philosophy not only for its particular materials, but equally for its philosophical program and its new systematic grounding. On the other hand,

---

[1] The *Schulphilosophie* remained Kant's major polemical context even after the completion of his *Critiques*. His attempts to break away from it continued to the end of the century, as testify Kant's *Fortschritte* and his current comments and replies to critics (cf. also G. Lehmann's "Einleitung," XX:479-483).

Kant's system is to *overcome* the historicality of philosophy and bring its process to a close. Through it, human reason will become fully explicated and known to itself and the series of past opinions will culminate in a philosophical *science*. Following the example of logic, mathematics, and the natural sciences, and partly relying on their achievements, Kant's revolution is to transform philosophy from historicized *doxa* into pure and timeless *episteme*, and thus to transcend its history.

Kant thus had a strong sense both of the historical nature of philosophy and of the new, trans-historical era that was opening. Even before Hegel, he was the first philosopher of the "end of philosophy" in the *historical* sense of the word. Many philosophers before him considered that their work had reached the final truth. But for them the history of previous philosophy was accidental, a contingent series of errors and opinions, unessential to the emergence of truth through their own work. Kant, on the other hand, situates his revolution at the end of a necessary process of gradual explication, a process that has made his own system possible and has been preserved and systematized by it. Kant's philosophy is the conclusion and overcoming of the inevitable historization of reason, its need to undergo a *process* of self-explication.

It is noteworthy that the *Critique of Pure Reason* ends with the hope that "before the end of the present century" (i.e., in less than twenty years!) philosophy will achieve "what many centuries have not been able to accomplish, namely, to secure for human reason complete satisfaction in regard to that with which it has all along so eagerly occupied itself" (*C1*, A 856/B 884).[2] But apart from these and similar remarks, Kant's awareness of the historicality of philosophy is also *systematized*. Indeed, careful examination

[2] The rest of the time was needed for finishing the *Metaphysics of Nature* and the *Metaphysics of Morals*, two substantive doctrines that had to be based upon the *Critiques* as an "essay on method." Kant more or less finished the second, but not the first.

will find in Kant a distinct if sketchy theory of the history of philosophy, as a basic mode of the history of reason in general. (It is also in this context that the term "the history of pure reason" is coined by Kant).

To reconstruct this theory we shall have to draw from both direct and indirect sources. Using the direct evidence in this chapter and the indirect evidence in the next, I shall start by expounding Kant's view of the *substance* of the history of philosophy—its alleged organic character, and its relation to the pure architectonic of reason. Upon this basis, Kant's program for writing a philosophical *historiography* of philosophy (as distinguished from an empirical one) should become more comprehensible. Then I shall have to face what may at first seem as counter-evidence to my thesis, explaining the difference between *historisch* and *geschichtlich* and bringing out the historical dimension of Kant's concept of "philosophizing."

To reinforce these results I shall turn in the next chapter to more indirect meta-philosophical contexts, showing how Kant's theory of the history of philosophy is at work both in the account he gives of the birth of the *Critique* and its unifying program, and in the *method* of philosophy, its final *composition*, and its relation to *other* sciences.[3]

It is worth noting that the major texts upon which my reconstruction relies are to be found in the *Critique of Pure Reason* itself.[4] This should not be surprising in view of

---

[3] Since my problem is to show that Kant's views of the history of philosophy are not only grounded in the system but also represent a persistent theme in his writings, some repetitive quotations will be inevitable. Also, let me remind the reader that for the *full* systematic argument, this chapter should be read in conjunction with the Introduction of this book, especially its second part.

[4] The major textual sources may be grouped as follows:
   (a) Kant's chapter on "The History of Pure Reason" in the first *Critique*, supplemented by the posthumous *Lose Blätter zu den Fortschritte der Metaphysik*.
   (b) Kant's chapter on "The Architectonic of Pure Reason" in the first *Critique*, supplemented by the Introduction to his later lectures on *Logic*, especially Sections I-V.

Kant's inclusion of the theory of the history of reason in the system of reason, and incorporation of it with the architectonic in the system's meta-philosophical framework.

The System of Reason Historicized

The History of Philosophy as an Organic Totality

The essence of Kant's view of the history of philosophy is given in the chapter on the "Architectonic of Pure Reason," and is supposed to be grounded by it. This succinct text contains some of the major points in Kant's meta-philosophy, including his concepts of system, rationality, and genuine philosophy. I shall discuss it from the point of view of the problem before us: the relation of philosophy to its history.

A central passage in the chapter reads:

> Systems seem to be formed in the manner of vermin [*Gewürme*] . . . from the mere confluence of assembled concepts, at first imperfect, and only gradually attaining to completeness; although *they one and all have their schema, as the original germ, in the self-development of reason alone.* Hence, not only is each system articulated in accordance with an idea, but, in addition, *they are one and all purposefully united in a system of human reason, as members of one whole* (*C1*: A 835/B 863; italics added).[5]

The history of philosophy is thus a latent totality, governed by the tension between the inherent architectonic of

---

(c) Kant's two prefaces (1781 and 1787) to the first *Critique* and parallel sections in the *Prolegomena* (1784).

(d) Kant's chapter on "The Discipline of Pure Reason" in the first *Critique*, supplemented by other references to the philosophical method.

(e) Kant's chapter on "The Interest of Reason in this Conflict" in the first *Critique*, and other references in the three *Critiques* to the structure, interests, and motivation of reason.

[5] I have made minor changes in the Kemp-Smith translation.

reason and its particular stage of manifestation. All philosophical systems expound the self-development of reason, from which they get their organizing schema, and they are thus all united in a single organic whole. However, this organic whole cannot emerge all at once. Because of the finitude of human reason (see Chapter One), it must undergo a process of historization:

> It is unfortunate that only after we have spent much time in the collection of materials in somewhat random fashion, at the suggestion of an idea lying hidden in our minds, and after we have, indeed, over a long period assembled the materials in a merely *technical* manner, does it first become possible to discern the idea in clearer light and to devise a whole architectonically, in accordance with the ends of reason (A 834-835/B 862-863).

Kant adds that "at the present time" it is already possible to devise the whole architectonic of human knowledge; but this is only because the history of philosophy, which is now coming to an end, has the same organic form as the final system that it brings to light. In other words, *the structure of the history of philosophy is inherently the same as that of the system of philosophy, although it must be concealed and become distorted in the process of its development.* This proto-Hegelian view is complemented by other texts,[6] which add the elements of *opposition* and *revolution* to the dynamics of the history of philosophy. To say that the development of reason is gradual does not mean that it is continuous. Instead it is characterized by periods of accumulation, contradiction, collapse, and radical innovation. It is true *in principle* that there can be no "polemic" and no "antithetic" in the field of reason (A 743/B 771; A 756/B 784);

---

[6] Especially the two prefaces to *C1* (especially A vii-xii, B xi-xii, B xiv-xvi), parallel sections in the *Prolegomena* (especially IV:256-258/3-5 and 367-368/116), and the chapter on "The Interest of Reason in this Conflict" in *C1*.

but such contradictions are inevitable in the *history* of philosophy—which is, as we shall see, the historicized form of the architectonic, where its single components emerge disjointedly and in seeming opposition to one another. Hence, the great controversies in the history of philosophy have their origin in the nature of pure reason. The conflicting principles and schools of thought represent different interests of reason, although they do so in partial, confused and one-sided ways. Thus they produce genuine *antinomies*, which lead to the breakdown of the respective systems and call for a new "revolution in the mode of thinking" (B xi-xii) to resolve them. Since reason, however, is fundamentally coherent, this is a sign that it had not been satisfactorily explicated. The breakdown of historical systems may temporarily turn philosophy into a "field full of ruins," i.e., aggregates of disunited concepts, the prey of skeptics who deny the very possibility of rationality. But it also produces a new "need of reason" to overcome this state through a new philosophical *revolution*, and this process continues as long as the new path of the *Critique*, which systematically reconciles the various interests of reason and enables its pure system to emerge in full, has not been found.

Thus, the endless conflicts between rationalists and empiricists, skeptics and dogmatists, hedonists and purists, Stoics and Epicureans, piecemeal and synoptic philosophers notwithstanding, all are historical members of a single organic whole; they are governed by the architectonic of reason and gradually bring its harmony to light. In this respect, Kant's *Critique* is supposed to open the way not just to another reconciling synthesis, but to the most comprehensive systematization of the ends of reason as these relate to one another in the pure paradigm of reason itself.[7] To under-

---

[7] Alexandre Kojève, in his posthumous *Kant* (Paris, 1973), also indicates the proto-Hegelian character of Kant's theory of the growth of philosophy. Kojève's Kant is as uniquely Kojèvian as is his Hegel; but on the point under discussion his interpretation does not depend on any special viewpoint, but on a faithful and attentive reading of the

THE HISTORY OF REASON MANIFESTED

stand this issue more fundamentally, we must now consider the architectonic.

The Architectonic as a System of Ends

The word *architectonic* suggests a plan or schematic design, such as that used in constructing buildings. It also suggests a functional relation between the construct and the set of *purposes* it is designed to serve. Kant employs both connotations when he uses the term metaphorically to denote "the art of constructing systems" in general (A 832/B 860); but he also makes it clear that in order to apply this metaphor to philosophy, further conditions must be met. In particular, all the parts of the system must be devised in relation to each other, and to their totality. And the system must be united by a central purpose that reflects an intrinsic end or interest of reason.

The key concept of the architectonic is thus "the essential (or intrinsic) ends of human reason." However, at first Kant defines the architectonic much more broadly, as "the doctrine of what is scientific in our knowledge" (A 832/B 860), and also, as we have seen, as the art of systematization in general. These two initial definitions are related, since only systematic unity can elevate a body of knowledge to the rank of a science.[8] Hence philosophy, too, must be system-

---

text, especially the appropriate sections in the "Methodology of Pure Reason." Like the present chapter, Kojève also approaches the history of reason from the viewpoint of the architectonic (59-60), and quoting some of the passages we do, he recognizes they present "une conception toute hégélienne de l'Histoire de la Philosophie" (60-61). Kojève, however, seems to go a step further, suggesting that for Kant, too, "le Système du Savoir pourrait aussi être exposé sous la forme de l'Histoire de la Philosophie" (61n.). This claim is too strong, for while Kant recognizes the history of philosophy as the historization of the pure architectonic, he views this historization as involving the work of distorting sensuous elements that, given Kant's dualism, must be purified in the final system as a condition for its being true and fully intelligible. This requirement also derives from the fact that the history of reason is no vindication of its outcome. but the latter must be justified *a priori*, independently of its genesis.

[8] It should be remembered that by the term *scientific* Kant does not

atic if it is to qualify as scientific. In other words, it cannot be an aggregate of piecemeal philosophical discoveries and particular concepts formed here and there, but must—as the current definition of philosophy puts it—become the *"system* of all philosophical knowledge," and give the latter "logical completeness" (A 838/B 866).[9] However, this is only the "scholastic" definition of philosophy, which is not sufficiently informative and overlooks a vital element. Granting that philosophy must be systematic, the problem is to know what *kind* of systematic form is adequate to philosophy. Is "logical completeness" sufficient or is it necessary to resort to a higher systematic organization, involving the concept of a purpose?

Kant's answer to this question is the crux of the architectonic. The proper systematic form of philosophy is indeed teleological. The scholastic definition overlooks the real significance of philosophy and reduces it to a dry academic and technical skill because it omits all reference to a purpose (*Logic,* IX:24/14). This would be legitimate if the purpose of philosophy were only a subjective addition that did not belong to the system itself. But this is precisely what the architectonic denies. The element of purpose spelled out in the ends of reason *belongs to the objective system of phi-*

---

understand a certain *kind* of knowledge, but a certain epistemic *status,* i.e., apodictic validity and certainty, that can be obtained by all the rationally founded disciplines, ethics and metaphysics no less than physics or mathematics. Indeed, the main attempt of the *Critique* is to establish philosophy as a "science" namely, to raise it to the epistemic rank other disciplines already enjoyed.

9 Practically the same definition is repeated in Kant's introduction to *Logic*: "Philosophy is the system of all philosophical knowledge, or of all rational knowledge through concepts" (IX:23/14). Thereby, however, philosophy is the system of the rational foundations of the other sciences as well, insofar as they are grounded philosophically. (I am using Abbott's translation of the Introduction to the *Logic,* although the Hartman-Schwarz translation is better in translating *Erkenntnis* as *cognition*—which can be used in the plural—instead of *knowledge,* since the parallel passages from the first *Critique* are also translated by Kemp-Smith as *knowledge.* When the distinction between the singular and the plural form is important, I used *piece* or *item of knowledge.*)

losophy and actually serves to articulate it. To be properly *systematized*, philosophy must therefore refer all branches of theory to the "essential ends of reason." It cannot be satisfied with discovering the foundations of the various disciplines, both philosophical and non-philosophical, without relating them to their ultimate *ends*; and it must not take these ends from extrinsic sources (like technology, or politics, or theology, or simple intellectual entertainment), but from the very nature of rationality as a self-sufficient interest.[10]

Hence the superior definition Kant gives philosophy according to its "world concept": philosophy is "the science of the relation of all knowledge to the essential ends of human reason" (A 839/B 867).[11] The architectonic of reason—the supreme rules of its systematization—requires that all its ingredients be referred to a set of rational *goals* or tasks that inhere in the rational attitude itself; and these must be pursued for their own sake and eventually become harmonized in relation to the highest good.[12]

[10] See Introduction.

[11] This definition is also repeated in the *Logic* (IX:23-24/14), where Kant remarks: "This high conception gives *dignity* (*Würde*) to philosophy, that is, an absolute value. And it is also indeed this alone which has *intrinsic* value, and which gives value to the other kinds of knowledge." Kant adds that whereas the scholastic definition presents philosophy as a matter of *skill*, the "world-concept" definition presents it as a matter of *wisdom*.

A little further on, Kant gives a broader version of the same definition, detailing the *plurality* and the *hierarchy* of the ends of reason under their *Endzweck* (i.e., the highest good; see pp. 11, 194 above): "Philosophy, in the latter sense, is the science of the relation of all knowledge and every use of reason to the ultimate end of human reason, to which, as supreme, all other ends are subordinated, and must be combined into unity with it" (IX:24/15).

[12] Positing the highest good as the supreme end of reason that systematizes all the others, introduces the primacy of pure practical reason into the definition of philosophy as wisdom. The same is given a strong formulation in *Verk.* (VIII:417-418), where Kant calls philosophy "the research of wisdom" (*Weisheitsforschung*), adding that "wisdom . . . is the agreement of the will with the final end (the highest good)." On this definition, wisdom is not a mode of knowledge but a certain *moral attitude*, a mode of the will.

Genuine and Pseudo-Philosophy

Given this architectonic view, Kant puts forth two conditions which distinguish genuine philosophy from what may be called pseudo-philosophy. In the first place, a philosophical system must be united by a focal purpose, a *"unity of the end, to which all parts relate and the idea of which they all stand in relation to one another."* Kant pictures this unity in strictly organistic terms, as the unity of an "animal body":

> The unity of the end to which all parts relate, and the idea of which they all stand in relation to another, makes it possible for us to determine from our knowledge of the other parts whether any part is missing, and to prevent any arbitrary addition . . . The whole is thus an organic unity (*articulatio*) and not an aggregate (*coacervatio*). It may grow from within . . . but not by external addition. . . . It is thus like an animal body, the growth of which is not by the addition of a new member, but by rendering each member, without change of proportion, stronger and more effective for its purposes (A 832-833/B 860-861).

Organic form is required because it expresses the highest ideal of rationality, as Kant states in other contexts as well:

> Pure speculative reason is a truly knit structure, wherein everything is an *organ*, the whole being for the sake of every part, and every part for the sake of all the others (C1:B xxxvii).

And again, in the *Prolegomena*:

> Pure reason is a sphere so separate and self-contained that we cannot touch a part without affecting all the rest . . . for as our judgment within this sphere cannot be corrected by anything without, the validity and use of every part depends upon the relation in which it

233

stands to all the rest within the domain of reason. As in the structure of an organized [*organisch*] body, the end of each member can only be deduced from the full conception of the whole. . . . In the sphere of this faculty you can determine and define either everything or nothing (IV:263/11).

The organic feature of reason is thus also the *specific* reason why, in philosophy, verification depends upon *complete* systematization. However, it should be noted immediately that Kant's organic ideal had to be greatly modified and restricted by the principles of his own critique of reason. Indeed, a strong and a weak organic model can be distinguished, and it can be shown that Kant had to declare the former the supreme ideal of rationality but the latter alone possible for man. The strong model implies complete transparency: each element of the system is not only justified but indeed deduced or formed by means of the others, without using any extrinsic additional material. This would, however, imply a form of intellectual intuition that man, being finite, cannot possess; and Kant must therefore admit of an element of *factual givenness* in the sphere of pure reason itself. For instance, the specific content and number of the categories or the material aspect of all rational principles cannot be deduced from or made fully intelligible in terms of the system but must be accepted from without as the "such and such" they are—or in Kant's own words, as *facts* of reason. Philosophy, therefore, involves a moment of sheer *discovery*, which cannot be reduced to any a *priori* principle; this is another reason it depends upon a historical process. However, once we admit of such irreducible facticity in the field of reason, we can still hold to a weaker model of organic unity, constructed as a functional interrelation among all its parts even if their material aspect is accepted from without.

And this is, indeed, the *critical* idea of organic unity to which Kant subscribes. As I have tried to show elsewhere,[13] the bold organic model is only a regulative idea, expressing an ideal form of intelligibility that cannot be attained by the human mind, and must therefore be limited and transformed into a more modest methodological principle. Kant's retreat from the strong to the weaker concept of organic system thus follows the dynamic of the *Critique* as a whole.

The crux of the first condition remains the "unity of the end" by which a philosophical system must be unified. But Kant adds a second condition, distinguishing between two sorts of unifying end. A system may be organized either "in terms of the essential ends of reason," in which case it is architectonic, or by "all kinds of optional external ends," that are only "empirically occasioned" (A 833/B 861). By the latter, Kant means the various objectives that might have governed a thinker's work: the pragmatic or technological utility of his system, its value as a purely intellectual pastime, its role in reinforcing religious dogma or the authority of government, and in general its use in reinforcing beliefs to which he is committed in advance. These are all instances of what might be called the heteronomy of reason;[14] and although such theories may as well be organized around a focal purpose, they are pseudo-philosophies. Their unity, Kant says, is merely "technical" because it is achieved by ends which are accidental from the viewpoint of reason, or even flatly counter-rational. Genuine philosophy, on the other hand, must be unified by a principle that expresses an *essential* end of reason, although when subject to historical limitations it may do so in a covert or incommensurate way. Hence, the only true members of the

[13] *Kant and the Renovation of Metaphysics* (Jerusalem, 1973; Hebrew); also in Systematic Philosophy: Ambitions and Critique," in: Dieter Henrich (ed.), *Ist Systematische Philosophie nöglich?* (Bonn, 1977).

[14] It is noteworthy that Kant includes here, beside the utilitarian use of reason or its subordination to external authorities, also cases of system-building that have merely intellectual or academic interest.

history of philosophy are those thinkers who work in the interests of reason alone and who give specific articulation to one or more of its intrinsic interests.

This applies even to skeptics who seem to end up with results destructive to reason.[15] Insofar as they arrive at these results by a rational procedure, putting the authority of reason above any other, they promote rationality as an end in itself and even contribute to its positive system; for the history of philosophy *needs* such duels and antinomies in order to produce positive solutions to them.

The Historization of the Architectonic

At this point Kant makes a further move, crucial to his theory of the history of philosophy. Since all genuine philosophical systems relate through their unifying principles to the single system of the ends of reason, not only is each system organized in itself, but in addition, they are "one and all" tacitly united as members of one organic totality, governed by the pure architectonic of reason. On the other hand, since each philosopher expresses the architectonic from his partial standpoint and in terms of his own cultural context, the history of philosophy must appear a concealed and distorted totality, breaking into diverse and opposing standpoints. Thus, *the history of philosophy is the historicized form of the architectonic of reason.* The *system* of philosophy and the *history* of philosophy have the same inherent form; but whereas the system expresses this form in its pure necessity, the history of philosophy must express it as a mixture of necessary and contingent elements.

Kant also describes the relation of genuine philosophers to the architectonic of reason in more technical terms, using the duality of idea and schema. The pure architectonic of reason is an idea that underlies the work of all genuine philosophers as an "original germ" (A 835/B 863). Each philosopher unwittingly represents this idea from his own stand-

15 Cf. Kant's remarks of Hume and Priestley (A 745/B 773) and the whole discussion in A 743-755/B 771-783.

point, by means of a schema (in the Kantian sense of the term),[16] which serves to unify the diverse concepts and principles assembled from his predecessors or from his own piecemeal discoveries. However, a schema is not commensurate with the idea that it is supposed to represent, for as long as the history of philosophy continues, "this idea lies hidden in reason, like a germ in which the parts are still undeveloped and barely recognizable" (A 834/B 862). To be clearly recognized the germ must have fully actualized itself and come to philosophical consciousness through the *Critique*; at this stage the schema becomes identical with the idea,[17] and the history of philosophy is consummated.

The End of Philosophy

This idea is reminiscent of Hegel's famous dictum, that the time has come for philosophy to give up the name *love* of knowledge (*philo-sophia*) and to become actual knowledge or wisdom (*sophia*).[18] Indeed, just as Kant anticipated Hegel in historicizing the Platonic concept of the love of wisdom, so he also preceded Hegel (and Marx) in putting forward the bold idea of the *end of philosophy*.

Kant is insistent and unhesitating on this point. His work was to "hand down to posterity the treasure of a metaphysics, that was purified by the *Critique* and thereby brought to a state of permanence" (B xxiv); it would shortly lead to the achievement of the goal of many centuries by bringing the quest of reason to "complete satisfaction" (A 856/ B 884); and, once completed, it would be "passed on to generations to come as a capital to which no addition can be made" (B xxiv).[19]

---

[16] A "schema" is the concretization of a rational concept, its manifestation in a quasi-empirical medium.

[17] In fact, the schema is *abolished*, and the idea emerges unmediated.

[18] *Phenomenology of the Mind*, trans. J. B. Baillie (New York, 1967), Preface.

[19] A similar idea is later reiterated in *Verk.* (VIII:413-422): The history of philosophy is marked by "wars," creating the illusion that no union of the opposite camps is possible; but this union is actually

It should be noticed that, because of reason's organic feature, the scientification of philosophy will *ipso facto* involve its full conceptual inventory. In the case of physics, its attainment of the epistemic status of science still leaves an open-ended task of particular discoveries; whereas philosophy, which is either a totality or "nothing at all," cannot attain scientific status unless it also attains material completeness:

> Metaphysics . . . is the only one of all the sciences that may promise to attain, in a short time and by a small but united effort, such completeness as will leave to posterity nothing but the role of arranging everything in *didactic* manner . . . without adding anything to its content.[20]

Kant explains that "it is not self-conceit" that gives him this confidence, but, once again, reason's organic feature. When the architectonic is realized "any attempt to change even the smallest part at once gives rise to contradictions, not only in the system but in human reason itself" (B xxxviii). In other words, any so-called progress would actually be a regression, a falling back into the typical flaws of the *history* of philosophy. But whereas these flaws were justifiable in the course of history, they are no longer justifiable after its completion. Former philosophers cannot be reproached for being entangled in contradictions, or for failing to establish philosophy as a science. Even with "the

---

achieved in the critical philosophy, which if understood will bring about "permanent state of peace" (*ibid.*, 416).

We may add that Kant is one of the first philosophers of knowledge to speak of it as advancing by means of theoretical *revolutions*. (The same is true of the history of morality.) But, unlike some neo-Kantians (and today, Kuhn), he believes in a final revolution, which will bring out the true paradigm of reason.

20 A xx. The word *only* is imprudent, for Kant believes that formal logic has reached material completion too. His actual comparison is between philosophy and the *natural* sciences.

greatest of all dogmatic philosophers"—a title with which Kant honors Wolff, whom he sees as standing at the threshold of the critique—"the blame lies not so much in himself, but in the dogmatic way of thinking prevalent in his day, with which the philosophers of his time, and of all previous times, have no right to reproach one another" (B xxxvi-xxxvii). These are not just courteous words; they reflect Kant's belief that philosophers, too, are children of their time. But this also means that after the architectonic of reason has come into full view, any departure from it must be viewed as anachronistic, indeed, as reactionary.

Kant versus Hegel

It is certainly interesting to find striking similarities between Kant's theory of the history of philosophy and that of Hegel. But it may be desirable at this point to state the major differences between them. Kant does not have a coherent theory to account for the rigorous duality of the empirical and the *a priori*, and for the schematization of the latter in the former. In other words, he does not have a dialectical logic to make both poles moments of a single developing whole. His theory of development is only *declared*, not substantiated by an adequate dynamic logic. This is also why Kant cannot, in the last analysis, account for the importance of *time* as a medium for the development of reason (see Introduction: "The Historical Antinomy," and the Epilogue). Indeed, it seems that all he can demonstrate is that all historical systems are latent moments of a totality; but he cannot show that their temporal sequence is of major importance. This he only states with reference to religion, not to philosophy, and here, too, it is a mere *assertion*. Finally, for Kant the history of previous philosophy plays no part whatever in vindicating the final system. The system of reason is justified by purely *a priori* means; while the process through which it was born might explain its cultural necessity, it does not explain its inherent truth.

Rational and Historical Knowledge: The Concept of Philosophizing

The unfounded belief that Kant regards the history of philosophy as philosophically irrelevant seems to stem from Kant's famous distinctions between rational and historical knowledge, and between philosophizing and learning philosophy. These distinctions are sometimes read as if philosophizing were opposed to studying the history of philosophy, and as if rational knowledge excluded all concern with history. But a few inconsistencies notwithstanding, careful reexamination of the text will show that the thrust of Kant's argument is exactly the opposite: rational knowledge can apply to the subject matter of history as well, and far from excluding the study of the history of philosophy, the concept of philosophizing is *based* upon it.

Historisch and *Geschichtlich*

Part of the confusion is caused by a terminological difficulty. There are two adjectives in German that are translated as "historical": *geschichtlich* and *historisch*.[21] Kant does not use them as synonyms, but reserves a different technical purpose for each. He uses the Germanic word *geschichtlich* (or *Geschichte*) to denote the subject matter of history, while the Greco-Latin form *historisch* is used irrespective of subject matter to denote a certain cognitive mode that can apply to *any* object of knowledge (both empirical and rational, ancient and contemporary).[22] By historical[h] Kant means an attitude that is merely empirical: lacking universal principles and rational necessity, and looking for knowledge through direct experience, accumulation of facts, narration, hearsay, or crude induction. The term *historisch* is chosen to invoke the original connotations of the Greek and Latin *historia*, meaning the search for information and

[21] The same goes for *rational*, which may be rendered in German as *vernünftig* or as *rational*.

[22] I shall therefore translate *historisch* as *historical*[h], and *geschichtlich* as *historical*[g].

the gathering of data, as in Aristotle's *Historia animalium*, or in the later *Historia naturalis*.[23] Accordingly, Kant defines historical[h] knowledge as knowledge from data (*ex datis*), as opposed to rational knowledge, which stems "from principles" (*ex principiis*).[24]

The notion of learning *ex datis* also has another connotation, which now has reference to the learner's *subjective state of mind*. He may either understand his object rationally or just repeat and record its particular elements as given. When the matter in hand is objectively only empirical, an aggregate of data that lacks necessary principles, the student is bound to lack true understanding, whatever his intention or intellectual aptitude. But even when the subject matter is objectively rational, he may still approach it without understanding, treating its principles as *particular* items or overlooking them altogether. In this case, his subjective attitude will merely be *historisch*, whatever the objective properties of the topic he is studying.

Kant stresses this subjective connotation of historical[h]:

> If we abstract from all objective content of knowledge, then, subjectively speaking, all knowledge is either historical[h] or rational. Historical[h] knowledge is *cognitio ex datis*, while rational knowledge is *cognitio ex principiis*. However a piece of knowledge may be originally given, the individual who possesses it will have it still as historical[h], if he knows it only as much and in the same measure as has been given to him from the outside—either by immediate experience, or by narration, or also by instruction (of general items of knowledge). Therefore, anyone who had strictly learnt a system of philosophy, such as Wolff's, even if he has in his head

[23] The same technical distinction between *historisch* and *geschichtlich* is to be found in Hegel. He, too, sees as *historisch* all knowledge that does not contain a *Begriff*, and is thus not rational—regardless of subject matter. Thus, anatomy is *historisch*, while history may well be *vernünftig*.

[24] A 835-836/B 863-864; Introduction to *Logic*, Sec. III (IX:22/12.)

and can count by his fingers all its principles, explanations, and proofs, together with the division of the whole body of doctrine, will nevertheless have nothing but a complete historical[h] knowledge of the Wolffian system; he knows and judges only as much as has been given to him. If we dispute him a definition, he does not know where to turn for another. He had formed himself in imitation of an alien reason,[25] i.e., with him knowledge has not arisen *out* of reason. . . . He has well grasped and retained, that is, learnt, and is merely a plaster cast of a living man (*C1*, A 835-836/B 863-864; my translation).

It is clear that the distinction rational-historical[h] is defined in terms of the subjective attitude of the learner, not in terms of the content of his subject matter. The grotesque portrait of the student who parrots a theory without understanding, unable to either criticize or to defend it, and alienating his mind by imitations of another's, does not apply to all concern with the history of philosophy, only to a specific form of it. Just as a rational system can be approached historically[h], by narrating its components as merely given, it can also be approached rationally, through the exercise of thought, which grasps the meaning and inner logic of the system by appropriating its universal principles. This would permit the student to reconstruct the author's further commitments and implications, to complete or correct the system in its own terms and—finally—to take a critical attitude:

Knowledge that is objectively rational . . . also deserves this name subjectively only when it is shaped by the universal sources of reason—sources that may lead also to criticism, and even to the disposal of what has been learnt—i.e., by principles (*C1*, A 836-837/B 864-865; my translation).

25 A play on words: *bilden* in German means to form, and *nachbilden* means to imitate. Kant says, "Er bildete sich nach fremder Vernunft."

Rational knowledge implies a spontaneous attitude of the mind rather than passive imitation. The learner has to be rationally creative, both in comprehending the details of the system through their universal meaning, and in adding a critical dimension to his understanding. Such a critical attitude, which Kant believes would be a natural result of rethinking the system out of one's own reason, involves a comparison between the principles of the system and the archetype of reason that is latent in the student's mind; and this would lead to discovering its flaws, and transcending the given system toward a more satisfactory position. As we shall see, this rational study of historical[g] systems is precisely what Kant understands by "philosophizing."[26]

"Philosophizing" and Learning Philosophy

Kant's famous dictum on learning philosophy reads:

> One can never learn philosophy (unless in historical[h] manner); in what regards reason, one can at most learn to *philosophize* (*C1*, A 837/B 865).

When explaining this dictum, Kant immediately revokes the imprudent word *never*. The inability to learn philosophy applies to the *history* of philosophy only until its final system has emerged:[27]

---

[26] The distinction rational/historical[h] is reiterated in Kant's introduction to the *Logic*. After using again the concepts of knowledge *ex datis* and knowledge *ex principiis*, the Introduction to the *Logic* continues:
We may . . . distinguish different kinds of knowledge as follows:
(1) According to their *objective* origin, that is, according to the source from which alone the knowledge can be drawn. In this respect all knowledge is either *rational* or *empirical*.
(2) According to their *subjective* origin, that is, according to the manner in which the knowledge can be acquired by the individual. From this point of view, knowledge is either *rational* or *historical*[h], no matter how it was obtained. Accordingly, it is possible for a thing to be *objectively* a piece of rational knowledge, which subjectively is *historical*[h]. (IX:22/12)
[27] We have seen that Kant expects his own system to be ready for "didactic" presentation (*C1*, A xx). This is all he leaves for future philosophers to do.

Philosophy is a mere idea of a possible science that nowhere exists *in concreto*, but to which, by many different paths, we endeavour to approximate, until the one true path, overgrown by the products of sensibility, has at least been discovered, and the image . . . has achieved likeness to the archetype. . . . *Until then* we cannot learn philosophy; for where is it, who is in possession of it, and how shall we be able to recognize it?[28] We can only learn *to philosophize, that is, to exercise the talent of reason, in accordance with its universal principles, on certain actually existing attempts at philosophy*, always reserving the right of reason to investigate, to confirm, or to reject these principles in their very sources. (A 838/B 866, italics added)

This passage summarizes the issue. The history[g] of philosophy is marked by various attempts to realize its latent archetype; but since this archetype is embedded in "the products of sensibility," it acquires an incongruent "image" in historical systems. *As long as* the history of philosophy continues, there is no scientific system of philosophy to be learnt. All we can do is philosophize, which means rethinking the doctrines of former philosophers, both from the viewpoint of their own principles, and from that of the latent "archetype" of reason, in comparison to which they are judged and, eventually, transcended. Rational rethinking of the history of philosophy is thus the core of the concept of philosophizing. Kant also states this in the *Introduction to Logic*:

He who desires to learn to philosophize must . . . regard all systems of philosophy as a *History[g] of the use of*

---

[28] This invokes the ancient sophistic problem put forth in the *Meno*, which Plato answered with the idea of recollection, as an intermediary between *episteme* and ignorance. For Kant, this intermediary is the concept of philosophizing based upon the *archetype* of reason and the history of its development.

reason, and as objects for the exercise of his own philosophical talent (IX:26/16).

Further Analysis and Comments

It may be observed that the concepts knowledge *ex datis* and knowledge *ex principiis* have implicit dual meanings, leading to minor inconsistencies without changing the basic picture. The concept knowledge *ex datis* means both (1) learning from particulars that lack universal principles, and (2) learning without understanding, by recording and imitating something as given. The first connotation refers to the objective methodological features of the subject matter at hand, the second to the learner's subjective attitude and state of mind. Both connotations are related, since a person can have subjective rational understanding only of a topic that is rationally intelligible. On the other hand, the imitative attitude is not confined to topics that are empirical *per se,* but may apply to rational subject matter as well.[29]

Learning *ex principiis* also has two meanings. It means knowledge by rational principles, and also creative or reproductive knowledge, gained by the exercise of one's own thinking. If the learner does so with a philosophical intention, Kant believes that his comprehension involves a critical rethinking of the system.

But here again, one ingredient may appear without the other. We may conceive of a form of learning *ex principiis* that suppresses the philosophical interest in favor of a purely scholarly one. The scholar would then be able to comprehend, reconstruct, correct and criticize the system *internally,* in terms of its own principles; but he would not measure its principles against the latent archetype of reason. Grasping the details of the system *ex principiis,* i.e., ra-

[29] Rationally intelligible subject matter is also, as we have seen, the total sequence of the history[g] of philosophy, not only singular systems within it; and this would allow for a *rational* historiography of philosophy.

tionally, he would be satisfied with mere comprehension, neither subscribing to the system nor transcending it. Such an attitude is certainly deficient; it violates the basic interest of reason and clearly cannot qualify as philosophizing. But equally clearly, it is not merely historical[h] and cannot be equated with the parroting student; for according to Kant's own definition, the scholar now learns the system *ex principiis*, exercising his active thinking and gaining internal subjective comprehension. Kant's tendency to confuse this case with historical[h] learning is therefore inconsistent. In fact, his definitions allow for an intermediary category between learning *ex datis* and philosophizing proper: I mean *rational scholarship*, a distinct form of learning *ex principiis* that should be recognized and admitted *per se*.

A graver inconsistency is perhaps to be found in Kant's statement in the *Logic*, that the study of philosophy will be historical[h] even after the pure system has been found.[30] The confusion seems to be of learning by imitation and learning by spontaneous re-production. Imitation is passive and external, and proceeds *ex datis*; while re-production may involve an original act of the mind, in which one produces a universally valid pattern from one's own thinking. The fact that I produce the same pattern as others is not a flaw but a sign of my rationality. To be rational, an attitude must fulfill both conditions: it must derive from a spontaneous act of the individual, and it must conform to a form shared by all. This synthesis of particularity and universality is the basic pattern of rationality in knowledge, ethics, and even esthetics, and it should apply in the field of learning as well. Indeed, Kant's theory of moral education, sketched in the last part of the second *Critique,* describes the formation of rational individuals by a similar dialectic: although stimulated by external examples, they end up by reproducing out of themselves a pattern of decision and behavior valid for all.

[30] Introduction to *Logic*, Sec. III, 25/16 (see also the word "never" in the quotation above).

And so, at the penalty of having to forsake his basic view of rationality (and autonomy), Kant must recognize the possibility of learning philosophy rationally as well, once its final system is culturally available.[31]

"A Philosophizing History of Philosophy"

The term "history" has two common uses, one referring to what the historian does (historiography), and one referring to what the historian writes about (substantive history). So far we have discussed the *substance* of the history of philosophy, showing its latent architectonic or organic nature. But Kant holds that this nature must also reflect on the field of historiography. He ends the *Critique* with a section, "The History of Pure Reason," delineating a further, still incomplete part of the system:

> This title stands here only to indicate a place remaining in the system, which must be filled in the future. I content myself with casting a cursory glance, from a transcendental viewpoint, namely, from the viewpoint of the nature of pure reason, on the whole of the works of those who have hitherto worked here—a whole which appears to my eye indeed as a building [*Gebäude*], but only in ruins (A 852/B 880).[32]

This programatic passage makes it clear that Kant has in mind a *philosophical* historiography of philosophy, written from a "transcendental," not an empirical point of view. It is made possible by the organic substance of the history of philosophy; and since it would be written from the standpoint "of the nature of pure reason," a philosophi-

---

[31] At the end of philosophy "philosophizing" would become identical with learning philosophy rationally, for exercising one's own mind upon the historically available *Critique* will no longer be expected to lead to its transcendence. (If such learning were impossible, the only fully rational person in history would be Kant!)

[32] I have re-translated the passage. Kemp-Smith omitted the word "the whole" (*das Ganze*), and rendered the term *Gebäude* in the plural, as "[many stately] structures."

cal historiography of philosophy would qualify as an integral part of the system of philosophy, and serve together with the Architectonic as its meta-philosophical theory. This is why Kant insists that a rational history of this kind *must* be added. On the other hand, it comes as the last step, as a complement that does not require the same innovative revolution necessary for the *Critique* itself. Once the nature of pure reason is completely brought to light, it will provide the paradigm by which one can turn back upon empirical history, grasp its holistic structure and trace the marks of the architectonic of reason within it.

Although Kant did not complete this missing part of his system, the *Critique* provides a sketch of what it should include. Its first part is to be a cross-school typology of philosophical stands and methods, selected in view of the basic interests of reason to which they give a historical manifestation. (From Kant's short account it is clear that he arranged this material in light of the major historical oppositions that his own system was supposed to reconcile.) The second and more difficult part is to distinguish the different philosophical periods and display the revolutions from which they sprang. Kant says that he will not himself discuss this issue, but he in fact deals with part of it when describing his own philosophical revolution, the cultural tension from which it arose, and the new era it initiated.

Kant never abandoned this program. Later in his career, when writing the competition essay on the progress of metaphysics since Leibniz and Wolff, he found himself dealing with a topic in the "history of reason"—suggested indeed by the Berlin academy but suiting his own approach. Moreover, the notes he wrote in preparation for this essay[33] in-

---

[33] The essay is "Welches sind die wirklichen Fortschritte, die die Metaphysik seit Leibnitzens und Wolf's Zeiten in Deutschland gemacht hat?" (XX:255-332). Only part of Kant's notes were used in F. T. Rink's posthumous edition of this work (Königsberg, 1804), but what remained of them was later found and also incorporated into the Academy Edition (XX:335-351). Their significance for Kant's view of the history of philosophy was brought to my attention by Hermann Lübbe's interest-

clude a section entitled "On a Philosophizing History of Philosophy" (XX:340). Explaining the difference between a rational and a merely historical[h] historiography of philosophy, Kant says:

> A historical[h] representation of philosophy tells the story how people have hitherto philosophized, and in what order. But *philosophy is a gradual development of human reason*, which could not have progressed—nor begun—in the empirical way, be it even through mere concepts (XX:340; italics added).

Hence the need for a philosophical historiography:

> A philosophical history[g] of philosophy is not itself historical[h],[34] or empirical, but rational, i.e., *a priori* possible. For even if it, too, puts forth facts of reason, it does not borrow them from the narration of history[g], but derives them, as a philosophical archaeology, from the nature of human reason (*ibid.*).

And further:

> A history[g] of philosophy is of such a special nature, that in it nothing can be told of what *has* happened, without knowing previously what *should* have happened. . . . For it is not the history[g] of opinions that arose here and there, but of reason that develops itself through concepts (XX:343).

Kant recognizes that *"one cannot write a history of things that did not occur"* (XX:342-343); his problem, therefore, is not to derive the historical states *a priori*, but to identify the developing pattern of reason *within* the diversity of empiri-

---

ing article "Philosophiegeschichte als Philosophie," in *Einsichten: Gerhard Krüger zum 60 Geburtstag* (Frankfurt am Main, 1962), 209-229, especially 211.

[34] In this text, the term *historical*[h] is used only in the first connotation of knowledge *ex datis* (see p. 245 above), corresponding to what the *Logic* calls empirical knowledge.

cal material, as he did in the case of religion and Bible hermeneutics. The signs of what "should have happened" must be discovered in what did happen, without eliminating the latter, but without accepting it as *merely* contingent. This is why no strict correspondence between the rational schema and the empirical history of philosophy can be found, although the former must be traceable in the latter.

For a while, Kant played with a bolder idea, for he asked "whether it is possible to construe the history of philosophy in mathematical manner" (XX:342). But as he realized, this is impossible, for one cannot account for the contingent aspect of empirical history by an *a priori* deduction (*ibid.*). Moreover, he found the mathematical model inappropriate to the system of philosophy itself,[35] let alone to its history. We are here confronted not with a deduction but with a *hermeneutic* task, in which the schema of reason is used for both discovery and reinterpretation.

Similarly, Kant has to reject the possibility of construing the history of philosophy as a neat temporal order. Had all the philosophers known the plan of reason in advance, "as if they had this schema before their eyes" when they set out to realize it, an orderly sequence of philosophical periods could have been the result (XX:342). But as we have seen, the plan of reason can be known only at the end, and each philosopher is groping after it in dim awareness. This gives the philosophical historian of philosophy a clear advantage not only over the empirical historian, but also over the great philosophers of the past: he can understand their systems better than they did themselves. But this also makes his hermeneutic task more difficult, for "he must not explain and determine [former philosophies] according to the description given by their founders" (*C1*: A 834/B 862) but —as Hegel actually did—reinterpret their meaning and expose their contribution "according to the idea . . . which is grounded in reason itself" (*ibid.*).

35 *C1*, A 712-738/B 740-766.

The execution of this program had to wait for Hegel, who realized it from his own philosophical viewpoint and on a grand, encyclopedic scale. Kant's failure to do so himself[36] may be due in part to his more limited historical scholarship and in part to his personal order of priorities. Judging that this was only a complementary part of the system, requiring less rational innovation (only a well-developed talent of *judgement*), he decided he had better leave it to others. But, programatically, when he again asks in his notes *"Ob die Geschichte der Philosophie selbst ein Theil der Philosophie seyn köñe"* (whether the history[g] of philosophy could itself be a part of philosophy, *LB*, 343), he certainly maintains the positive answer given in the first *Critique*; for, as he adds, "This is not the history[g] of opinions that arose here and there, but of reason that develops itself through concepts."

[36] A short sketch in the Introduction to the *Logic* (Section IV, ix:189-196/17-23) is too meager and superficial to qualify even as an attempt.

CHAPTER VII

THE ROLE OF HISTORY
IN THE PROGRAM, METHOD,
AND COMPOSITION
OF THE CRITICAL SYSTEM

Until now I have used Kant's more or less direct references to the history of philosophy, to show that he had a
distinct (if incomplete) theory on this matter, and to trace
its relation to the pure architectonic of reason. This conclusion will be reinforced as we turn to other metaphilosophi-
cal issues that also suggest, although indirectly, the relevance of the history of philosophy to the pure system of
philosophy. First of these is Kant's account of the emergence
of his philosophical *program* from the special situation of
his culture. Other issues concern the role of history in the
method of philosophy, in its final composition, and in its
relation to other sciences.

The Birth of the Critique from Opposing
Interests of Reason[1]

Kant's program was to give metaphysics "a new birth"
(*Prol.*, IV:367/115), by establishing it as a science. The new
metaphysics was to relate to the old as chemistry relates to
alchemy, or astronomy to astrology (IV:366/115). What
Aristotle did to formal logic, Euclid to geometry, and Newton (and, in Kant's view, Bacon) to the natural sciences, the
Critique is to do to metaphysics. In each case, a "revolution
in the mode of thinking" raised a given discipline to the

---

[1] I have discussed this topic at some length in my book *Kant and the
Renovation of Metaphysics* (Jerusalem, 1973; in Hebrew).

status of science and ended its "groping in the dark." Similarly, Kant's Copernican revolution would overcome the history of philosophy, partly on the basis of the other sciences (e.g., using mathematics and physics in the regressive transcendental argument, and using formal logic in deducing the categories) and transform it into timeless *epistēmē*.

In the language of the architectonic, this program would qualify as the unifying end of Kant's work; and it is noteworthy that, on all three occasions in which he accounts for this program,[2] Kant does so in basically historical terms. The unfiying purpose of the *Critique* is taken—as it should be—from the "essential ends of reason," not as they stand abstractly in themselves, but in the particular form they assume in Kant's own philosophical culture. This form is marked by a special antinomy between two rationally necessary interests: the perennial *metaphysical* interest of reason on one hand, and its *critical* interest, born of the advance of the modern sciences and the spirit of the Enlightenment on the other.

The metaphysical interest is primordial; it has operated in human reason throughout its evolution, and "would survive even if all other sciences were swallowed in the abyss of an all-destroying barbarism" (*C₁*, B xiv). This interest has shown itself in a variety of forms, from myth to primitive religion, then in theology, dogmatic rationalism, and finally, critical rationalism. The critical interest, on the other hand, does not emerge to consciousness before a certain stage in the evolution of reason, and it is thus basically *modern* in character. Although it, too, inheres in the pure archetype of reason, its emergence presupposes a high degree of cultural maturation, exemplified in the method of the new sciences, in modern empiricism, and in the general principle of the enlightenment, which demand that reason *educate* itself autonomously, refraining both from appeal to external authorities and from unrestrained internal specula-

[2] The Preface to *C₁*, A (1781); the *Prolegomena* (1783); and the Preface to *C₁*, B (1787).

tion. Evident in the conflicts between empiricism and rationalism, and sharpened by the opposition of dogmatism and skepticism, between a Hume and a Leibniz, this modern antinomy creates a "need of reason,"[3] to find a new path by which the opposites can be checked and reconciled. Since all previous ways have by now been tried and exhausted, since a great amount of conceptual material has been accumulated bit by bit in the process, and since the norms of order and systematic rigor have had their educational effect, the time is ripe for Kant's own "revolution in the mode of thinking"—the Copernican revolution—to create the final synthesis by reversing traditional ontology (and ethics).

This is the message of Kant's main programmatic texts. In the preface to the first edition of the first *Critique* he starts by describing the degenerate state of metaphysics in his day. "Time was when metaphysics was entitled the Queen of All the Sciences," a title it deserves by the nature of its tasks. "Now, however, the changed fashion of the time brings her only scorn . . ." (A viii). This attitude involves a form of repression and self-deceit, for "it is futile to pretend [*erkünsteln*] to be indifferent to such enquiries, the object of which can never be indifferent to human nature" (*ibid.*). However, Kant does not really blame those who ignore metaphysics; he understands them and in a way recognizes their merit. Repression of the metaphysical interest (for this is all the pretended indifference amounts to) is a distortion in reason; only it does not result from shallowness or individual caprice, but from a tension inherent in the spirit of the age. This present indifference to metaphysics "is not produced by lightness of mind, but by *judgement of the age*, which has matured and no longer tolerates being put off with illusory modes of knowledge (A xi). "Our age," Kant says, "is the genuine [*eigentlich*] Age of Criticism, to which everything must submit," including the most "majestic" institutions of religion and political authority (A xi n.)

[3] Kant even speaks of an "irresistible necessity," and a "pressing want" (*Prol.*, IV:367/116).

as well as reason's own product, i.e., metaphysics. On the other hand, it is precisely this critical interest of reason that leads, in the present state of affairs, to the distortion of another fundamental interest; and this antinomy cannot be resolved unless the power of criticism is turned upon reason itself.

> This [situation] calls upon reason to undertake anew the most difficult of all its tasks—that of knowing itself —and to institute a tribunal that will assure to reason its legitimate claims while dismissing its groundless pretensions; not by enforced decrees, but in accordance with its eternal and unalterable laws. This tribunal is the critique of reason itself (A xi).

As we know, self-limitation by the inherent laws of reason is Kant's definition of autonomy; thus the critique will be not only an act of self-knowledge, but also an act of autonomy that, prior to ethics, takes place in the *cognitive* field. Furthermore, we see that Kant offers the *Critique* not just as a timeless truth, as Spinoza presents his system, but equally as a form of cultural emancipation, i.e., as a means of liberating philosophical culture from the antinomic impasse in which it is caught, which forces the enlightened individual to sacrifice one fundamental aspect of his rationality in favor of another.[4]

The Prolegomena

The same antinomy recurs in the *Prolegomena*,[5] where the historical context of the birth of *Critique* is stressed even more:

---

[4] As indicated, I do not claim that Kant assigned this "need of reason" a role in *justifying* his new philosophy. The truth of the *Critique* is independent of the conditions of its *birth*, which cannot (in contrast to Hegel's method) play a part in its verification.

[5] In the opening sections (esp. IV:255-257/3-5), and in the beginning of the section: "Solution of the General Question of the *Prolegomena*" (IV:365-367/114-116).

All false art, all vain wisdom, lasts its time but finally destroys itself, and its highest culture is also the epoch of its decay (IV:366/115).

From this generalization and diagnosis of his own culture, Kant concludes that "the period of the downfall of all dogmatic metaphysics has undoubtedly arrived" (IV:367/115-116). Having reached its apex in the rigor, method, and comprehensiveness of Wolff,[6] it is now a mere shadow, sustained by institutional inducements—academies, prizes, and "the old arrangement of our universities"—but not by living thought. Indeed, an enlightened man must, perhaps despite himself, avoid accepting compliments like "great metaphysician" (*ibid.*, 366/115). For a while the metaphysical interest has been paralyzed; but this is only a transitory state, the "point of indifference" between opposite trends. The next stage must inevitably be—Kant speaks of an *"irresistible law of necessity"*[7]—the critical rebirth of metaphysics:

> That the human mind will ever give up metaphysical researches is as little to be expected, as that we, to avoid inhaling impure air, should prefer to give up breathing altogether. There will, therefore, always be metaphysics in the world; nay, everyone, especially every reflective man, will have it, and for want of a recognized standard, will shape it for himself after his own pattern. *What has hitherto been called metaphysics cannot satisfy any critical mind; but to forego it entirely is impossible. Therefore, a critique of pure reason itself must be attempted* . . . because there is no other means of supplying this pressing want which is more than mere thirst for knowledge (IV:367/116; italics added).

This passage, especially the italicized sentence, summarizes the antinomy that gave birth to the *Critique*. While most emphatically stressing the unalienable character of

---

[6] Cf. B xxxvi.   [7] Italics in the original.

metaphysics (it is to the rational man as breathing is to the body), Kant again justifies those who reject (or repress) metaphysics in its present form, for they do so out of "a critical mind." Hence the "pressing want" (or need: *Bedürfnis*) of reason for the *Critique*, and also—Kant believes —the ground for predicting its cultural success:

> I pledge myself that nobody who has thought through and grasped[8] the principles of the critique . . . will ever return to that old and sophistical pseudo-science; but will rather with a certain delight look forward to metaphysics, which is now in his power (IV:366/115).

This overreaching optimism is based not only on the abstract truth of the *Critique* but, as we see, on historical conditions and on the emancipating effect the *Critique* will have upon the individual. Satisfying "a want that is more than mere thirst for truth," it has a formative and liberating influence and allows the critical man to develop *all* the aspects of his rationality in a coherent and balanced way.

The Historical Necessity

Kant's claim that the birth and spread of the critical philosophy express "an irresistible law of necessity," contains an interesting ambiguity. In one respect he may mean the logical necessity of an inference: if his premises are true, then the *need* for a critique follows as a consequence. But Kant also wants to say that the *historical* fact that someone drew this inference and actually produced a critique, and the expectation that others would follow him, is also governed by "a law of necessity." This is an altogether different form of necessity, which may be called historical and, with some reservations, also empirical; for it refers to essential drives of the human mind as these manifest themselves in actual time. This ambivalence is characteristic of Kant's references to the "needs," "aspirations," etc. of reason in gen-

[8] Notice the similarity of this wording to Kant's definition of "rational" learning.

eral. His usage of a semi-naturalistic vocabulary is not psychological, but has reference to non-empirical features of the mind; for instance the categories are considered modes of unification. But this raises the question of the relation of the transcendental evolution of the mind to concrete cultural states in time. How does the one manifest itself in the other? This problem is a special variant of Kant's general problem of representation and schematism: it has its origin in his rigid dualism, and I have already argued that Kant has no satisfactory solution for it.[9] But the recognition of this problem is no ground for overlooking the genuine historical context that Kant ascribes to the history of reason, and within it, to the rise of his own critical philosophy.

The Solution of the Antinomy

How does the critical system finally solve the antinomy from which it arises? Although the final harmony is attained only in the field of practice, three essential steps are already taken in the sphere of knowledge. First, reason actualizes its autonomy from external authorities not only negatively, but also positively, by an act of self-limitation. Secondly, and more specifically, it reconciles the metaphysical and the critical interests by creating a new, transcendental ontology. Metaphysics has to do with supersensibles and with the problem of existence, while the critical interest is here expressed in the form of the empiricist principle, which bars all claims of existence where no relevant observations can be supplied. How can the two be reconciled? Kant's answer, as we know, is that transcendental science does not claim to know *a priori* any separate supersensible *entities*, either beyond nature or within it, but that it does claim to know the *a priori*, or supersensible, existence-*conditions* of all empirical existents. As a result of the Copernican revolution, the synthetic-logical conditions for correctly describing an objective state of affairs are equally the onto-

[9] See conclusion of the Introductory Chapter: "The Historical Antinomy and Historical Schematism," and the Epilogue.

logical conditions for this state of affairs to *be* what it is (and what the description claims that it is); and thus, all analysis of the *a priori* structure of knowledge *ipso facto* becomes an analysis of the *a priori* (super-empirical) structure of known *reality*. However, the metaphysical knowledge gained thereby does not have reference to any particular existent, only to the sum total of the *a priori* conditions for all natural existents or what Kant calls "nature in the formal sense" (*Prol.*, IV:318/65). Therefore, the metaphysical interest is satisfied critically, and the same critical metaphysics also does justice to the empiricist claim. Moreover, since one of the *a priori* conditions of natural existence is observability, the critical principle, which formerly functioned as a mere empiricist dogma, now finds its proper place and "deduction" within the new metaphysics, as a *non*-empirical condition for the existence of natural objects.

The third step is taken in the Dialectic. Although the supreme objects of traditional metaphysics (God, the soul, the cosmos as a whole) must be declared cognitively problematic, this negative result does a positive service to the practical interest of reason by barring the possibility of heteronomous morality based upon the will of a transcendent God, and thus by clearing the way for a moral law that man legislates himself.

The final harmonization of all the interests of reason, however, is attained in the field of moral history by projecting the ideal of the highest good as the totalization of all man's rational endeavors. But this primacy of practical reason does not mean that the other interests of reason are simply subordinated to the moral ideal, as if we could distort truth, or declare an ugly work of art beautiful, only because it served some moral interests. This, indeed, would be another violation of the critical interest and a form of heteronomy. All regional interests of reason (in knowledge, ethics, and esthetics) must follow only their immanent criteria. But indirectly, knowledge and esthetics also serve "the moral destiny of man": the first by refraining from judgement on transcendent issues, thus making a form of rational faith possible (see Chapter Two), and the second by serving as a symbol for morality.

History and the Composition of the System

The system of philosophy also depends upon its history in a material way. We have seen that philosophy cannot become scientific unless its full conceptual inventory is discovered and "deduced." But this deduction concerns the order and unifying principles of the concepts, not their particular content. For their material side, the ingredients of the system depend upon a huge task of preparation that involves their piecemeal discovery or recovery from the "ruins" of former systems and from *a priori* disciplines. To give but a few examples, it is well known that Kant arranged his table of categories with reference to the forms of judgement in formal logic and to the ontological categories derived from the Aristotelian tradition. Similarly, his picture of the empirical mind is based upon Locke's; his account of transcendental consciousness presupposes Descartes' "I think" and Leibniz's "apperception"; and the distinction between analytic and synthetic judgements reformulates the discoveries of Hume and Leibniz. Indeed, the whole *Critique* abounds in borrowed concepts and distinctions, which it assimilates into its own texture.[10] The first antinomies summarize the historical paradoxes that have haunted philosophy since Zeno, assigning them a systematic place and origin in reason; and the rest of the Dialectic does the same for other perennial philosophical themes—God, the soul, and free will. The same is again true of the other *Critiques*, where the classical arguments of hedonism and purism, mechanism and teleology, freedom

[10] Only a few particular concepts are genuine Kantian formations, such as pure intuition or schematism; and in most of these cases, the alleged discovery is due to internal heuristic rules, i.e., to the need to account for other concepts or to fill missing parts in the system.

and legal restriction, and so forth are summarized and systematized. A thorough examination of the three *Critiques* will, in fact, render a whole encyclopedia of historical concepts reduced to their essential form and incorporated in the pure system of reason.

Kant is clearly aware of his great material debt to the history of philosophy. When he claims that the time had come for scientific philosophy, he explains this in part "in view of the great amount of material that has been collected, or that can be obtained from the ruins of ancient systems" (*C1*, A 835/B 863). His own role consists not so much in material innovation as in revolutionizing the *foundations* of philosophy, and upon this basis, in *re-integrating* the accumulated wealth of the past within a new systematic totality.

The second task extends far beyond the scope of the *Critiques*, which were to function only as a "propaedeutic" (*C1*, A 841/B 869) or "an essay on method" (B xxii). Once the original *a priori* concepts of nature and of moral action have been laid down by the *Critiques*, a great number of derived[11] *a priori* concepts are to follow, forming the two *material* branches of philosophy—the metaphysics of nature and the metaphysics of morals. Again, the content of these two disciplines was to be borrowed from the vast wealth of traditional metaphysics as well as from the political, moral and educational insights of the Enlightenment: motion and force, absolute and relative space, matter and impenetrability, and, in ethics, virtue and conscience, friendship and family, republicanism, property, punishment, and so forth, constitute the actual subject matter of metaphysics, its material flesh and blood. These concepts are certainly to be selected, organized and modified in accordance with the new philosophical foundations; but it is finally in the complete set of these concepts that the goal of the new metaphysics consists, and for which the *Critique* was only a preparation.

---

[11] On the distinction between "original" and "derived" concepts, see *C1*, A 81-82/B 107-108.

It may be ironic that Kant does not consider this part of his task—the most important *per se* from his own point of view—as particularly interesting; for being "derived," it does not require the same originality and innovation as the *Critiques*. This may be part of the reason why Kant never actually finished this task "by the end of the century," as he proposed to do. His metaphysics of nature are meager; and only in the metaphysics of *Sitten* (i.e., particular ethical, legal, and political principles) did he produce a fairly thorough body of work. But there is no doubt that, programmatically, the system is designed from a really *encyclopedic* point of view. (It has been said of Kant that there was almost no category in the dogmatic ontology of Wolff that he did not wish to reintegrate—critically—in his own system). In this respect Kant's radicalism is tradition-oriented; he breaks away from the the past while looking back to it, and his revolutionary act is designed not to do away with the wealth of traditional philosophy, but to retain and reassimilate it within a new and higher organization.

History and the Method of Philosophy

The dependence of philosophy on its own history is also shown in Kant's conception of the philosophical method, especially in (a) his rejection of the deductive (mathematical) model and in (b) his claim that an element of material opacity—requiring sheer discovery—is inevitable in the field of reason itself. (a) Kant flatly rejects Descartes' prescription of a single methodological model to all branches of knowledge. Each discipline must become scientific by its own method, by a method adequate to its epistemic origins and to its subject matter. Geometry and other formal systems require linear deduction; physics and the other natural sciences are based upon empirical synthesis; while philosophy presupposes the *self*-explication of reason, where tentative discoveries and definitions are gradually corrected and transformed. This excludes the classical *ordo geomet-*

rico, which starts from fully defined concepts (stipulated, or "made" by itself: *C1*, A 730/B 758) and from absolutely true propositions (axioms), and transmits the same values of clarity and conclusiveness to all further steps in a linear process. The deductive chain requires no additional material as it progresses; it leaves behind it no opaque residues; and it does not need to retrace its steps or to consider, even vaguely, its future horizons. At any stage of the deduction, all concepts are exhaustively clear and all theorems have conclusive truth value.[12]

In contrast, philosophy starts from an indistinct context of concepts and relations, which has to turn back upon itself and be explicated gradually. It therefore has no fixed axioms and definitions, and attains full clarity and validity only at the *end*. As the self-explication of reason, philosophy has nothing to rely upon, be it external data or internal first principles, except reason itself—in its still rudimentary and badly articulated shape, but with all the richness of its latent concepts and forms. Its march does not, therefore, resemble that of a linear deduction, where every item emerges immediately and discretely, fully clear and verified. It is more like bringing a blurred context, a latent totality, into clearer focus, discerning its features while reshuffling them by rules that derive from the developing system itself. This makes every progression a matter of regression; the movement must leave residues of obscurity and ambiguity behind it; and every new achievement immediately turns back, revising what went on before or shedding new light upon it. In philosophy, Kant says, definitions are not the beginning,

---

[12] This is the classical view of the *ordo geometrico*. Today we may no longer concur with this ideal picture. Realizing that primitive terms are arbitrary, not intuitively clear; that axioms are interchangeable; that by following the rules of inference we may still end up in contradictions; and that there is, therefore, some point in considering the horizons of the system in advance (at least when choosing its axioms), we may no longer subscribe to Kant's ideal picture. For him neither Gödel nor the interchangeability of deductive calculi were imaginable. But this does not essentially change the issue.

but the conclusion (*C1*, A 731/B 759),[13] and the incomplete explication must precede the complete explanation (A 730/B 758). But just as we do not start with fixed and final principles, so we do not start in a void. Knowledge springs from blurred knowledge, not *ex nihilo*; as rational creatures, we reside *ab initio* in the sphere of reflection and possess the ability to reason even if we do so in confused fashion. This is shown by the very possibility to philosophize, for "if we could make no use of a concept till we had defined it, all philosophy would be in a pitiable plight" (A 731n./B 759 n.).[14] And just as the gradual movement of self-explication is the essence of the *history* of philosophy,[15] it is also the governing principle in the *method* of philosophy, which excludes all appeals to external experience or to the deductive mathematical model.

In this Kant not only establishes a certain similarity between the two, but actually gives the history of philosophy a distinct methodological import. This will become more specifically evident as we reexamine the problem of *rational contents*. A major reason for barring the deductive model from philosophy is that the full material content of the various concepts cannot be derived in philosophy from previous elements. To be able to do so indicates that man is endowed with intellectual intuition. As Kant makes clear, the fact that he has to borrow piecemeal contents from the history of logic, of ontology, and so forth is not a flaw in the system, or even an accidental shortcoming, but a major

---

13 Kant has a *theoretical* definition in mind, not a stipulative one. The former contains objective constraints and must conform to the nature of some subject matter—in this case, the universal features of rationality.

14 This is Kant's version of Plato's *anamnesis*. As *Meno* showed, any theory of learning or of rational growth must presuppose a variant of this theory.

15 Cf. the previous chapter, including Kant's assertions that "philosophy is the gradual development of human reason" (*LB*, XX:340); that "the history of philosophy is the history of reason that develops itself through concepts" (*ibid.*, 343); that all philosophical systems "have their schema, as the original germ, in the self-development of reason alone" (*C1*: A 835/B 863), etc.

expression of the finitude of reason. The deduction of the categories means that they are fully discovered (Metaphysical Deduction) and justified (Transcendental Deduction) according to their unifying principles and *a priori* ground in pure consciousness. But why they have the particular content and number they do is in principle an opaque "fact of reason," something to be simply encountered or discovered, which cannot be made intelligible *per se*. Similarly, discovering particular epistemological functions, the types of judgement, the role of memory, imagination, or the pursuit of happiness, constitutes a vast material domain that is not derived by pure deduction but revealed or encountered by a kind of pure observation that can perhaps be called phenomenological. The need to rely upon such material makes the method of philosophy depend even more specifically upon its history, namely, upon the vast cumulative work performed throughout the history of reason.

The History of Philosophy and Other Sciences

Just as the system of philosophy depends on its own history, so it depends on the history of *other* sciences. There is an explicable *ordo cognoscendi* in the sequence in which the different disciplines attain scientific status. It may be deplorable, almost "ridiculous,"[16] that the most important and fundamental science, philosophy, should come last; but this is the natural order of things. In order to grasp the foundations of all knowledge in their purity, we must first have some actual knowledge, or other forms of cultural experience, in which they are involved. This holds true for philosophy as well as for the other rational, i.e., *a priori* disciplines: logic and mathematics. All of them presuppose some cultural products or experiences in which their rules are embodied and from which they can be extricated by reflection in their pure form. This procedure does not abolish the *a priori* nature of the discipline itself, nor does it pre-

16 *Prol.*, IV:256/4.

vent it from following a progressive and even deductive method internally. In other words, the substantive experience precedes its conceptualization in terms of the historical *ordo cognoscendi* without affecting the internal method and justification of the science it invokes.

Mathematics and formal logic,[17] the first disciplines to attain scientific status, presuppose pragmatic experience (measurement, disputation) but not the existence of other *sciences*. Mathematics has been scientific "since the earliest times in the history of human reason" (*C1*, B x). At first it was embedded in imagery and pragmatic usage (Egypt), but then the Greeks had the revolutionary insight that mathematical objects were constructed by reason itself, and so could be studied and exhausted *a priori*, without relying on observation. A similar revolution occurred in logic, where reason produces no objects at all, only a system of formal relations that apply indifferently to all objects. The restricted scope of these disciplines, together with their internal deductive method—and the fact that they did not presuppose other sciences—made them fairly self-sufficient and allowed for their early scientification.

The case of physics is much more complex, for it had to discover rational necessity in the empirical world itself. The nature of the problem is such that this cannot either be done *a priori*, by mere speculation, or by crude and qualitative induction; both ways have been variously tried and proved futile. It is only when the study of nature submits to *guided observation* (i.e., experiment: *C1*, B xii-xiii) and to quantification that the way is opened to its becoming a science; and this represents a much more mature, and dependent, stage in the history of reason. The success of Newtonian science was not only a revolutionary coup; it also provided a new kind of experience, and a new cultural

17 By formal logic Kant understands mainly the Aristotelian syllogistic; and by mathematics he understands above all geometry. The great advances in logic and mathematics we know today were inconceivable in Kant's time.

product, that in substance contained the new insights of reason with regard to methodology and metaphysics; and these had still to be elucidated and grounded *a priori*. In the texture of modern empirical science, quantified data combine with the rules of formal and of *synthetic logic* (metaphysics) to produce a unified world of experience. But the metaphysical principles are only used; they operate in the synthesis without being justified and grounded by the *a priori* structure of reason (in Kant's terms: without a "deduction"). This defines the task of critical metaphysics and immediately makes it possible. It has to explicate the conceptual framework of objective experience, which leads the *products* of reason back to their *origin* in transcendental consciousness. This procedure provides the empirical sciences with their foundations. But—more important for Kant— it opens the way for metaphysics to attain the same success as physics, i.e., the status of a science.

This is not only the essence of Kant's regressive transcendental argument,[18] but also a prerequisite for the *Critique* as a whole. Internally, the system of reason may be organized and justified by its own means. But historically the *Critique* would not have had a ground for arising, unless the kind of experience of which it is the pure conceptualization already existed. This does not diminish its *a priori* character *per se*, or prevent it from being justified by a *progressive* transcendental deduction. (Indeed, within the system itself, the regressive argument is secondary to the progressive.) But it indicates that, according to the historical *ordo cognoscendi*, we discover the pure forms of our mind not in the abstract, by some sudden insight, but through

18 By "regressive" and "progressive" arguments I mean what Kant calls in the *Prolegomena* the "synthetic" and "analytic" methods. The first starts from the existence of an apodictic science of nature, and looks for the *a priori* conditions that alone make it possible. The second starts from the reflective thought "I think" and looks for its preconditions. Both investigations end up with the *same set* of conditions, establishing a mutual dependence between the identity of the ego and the possibility of an objective world of experience.

their embodiment in the actual products of culture and knowledge which they make possible.[19]

A reference to Hegel again suggests itself. Hegel conceives of all philosophy as the conceptualization of the objective products of the spirit. For him the substance of a given culture and its subjective self-consciousness are two aspects of the same *Sache*; Kant, however, working with a transcendental rather than a dialectical model, conceives of philosophy as a distinct meta-theory, over and above the substantive experience to which it relates by the pure and one-sided relation of *grounding*. Moreover, while Hegel applies his regressive model to all periods and forms of culture (each *Zeitgeist* has its proper philosophy as well as its religion, art, and political culture), in Kant the model applies only to the last stage of scientification, and only to the relation of philosophy and the sciences on one hand, and to moral experience on the other.

The End of Philosophy and the Infinity of Praxis

In conclusion, we see that Kant suggests the historicality of philosophy both directly by an explicit theory, and indirectly by assigning it various meta-philosophical roles in the method, the program, and the final composition of the system. The history of philosophy is thus made an essential form of the history of reason in general. Kant's account of it in essence resembles his accounts of the history of religion and politics, where a latent rational plan is gradually unfolded, although its promoters are not fully aware of it, and thus engage in opposition and contradictions. But it should be born in mind that the history of philosophy is only a prerequisite for the history of reason in the practical sense.

---

[19] This also applies to morality and religion. As the *Foundations* makes clear, the pure moral law is explicated from actual moral experience, reflected even in popular consciousness; and in the *Religion* we see that the religion of reason is first embedded in the various historical churches, before it attains full explication (see Chapter Five).

With the rise of the *Critiques,* the complete theory of rationality is brought to consciousness. Now it is possible to look back upon the history, not only of philosophy, but also of religion and politics, and find the latent paradigm unwittingly produced in them. In politics we find that what actual history has brought about, through the dialectic of conflict, violence and self-interest, conforms teleologically to the plan that reason itself recommends—as we now know by its explication. Similarly, knowing the real significance of all religion, we can now discern in the historical churches a pattern of rational morality, towards which their founders and adherents were groping in their various sensuous ways. However, with the full theoretical explication of these histories, philosophy itself ends, while in politics, religion, and above all in ethics, a radically new era begins.

With the birth of the *Critiques,* and with the Enlightenment in general, we are already able to understand our history, what we have been doing all along and what we *ought* to be doing; and so, henceforth, there is no longer a rational justification for latent and embedded action. From this point onwards, once the light of reason has dawned consciously, moral history ought to be forwarded by a clear design and by a rational intention; its ideal goal, the highest good on earth, must be pursued *intentionally,* both in its ethical and political dimensions; and this implies that a rational man henceforth may not escape into his own private morality or only react to particular moral problems that occur in his life, but he must also initiate global changes in the world—ethical, political, and educational reforms— the object of which is not just that he should become good, but, ultimately, the goodness of the world-order as a whole.

This sheds new light on the primacy of pure practical reason. It is not only a methodological principle ("You may rationally believe in a cognitive proposition that cannot be decided cognitively, if and only if this belief is necessary for moral action in a concrete situation that you face"); it also means that, historically, the ultimate goal of man (his destiny) is not knowledge, but the moral transformation of the world. In Hegel, social and political action are subordinated, as conditions, to the ultimate end of speculation, by which they are *aufgehoben*. Hegel thus historicized the Aristotelian ideal of absolute knowledge, making philosophical knowledge the supreme stage in the history of the world spirit. One does not attain complete philosophical self-knowledge unless the world has already become rational in praxis as well; and this self-knowledge, not social action or political culture, is the ultimate actualization of spirit. For Kant, on the contrary, self-knowledge is a prerequisite for rational action, not its result. When the history of philosophy is consummated, the destiny of man is not yet achieved. Instead, man now understands for the first time the meaning of his own history, and thereby he becomes aware of the immense—even infinite—historical task that still lies *ahead* of him: to shape the world itself as a "highest good."

EPILOGUE

The Historical Antinomy Reexamined

I hope the preceding chapters (including the Introduction) have made it sufficiently manifest that the concept of rational history is both genuine and central in Kant's system. It pervades Kant's theories of ethics, religion, politics, education, science, and philosophy. It determines man's special position in the universe, his infinite destiny and the final end of creation itself. Methodologically, it provides the system with a focal end-of-reason (the highest good), by which all branches of philosophy are to be united architectonically. And, far from being imposed upon the system from without, it is rooted in the fundamental features of rationality as Kant conceives of them: the finitude of human reason; its interested character; its need to undergo a process of self-explication; its being constituted by the rational subject (rather than being given to him ready-made); and—with respect to praxis—its being radically external to nature, yet demanding to imprint itself upon nature in the form of an ought.

And yet, in maintaining his concept of the history of reason, Kant also has fundamental difficulties, for unlike Hegel, he cannot allow for the *temporalization* of reason, nor —more broadly speaking—can he admit of an affinity between pure reason and its opposite, empirical reality. The first and narrower difficulty gives rise to an actual antinomy in Kant: while the concept of a history of reason is systematically *indispensable*, from another viewpoint (that of time) it is *untenable*. The broader difficulty does not involve a strict contradiction, but a weaker form of incoherence, which we called the problem of *historical schema-*

tism:[1] Since no satisfactory bridge is available between reason and the empirical world, rational history and empirical history cannot be united in a single process, and Kant's theory of the history of reason is not fully accounted for in terms of the system in which it necessarily arises.

For brevity's sake I shall refer to both forms of the problem as the *historical antinomy.*[2] Throughout this book I had to stress the "thesis" side of this antinomy, i.e., the central and indispensable place of the concept of rational history in Kant: this is the most neglected part of the picture, which Kantian scholarship was late (if not reluctant) to recognize. But I cannot conclude without pointing out the antinomic situation itself and survey in short the side of the "antithesis" as well—namely, the grounds for the systematic untenability of the history of reason in Kant.

In order to do this I propose to go back to the various topics discussed in the book and sum up the difficulties they raise, not as a simple list, but as variants of a central problematic. In the final analysis, most of the important objections go back to Kant's radical dualism, which (short of transcendent postulates and *deus ex machina* solutions) prevents him from seeing rational history and empirical history as mediating each other in a single dynamic whole. This will also define the major difference between Kant and Hegel on our subject.

The Highest Good and the Historical Imperative
(Chapter One)

Discussing the possible objections to the imperative to promote the highest good, we have seen that, although it does not necessarily involve heteronomy (as some critics have charged), it does introduce a systematic gap between both parts of Kant's theory of practice. There is no continu-

---

[1] See Introduction, pp. 21-22.

[2] Even so one should remember that admitting an antinomy implies that both sides are equally necessary from a systematic viewpoint, and that neither one can be dismissed as spurious or as illegitimate.

ous passage from the formal to the material imperative and, what is more, from the narrow concept of rational will implied by the first to the broader and more concrete rational will implied by the second.[3] We have also located the exact point of this leap: it occurs when the highest good is made the object of duty. This constitutes by implication a new concept of moral will, for which the highest good with *both* its systems, the rational as well as the empirical, becomes a *rational* end in itself.

This turn is crucial for the evolution of Kant's theory of praxis. It leads from personal morality to the vision of a moralized nature, from reaction to particular circumstances to initiation of global changes in the world, from a morality of single acts to their totalization in view of a historical ideal. But this turn has no sufficient ground in what precedes it, and in addition, it leaves unclear what is the *single* object of the will and who is the *one* will that wills this object. Actual unity has not been achieved either on the side of the object or on the side of the subject. The willing subject, man, remains split between two radically different principles of will; and the object, the highest good, is only an external juxtaposition or correspondence of components that retain their fundamental alienness even within their alleged synthesis.

If we ask what makes the passage from the first to the second stage of praxis so hard to explain, we must come to two fundamental features of Kant's ethics: the split in man's principle of will and the interpretation of practical reason in terms of an ought, that is, as extrinsic to the world and having to remold it from without. Both these features are variants of the basic dualism of reason and nature. As a dual creature, belonging at once to opposite worlds, man is torn in his very existence. His natural will has one object, his rational will quite another. What can make an actually single object of both? And how can the combined object be-

[3] See above, pp. 43-48.

come *rational in itself*: in Kantian terms, the object of an ought? Had reason been conceived as intrinsic to the empirical world, had each been grasped as mediating the other within a single process, these difficulties would not have arisen; but then we would be discussing Hegel, not Kant. Kant certainly cannot afford to renounce his view of reason as extrinsic to nature and the mutual exclusion of spontaneity and receptivity, for this would undermine the critique not only in ethics but in the other branches as well. It is therefore no occasional difficulty, but an essential one, which affects his construal of the highest good as a fully coherent and self-sustained theory of historical praxis.

The Postulate of God (Chapter Two)

In speaking of a "self-sustained" theory I have a further difficulty in mind: the need to use a transcendent postulate in order to ensure that the highest good is possible. This is a further problem, for even supposing that the highest good is an object of duty, the system itself has no sufficient ground for explaining its possibility.[4] The historical synthesis implied in the highest good cannot be achieved by the *self-*evolution of nature toward its own rationalization.[5] It requires that man, in his conscious action, *imprint* (from without) the goals and precepts of his reason upon a basically alien and indifferent nature. But since no material affinity can be admitted between nature and reason, there is nothing to guarantee that the historical synthesis is not an intrinsically futile adventure. Suppose that nature, following its own mechanical laws, is primordially such that it cannot lend itself to moral reshaping by man, but must frustrate and negate any such attempt? The basic rules of the critical system cannot preclude this possibility, since it is they themselves which establish it. It follows that the system cannot account for the feasibility of the historical ideal it

---

[4] See above, pp. 83-88.
[5] As we have seen, the cunning of nature has no moral value in itself, and can attain but an external "copy" of morality.

requires, unless it *suspends* the basic rules of criticism and postulates, as an extrinsic principle, some common ground of nature and freedom, a principle that our ontology cannot admit and yet that may be admitted "from a practical point of view."

In addition to suspending the basic rules of criticism by way of an extrinsic postulate, Kant's recourse to the concept of God incurs a further systematic price. The whole thrust of the Copernican revolution runs contrary to assigning to God a determinative role in the system. As against former theology and philosophy, God has no longer a part to play ensuring knowledge, prescribing moral commands, bridging body and mind, providing *ab initio* the "best world," or even evoking religious awe. It is the human mind itself, in its spontaneous capacity, that must now fulfill all these functions. It provides the foundations of knowledge and ethics, of nature and action, of beauty, sublimity, even of sanctity and religious awe; and, equally, it has to supply *of itself* the necessary mediation between its various modes of operation (i.e., provide its own "schematism"). This is the systematic expression of the creative autonomy of human reason—Kant's most important single principle. While Descartes had to relegate to God the task of bridging the mind and the external objects, Kant's revolution forgoes such transcendent mediation by making the objects themselves constituted by the pure forms of the mind. While Leibniz had to rely on God for providing the "best world" as a *pre-*established harmony between the realms of nature and grace, Kant's revolution transfers to man the task of *producing* this harmony by way of his action and practical reason. Cartesians have postulated God as the link between man's heterogeneous functions (for them, body and mind); Kant, when confronted with his *own* problem of schematism, seeks to solve it by the immanent faculties of the mind itself (judgement, productive imagination, etc.). It is only with respect to the problem of historical schematism in this particular form, i.e., the need to establish an affinity between nature and reason in the face of opposing critical presuppositions, that Kant, too, reverts to a *deus ex machina* solution, following a tradition his whole philosophy was trying to reverse.

Unfortunately, even paying this high price does not actually solve Kant's problem, for if we strip the concept of God of all subjective addenda, as Kant says we must, the postulate of *God's* existence becomes functionally redundant. It only repeats that the highest good is possible through human action, but does not explain *how* this is possible. Faced with the imperative to promote the highest good and with the principle that duty implies ability, Kant had to conclude that, whatever the basic assumptions of the critique, man must be able to promote the highest good. This was a purely moral deduction that Kant sought, however, to complete with an ontological *explanation*; and for this purpose he postulates "the existence of God" as the transcendent source, by which an affinity is established between nature and human freedom. Yet Kant admits that even as a postulate, we may not conceive of God in the traditional way, as a super-subject or independent entity endowed with understanding and will, who has created both nature and human freedom with an eye to their eventual reunification. All that the objective part of the postulate allows us to assert is an indefinite factor, a mere "something" that ensures the possibility of the highest good.[6] But this only reiterates the *explanandum* without supplying it with an explanation. Saying that the highest good is possible and saying there is "something" that makes it possible amounts to the same thing.[7]

[6] See above, pp. 89-90, 118-121.

[7] Kant's problem in this respect is a variety of his need to use a transcendent postulate at all. The primacy of pure practical reason allows him to postulate only as much as is strictly necessary to give meaning to the imperative to promote the highest good. But how much is that much? If what is required is a detailed ontological scheme which spells out exactly how the highest good is to be conceived as possible, then the primacy principle might have sanctioned picturing God as an

The Cunning of Nature (Chapters Three and Four)

A striking example of the split between rational and empirical history is given in Kant's struggle with the theory of the cunning of nature. He does attribute to nature a principle of self-overcoming, whereby a semirational pattern emerges; but he cannot make it the vehicle of rational progress in the proper sense, nor can he allow the cunning of nature an exclusive role even in the production of external institutions.[8] Strictly speaking, reason is alien to nature; it does not work in and through it, but must confront and remold it from without. No other form of rationality is recognized in the field of action; and therefore, even if by a striking correspondence a semirational system is found to have been produced by the natural course itself, this must be branded as mere "legality," the fruit of a blind contrivance of nature which has, as such, no truly rational import.

Moreover, this stepbrother of rationality must also be considered the illegitimate child of *nature*; for its springing off the natural course as such cannot be accounted for in terms of the critical system. True, we have seen that Kant can avoid the dogmatic character of his thesis by placing it, with due restrictions, within the framework of his reflective teleology. But from a wider systematic viewpoint the cunning of nature is not fully integrated in the rest of the system, since it cannot be linked with rational history proper, and its very occurrence remains inexplicable. In the absence of a common ground for nature and reason, and without using dialectical logic, how can we explain that this won-

---

actual super-subject who had created both nature and man; but this "maximal" interpretation of the postulate would have presented further problems for Kant. However, *if all that man needs in order to act is the bare assurance that his efforts are not doomed to futility, then this assurance is also all that the postulate may assert objectively.* Kant clearly opts for this minimal interpretation of the postulate, avoiding further complications, yet at the same time making all further explanations redundant.

[8] See above, pp. 170-177, 194-196.

drous correspondence takes place *within nature itself and by its sole and immanent agency?* Grounded in violence, conflict, and self-interest (that is, for Kant, in the strict opposite of rationality), the products of culture can bear the external marks of reason only accidentally, as a purely contingent fact, whose initial probability is infinitesimally low. If despite this low probability nature happens to produce of itself the same kind of legal institutions that reason, too, would have recommended, this must be seen as a happy chance, a mere coincidence that the system cannot explain. Moreover, this contingent correspondence is discovered *ex post facto*, and applies only to the past; with regard to the future, its *a priori* probability remains very slim (for the basic duality persists at every stage of the development), and so we have no valid ground for historical prediction, much less for a solid guarantee of political progress in the future.[9]

These difficulties must lead us to concede that our efforts to integrate the cunning of nature within Kant's broader system of history can succeed only in part. We have certainly removed the graver objection that views the cunning of nature as a dogmatic principle of teleology. But we are left with two independent systems, natural history (culture) and rational history, which may complement each other externally, but which have no internal mediation between them. Whatever nature produced of itself is one thing; whatever practical reason effects is quite another; and both principles

[9] This also speaks against Kant's alleged "guarantee" of political progress in the future (in *PP*, First Supplement). The doubtful position of culture can be seen from another angle as well. While Kant joins other writers in presenting culture as qualitatively different from nature and as opposing it, his opposition between culture and nature is not genuine, for in the final analysis both belong to the same homogeneous domain, and both stand in strict opposition to *reason*. Culture represents only an inner dialectic within the realm of nature itself; and its sublimating effects are no more rational and no less empirical than, say, the "elevated" passions of love, generosity, etc. in the field of ethics. And so, while culture is supposed to mediate between nature and reason, or even be their mutual product, the basic terms of the system block this role, forcing culture back to one side of the actual dichotomy.

must be radically severed. This particular split between empirical and rational history again reflects Kant's basic dualism, not only in general, but in the more specific form of identifying the rationality of action with an ought. As an ought, reason cannot grow out of the inner dialectic (and self-overcoming) of nature itself; it is not embedded in the actual behavior of men, acting naturally by passion and ambition, as in Hegel, but is rather opposed to the natural course of the world. The proper relation of reason to empirical reality is that of *subsumption*; rather than being explicated from within this world, reason seeks to subordinate it from without to its own transcendental precepts; and since this view is crucial to Kant's practical philosophy (without it, his rigorous ethics will collapse, and all will become heteronomy), it is again no accidental reason, but a *fundamental* one, which makes inevitable the split between rational and empirical history, as seen from the viewpoint of the cunning-of-nature theory.

The History of Religion (Chapter Five)

A much more daring attempt to unite the history of reason with empirical history is found in Kant's account of religion, its history and critique. All religions are varieties of a single principle, the religion of reason or pure morality, which they express in different degrees of inadequacy and sensuous cover (myths, symbols, fanaticism, crude cults, etc.); and it is *within* the actual religions that pure moral consciousness gradually awakens and becomes explicated to itself. This conception, even more than the cunning of nature, brings Kant close to the Hegelian model; for now he pictures the pure religion of reason as actually *embedded* in the various religious cults; and *the empirical history of religion becomes the medium or "vehicle" of the history of reason proper.*

This conception evokes, however, a number of difficulties, some of which Kant is able to solve only at the price of leaving the others insoluble. The first objection is that in placing the history of reason *within* the empirical history of religion, Kant has given up his crucial notion of reason as an ought confronting nature. To this Kant would answer that what we call the "empirical" history of religion is not strictly empirical, but already a combined product of reason and nature. It represents the work of practical reason, embedded in the precepts of the various religions, in affecting the real world, that is, in shaping the actual practice of individuals and whole societies bound by a certain religion. We have seen that, according to Kant, all religions are based on the sole principle of duty; their true import is normative, taking the form of *absolute commands*; and these commands, erroneously ascribed to a transcendent lawgiver, express the precepts of practical reason in various distorted ways. Therefore, Kant may argue, even the "empirical" or positive religions incorporate a principle opposing raw nature; and while they embody the precepts of reason in inadequate and sensuously affected forms, their history is not simply natural but, *ab initio*, it is that of a *remolding encounter* between practical reason and nature.

But this encounter is also the medium in which pure moral consciousness emerges and becomes explicated to itself. And here a second objection arises: The moral law is a fact of reason belonging to every rational being; how, then, can it have a history? Kant would reply that although a moral consciousness inheres in principle in every man, its latent paradigm is not immediately recognized but must undergo a process of awakening and self-recognition. Moreover, this process cannot take place in the void, but must occur through the *actual effects* that moral consciousness has on the world in different stages of its awakening. Since these effects were mostly guided by the various religious traditions, the history of religion is the most important practical substrate for the rise of pure moral consciousness. The role of the philosopher is to recognize it as such and, instead of simply dismissing this history as a series of mere superstitions, to enhance the process further by a proper *critique* of religion and by reinterpretation of its sacred documents.

Kant can meet these objections only by committing himself to a theory he cannot maintain. The positive history of religion can serve as a vehicle for rational history only because, from the start, it is a combined product of reason and nature, and because the pure paradigm of morality is supposed to be embedded in its sensuous cover. But in order to maintain these notions Kant would have to admit that a rational content can be contained in partial or "impure" forms in a nonrational medium (sensibility, imagination, etc.), such that its becoming purely rational is only a change in degree, or a mere alteration of form that leaves the content essentially the same. This conception may be in place in the systems of Hegel, Leibniz and also Aristotle, but it is at odds with Kant's own critique. In Kantian terms, the rational and the nonrational differ not in degree or in form, but in *kind*; they are not two stages along a single scale, but two heterogeneous and mutually exclusive principles. Therefore, there is no way for the second to contain the first, or for the first to be embedded, however distortedly, in the "sensuous cover" of the second.

It should be noticed that the relation of embeddedness is not a proper form of schematism, the only mediation between the rational and the nonrational admissible in Kant. In schematizing a rational concept we are supposed to translate its full rational import into some intuitional medium such that both will remain purely homogeneous in their respective domains. The schematizing medium must represent (*darstellen*) the rational content in its own way, with no confusion of the elements. In the case of the historical religions, however, no such *Darstellung* is involved, but a pure and simple *mixture* of the elements (which must, in strict Kantian terms, be dismissed as purely non-rational); and from this point of view Kant's theory is incongruous with a basic dichotomy of his system.

Kant's actual difficulty is, therefore, that in viewing reason as initially embedded in the positive religions, he must relax the rigid heterogeneity of the elements that gives his system its distinct critical character. The critique does not subscribe to the Aristotelian tradition, for which rational concepts are mediated by an image and have a sensuous substrate from which they rise. Even more specifically, the critique is opposed to the doctrine of Leibniz, who established a continuity between the sensuous and the rational, both being different stages of the same principle; and it equally rejects the Hegelian variety of this theory, which makes the continuity dialectical rather than simple. And yet, when construing the history of religion as containing practical reason under a sensuous cover, Kant comes closer to the Hegelian model while departing from a basic distinction of his own.

The impropriety of the notion of embeddedness as a form of historical schematism is not the only difficulty. A more specific, and even graver objection relates to *time*. *Per se*, there is nothing objectionable in allowing for a process of of rational awakening, by which the pure paradigm of rationality in consciousness becomes more and more explicit. But the inevitable question is: How shall we explain the growth of rationality as a *temporal* sequence? What is the relation between the various stands of pure consciousness and actual states in time? From Moses to Jesus, Mohammed, and Luther, the actual history of religion takes place through real persons in their respective generations. It involves the work of prophets and popes, Byzantine rulers and medieval monks, German reformers and modern zealots, as well as the daily actions and habitual behavior of innumerable believers. If the history of reason is to take place within this necessary medium, how shall we account for the *temporalization of reason*—when the Kantian system precludes this notion in advance?

Here we touch upon the historical antinomy in the narrow sense. While having to assert, on other grounds, that a history of reason is indispensable, Kant cannot reconcile this view to his theory of time. Time mediates the application of the forms of the understanding (*Verstand*: the categories and the synthetic-logical principles) to perceivable data; but it cannot, by definition, schematize the ideas of reason (*Vernunft*). Strictly speaking, an idea has no adequate representation, or *Darstellung*; it can only have external copies in the empirical world, but these (as we have seen, for instance, in the case of legal institutions) cannot capture the essential import of reason or represent it adequately in their own domain. Moreover, as a form of intuition, time is not of the same ontic order as the pure stands and forms of reason. Time is constitutive only in the phenomenal world,[10] while the proper sphere of reason is noumenal, lying beyond all temporalized experience. Therefore, no possible relation can exist between shifts in man's pure rational consciousness and changes in his temporalized experience. We are left again with two separate systems, each having a dynamic of its own. But the problem is now even more serious, since these two systems are alleged to *actually* mediate each other, while on the other hand—as implied in Kant's theory of time—they are presented as *incapable* of such mediation.

The History of Philosophy (Chapters Six and Seven)

A similar objection applies to Kant's construal of the history of philosophy. As we have seen, this history is the historization of the pure architectonic of reason. Here again a pure paradigm of rationality is breaking from under the "products of sensibility" toward its coherent explication in the *Critique*. Although apparently an aggregate, the history of philosophy is a covert totality, as it also is in Hegel, with each particular system expressing some interest of reason in confused and one-sided manner; and their antinomies, collapses and resystematizations are all anchored in the pure architectonic of reason. This progress is consummated, and transcends its historicality, only with the appearance of phi-

---

[10] From this viewpoint, time will be of the same ontic order as the categories of the understanding, for both are constitutive of empirical objects and states and belong to their ontic makeup. This is, however, not true of the Ideas of reason.

losophy as science, where the pure paradigm and its conscious articulation become one.

To maintain this theory Kant would have first, to assume some nontemporal processuality of the pure ego, a mode of change or development obtaining in the transcendental sphere as such; and second, to show that this pure development can be embodied or schematized in the sphere of temporal experience. But only the first idea can and does have a legitimate place in Kant's system; the second remains untenable.

Ascribing a supra-temporal processuality to the pure self is crucial to Kant and not as odd historically as it may first appear. Ever since the Greeks, philosophers have distinguished variously between time and some pure processuality of being (or of the mind) of which time is only a phenomenal expression. From Aristotle to the Neoplatonists to Spinoza; from Schopenhauer to Bergson and Whitehead; and from Fichte to Husserl, a variety of this distinction seemed necessary to thinkers of different schools. Kant does not restate it explicitly, but he implies it strongly in central parts of his system. For instance, all the cases of *growth in rationality*—as education, or as our own topic of the history of reason—involve such a pure dynamic of the self. But even where no ascent is involved, when out of purely rational grounds consciousness takes a stand, adopts or rejects a rule, takes an option, etc., we have again a pure dynamic of the self, i.e., changes in the posture of *pure* consciousness that take place on the transcendental plane and stand in problematic relation to the empirical person and to time. Moreover, Kant's discussion of the unity of apperception in the first *Critique* presents the ego as an *activity*, a pure subjective function expressing itself in the various *a priori* functions of the mind, including its time-engendering function. As the original synthesis of the manifold, it underlies all other forms of synthesis, including that of time itself, and is presupposed by them. Moreover, since

284

it is an *activity*, not a substance, the transcendental ego depends upon its actual unification of the manifold.

The latter claim is made more explicitly in the Transcendental Deduction. As against Descartes, Kant denies that the identity of the ego is given beforehand, prior to its unification of the manifold of impressions into an objective world. The identity of the ego is rather *actualized* by fulfilling this function; it is not ready-made, but constitutes itself as a *result* of its pure operation. By synthesizing the many data in categorizable ways, the ego not only makes possible a universally valid experience, but also reconstitutes its own identity and individuation. Thus, the idea of a pure processuality, pertaining to the transcendental ego as such, occupies a central place in Kant's most important argument in the first *Critique*, to the point that his whole Copernican reversal hinges upon it.

The pure processuality of the ego does certainly not take place in time. It is the most primordial function of the mind that time, too, ultimately presupposes. As such it is analogous to the pure development involved in the "history of reason"; and if Kant sought the systematic locus for the latter idea, he might find it in his notion of the pure becoming of the transcendental ego.

However, showing that this idea is central or legitimate in Kant will not solve the historical antinomy, but rather restate it. For the problem remains: How can pure changes in consciousness be temporalized and expressed as changes in empirical persons, states of culture, etc.? This question, as we have seen, cannot find an answer in the Kantian framework, and so we are left again with two parallel systems—the pure history of reason on the one hand, and the empirical history of philosophy on the other.

Kant's failure to schematize the history of reason is dramatized by his illegitimate use of the term *schema* in referring to the historical systems of philosophy. We have seen that he pictures the ascent of philosophy as a tension between

285

the pure "monogram" of the architectonic and the "schema" that each philosopher makes of it, however dimly, when construing his own one-sided system. By so using the term *schema* Kant may give the impression that there is, after all, a schematization of the architectonic within the actual history. But we have seen that a partial, one-sided, or sensuously affected representation of a pure rational model cannot properly count as its schema. A schema, by definition, must capture the full import of the rational model, not a dim or one-sided aspect of it; and it must represent it in its own medium without confusion of the elements. Kant's construal of the history of philosophy does not, however, meet these requirements, but makes him fall back again upon the Leibnizian pattern of development, which is untenable in Kantian terms.

To conclude, the history of philosophy cannot be made to represent, as a covert totality, the history of reason proper as long as no bridging principle exists between pure changes in consciousness and actual states in time. This problem makes us conclude that while on certain grounds a history of reason is indispensable for Kant, on other grounds it is impossible. And the effects of the same problem on other areas—making impossible the representation in time of the process of education, or of any other change in the stand of the rational self—only indicate that this is not an accidental problem in Kant but a variant of the most fundamental difficulty in his system.

We cannot leave the matter of the history of philosophy without further words of criticism concerning Kant's conception of the end of philosophy. Kant may be right in claiming that philosophy must be the self-explication of reason, in which human subjectivity is elucidated to itself with respect to its experiencing. He may be right in adding, correspondingly, that "reason" does not mean a frozen set of rules and structures, but the subjective, interested activity that produces and structures itself in them. Yet all this should lead him at least to *question* the ancient philosophical dogma, that there is, at the end, some pure, eternal system of truth, awaiting revelation once and for all. This belief certainly pervades the history of philosophy, and is shared by all the classical rationalists. Yet their failure to find such a system may not be simply due to intellectual limitations, or to the fact that the time was not ripe, but to the misguided goal they had set to themselves. A more radical criticism than Kant's will have to identify in this goal another form of metaphysical quest, which critical reason should both pronounce as inevitable and yet as misleading and calling for transformation. Doing so will lead us beyond Kant's philosophy, while using his own critical procedure. I cannot here justify this neo-criticism in full; but let me point out, that if there is, today, an advance in the critical consciousness, it lies in the recognition that theoretical reflection and orientation of our experience is not necessarily dependent on unique theories, that capture the truth, as it were, *sub specia aeternitatis*; they are rather culture-bound and open to alteration and revisions. This will mean that "reason" is self-transcending; its actual shapes are open to restructuring, in relation to the changing cultural experience; or to use Kant's own language, a "regulative" idea of philosophy must here take the place of the speculative quest for a final system.

The Primacy of Praxis and the Postulates

When Kant suspends the basic rules of the critique by postulating the existence of God as a common origin for receptivity and spontaneity, he certainly has a meta-theory justifying this procedure. This theory, the primacy of pure practical reason, is too important an issue for a summary discussion. But for the purpose of this epilogue a few objections to it may be listed. The main questions are: What are the grounds for this theory itself? And even if we admit the theory, how far does its force reach?

As a background for this discussion I should like to draw

a distinction between what may be called the *doctrinal* sense of the primacy of pure practical reason and its *methodological* use. By the first I mean the philosophical doctrine portraying reason as a system of interests and placing the practical interest at the top of the hierarchy. This includes Kant's idea that the metaphysical interest of reason attains adequate satisfaction in the field of praxis. By the second I mean the methodological rule sanctioning, on certain occasions, the acceptance of cognitive propositions that cannot, in principle, be proved cognitively. I suggest that the doctrinal sense of the primacy of pure practical reason is logically independent of its methodological use (although not vice versa), and one could, therefore, maintain the first without accepting the dubious procedure involved in the second.

To illustrate the utility of this distinction let us imagine a hypothetical argument between an ardent Kantian and an unsympathetic critic. The Kantian will argue that, given the theory of the primacy of pure practical reason, using a postulate is not, after all, extrinsic to the system but rooted within it. The critic will retort that the primacy of pure practical reason itself is an artificial expedient, devised to solve an *ad hoc* difficulty. When the need arises, any theory can proclaim certain exceptions to its rules, and even supply a new rule for generalizing them; but this should not make the exceptions any less arbitrary or any more coherent in terms of the system.

Who is right? The critic is certainly wrong, at least in his first statement. Whoever sees the primacy of pure practical reason as an *ad hoc* expedient misses a vital aspect of Kant's philosophy and is being blind to the central place it has in Kant *regardless of its function in justifying the postulates.* But this does not put the ardent Kantian in the right, since the central place of the primacy principle applies to its doctrinal sense, not necessarily to its methodological use. In other words, using a postulate to suspend the basic rules of the *Critique* remains objectionable even if one admits that reason attains its ultimate end in the field of praxis. (This would mean: in action proper, not in speculation about the nature of the universe on the basis of moral deductions.) Let us examine both aspects of the primacy of pure practical reason in greater detail.

The Doctrinal Sense

That the doctrine of the primacy of pure practical reason has deeper reasons in Kant than his need to overcome a particular difficulty is clearly seen from two complementary viewpoints: the Architectonic of reason and the direction of the critical move. The Architectonic belongs to the fundamental descriptive inventory of the system, namely to the same descriptive layer of the critique investigating the structure and forms of reason. As we have seen, Kant in the Architectonic defines rationality as a goal-oriented activity, pursuing its own essential ends. These ends culminate in the supreme end of moral practice, which also provides the systematizing factor for the whole system of reason, and establishes the meaning of philosophy itself in the genuine sense.[11] Therefore, saying that the whole rational endeavor of man attains its climax in moral practice is no occasional dictum (or expedient), but a fundamental principle, enjoying the same primordial status as other descriptive presuppositions of the critique (including the distinction between spontaneity and receptivity).

The same can be seen from the direction of the critical move. The critique of reason frustrates the ultimate rational goals in the cognitive sphere, but redirects them to the sphere of praxis as their positive and legitimate domain. It is not in knowledge but in action that the ultimate metaphysical interest of reason will find its adequate expression and even satisfaction. Hence the new concept of a *metaphysics of moral practice (Sitten)* established by this move. In this transformation of the metaphysical interest from a means of absolute knowledge into a principle of *will*,

[11] See pp. 11, 20-21, 230-233.

Kant sees the apex of the critique of reason, expressing again the primacy of pure practical reason in the doctrinal sense. The unconditioned and the total, which we cannot approach by knowledge, can be *created* by moral action and by the totalization of the particular acts in light of a comprehensive historical goal. The unconditioned takes the form of the *absolute law* of the will, the categorical imperative, and the total is given in the form of the *ultimate end* of the will, the highest good. Moreover, a variant of the same move is given in the critique of religion, which denies to religion any cognitive significance and transforms its full import—including the religious qualities of sanctity, awe, sublimity, etc.—to the sphere of moral-historical action.

It should be noticed that Kant's move has no skeptical character. Skeptics from the Sophists to Hume have also declared the primacy of practice, although not as a systematic continuation of knowledge but rather as a leap and a break from it. But by opting for the practical needs of life, they have stepped outside the system of reason, and their concept of interests has been duly pragmatic or utilitarian. For Kant, the move is supposed to take place *within* the system of reason itself and be grounded in its own architectonic. It is a move from one function of rationality to another, compensating for the failure of the first and sublimating the intellectual drive underlying this failure.[12]

But here the doubt arises: Is this a proper sublimation of the metaphysical interest of reason or rather a means for its repression? Psychologically the ultimate metaphysical queries of the mind can certainly be submerged in the hum-

---

[12] Here a comparison between Kant, Hegel, and Marx may be suggested. Kant, like Marx and unlike Hegel, opts for the primacy of the will over the understanding. And since the will projects ideals that reality does not meet, it turns out to be a principle demanding to change and transform the world in light of an ideal. What is the position of *understanding* the world within this relation? In Hegel, action to change the world is a *prerequisite* for understanding it; in Marx it is a *consequence* of having understood it; whereas in Kant it appears as a *compensation* for failing to understand it.

drum of practical life, in zealous moral and social action, or, as Kant finally suggests, in the vision of a moral world. Indeed, Kant's pattern shows in the great movements and ideologies of secular messianism following his time; and his model also has interesting affinities with the modern phenomenon of *sacralization*—the replacement of religious attitudes and of ultimate metaphysical concerns by absolutist historical ideals. But the question is not psychological. Kant claims that his move is rooted in the architectonic of reason as a transcendental paradigm, defining the proper relation between the interests of the reason; and this paradigm can be challenged on the same non-empirical level. A rival theory of the architectonic might claim that the queries about being as such, about the ultimate ground of the universe and the individual's existence within it, constitute a *sui generis* interest of reason, irreducible and untransformable to the sphere of any other. In this view, Kant's attempt to satisfy the metaphysical interest by turning its force into practical concerns is not proper sublimation of the interest but rather a form of repression or self-alienation.

This seems a basic phenomenological problem that no prior deduction can solve. What are the genuine interests and "essential ends" of philosophizing—and what are the inner limits for transforming the one into the other? Philosophers from Plato to Hegel and from Aristotle to Heidegger have maintained that there is a primordial metaphysical interest, concerned with being as such; and Heidegger even claims that this interest is not only the essence of philosophy but is constitutive of the human *Dasein* as such; we *exist* as this concern and do not just "have" it. Other philosophers, like Wittgenstein, have seen this interest as a distortion, the product of linguistic and other fallacies of which philosophy should rather "cure" us. Kant is radically opposed to such alleged therapeutics. For him, the cognitive metaphysical queries remain rational and meaningful even after the fallacies of pure reason have been uncovered and the objects of the queries declared unattainable. The tension between the rationally meaningful question and the rationally impossible answer is a typical result of the critique of reason, reflecting the limits of human rationality (its being an *inherently unsatisfiable* interest) and bringing back, thereby, to man's consciousness the fact of his finitude.

And yet, in turning the full force of the metaphysical concerns from ontology to ethics and history, Kant denies the cognitive metaphysical interest not only priority, but also a *sui generis* character on equal footing. Based on the primacy of pure practical reason in its doctrinal sense, Kant's move undermines the autonomy of man's existential queries—the sign and product of his finitude—disguising them as practical concerns and submerging them in the tumult of social action and in utopian vision; and this, to borrow again a term from Heidegger, is a form of the "forgetfulness of being." Or, putting the matter in Kant's own terminology, instead of actualizing the inherent architectonic of reason, this program is bound to repress and distort an essential interest of reason.[13]

Summing up the doctrinal sense of the primacy of pure

[13] In his otherwise suggestive and interesting interpretation, Lucien Goldmann (*La Communauté humaine et l'univers chez Kant*, Paris, 1948) criticizes Kant for failing to hold a position that we, on the contrary, have found him to maintain and even to press too hard. Goldmann states justly that "we find in Kant almost all the elements of a philosophy of history" (228, my translation), adding later that in this Kant anticipates Hegel, Marx and Lukacs (Goldmann's own philosophical mentor). But he misses the point when he claims that Kant finally escaped from history into the transcendent and super-natural domain of religion, since Kant in fact did the opposite, reducing religion itself to the domain of moral history, and even trying to transform the metaphysical and religious interests into moral-historical concerns. Goldmann also adheres to the erroneous view that according to Kant it is God, not man, who has to realize the highest good (p. 242), and he sees the highest good as an other-worldly ideal with no implications for present-day action. To Goldmann, a Marxian thinker, Kant's alleged escape from history to transcendent religion is a form of alienation; but I suspect that Goldmann falls here victim to a much too rigid Marxist scheme that he imposes on Kant *a priori*.

practical reason, we may say it states that (a) reason is a hierarchy of interests; (b) it attains its supreme goal in praxis; (c) its metaphysical interest can be fully satisfied by being transformed to a moral-historical ideal. Having criticized the last point, let me point out that the concept of an interest of reason itself is adequate and fruitful. It suggests a view of rationality which retains the element of *eros* within the element of *logos*; it construes reason as a subjective activity, not as an independent Platonic form; it portrays the rational activity as *self*-structuring and *self*-constitutive, not as dependent on an external paradigm; and it does justice to the finitude of man within the concept of rationality itself. Moreover, this concept implies a much-needed distinction between instrumental rationality (intelligence) and reason as an end in itself; and thereby it does justice to another typical human feature, namely, that man *qua rational* is *interested* to break away from the bond of natural needs and purely utilitarian values, not by simply deferring them, but by sacrificing them to something considered a value per se. The main objection to Kant's concept refers, again, to the split it involves between "pure" reason and actual life. Reason is confined to its own transcendental sphere; it does not pervade the totality of life or express itself in the rest of our human functions, but only conjoins them as a foreign element; and man, the *animal rationale*, is thus artificially construed as an external conjunction: "animal" + "reason."[14]

[14] This construal, to be sure, is not specific to Kant but has powerful roots in Christianity and other religions on the one hand, and the major part of the history of philosophy on the other. The alternative would be, however, to recognize man as rational *in his very animality*, including his bodily functions, and thereby redefine both terms of the conjunction. A move toward a more concrete view of rationality is made in Hegel's dialectic, where reason operates and can develop only through the "lower" functions and actual life. And Merleau-Ponty and other phenomenologists take the even more daring (and promising) view that the body, far from being of "animal" character, is itself the *pour-soi* in the genuine human sense, i.e., the locus of actual subjectivity.

The Methodological Use of the Primacy of Pure Practical Reason

Even admitting that human rationality attains its supreme goal in the field of practice—the doctrinal sense of the primacy of pure practical reason—no necessary consequence follows with respect to Kant's method of practical postulation—the methodological use of the primacy of pure practical reason. This method sanctions as rational the belief in certain cognitive propositions that (a) are cognitively undecidable, that is, can neither be proved nor disproved by other cognitive propositions; (b) can be shown to state necessary conditions for the possibility of moral action of a certain kind; and (c) are accepted by the believer in the context, and for the sake, of actual moral practice, not as a mere theory *about* practice. Kant claims that when these conditions are fulfilled, we may accept the propositions in question with the same degree of assurance that a religious believer would have accepted them from his own, nonrational motives; but ours will be a perfectly *rational* attitude described as "rational faith."

The comparison with a religious believer is more than relevant, for although Kant's rule for moral postulation has a generalized form, the actual postulates it yields turn out to be specifically related to traditional themes of theology: God, immortality, and the freedom of the will. (Even the tacit extension of the postulates we discovered in Bible hermeneutics applies to religion and its criticism.) This is no accident, for Kant actually seeks to provide in the postulates a rational and criticized version of the great metaphysical issues that the history of both religion and philosophy manifest. The deep roots of this attempt in Kant lie beyond this Epilogue, but we should point out that the postulates share other similarities. They are designed to establish in certain ways a link between morality and the actual world, and they do so by going counter to the basic assumptions of the critical dualism that they claim to suspend.

Indeed, what the postulates permit to affirm should have been regarded by the critique under regular conditions—had the method of practical postulation not interfered—as absurd and irrational, a complete systematic mystery. That the noumenal will can intervene in the mechanical course of nature and imprint its designs upon it[15] is no less mysterious and irrational, in terms of the critical dualism, than the notion of particular divine Providence—to Kant the "*salto mortale* of human reason.*" That there is a common source for nature and reason, or receptivity and spontaneity (God), conflicts with the critique's basic assumption to the contrary; and that man can have indefinite existence conflicts with his definition as a *finite* rational being—another fundamental principle of the critique. (It also involves the mystery of atonement: the undoing of past deeds and the reversibility of an immoral career.)[16] It is manifest, there-

---

[15] This is Kant's positive sense of freedom; its negative sense is only the indeterminacy of the will by the natural processes. While the latter is *not* inconceivable in terms of the systematic dualism, the former is.

[16] The postulate of immortality is the most problematic in Kant's own terms and the least adequate to its intended purpose. Apparently this postulate is related only to the *personal* highest good. But what precisely does it ensure? It certainly cannot ensure reward, since reward is empirical happiness, and this will involve the immortality of the body, not only of the soul. But the postulate can also not ensure the attainment of virtue. Virtue is defined as moral conduct throughout a lifetime, or as closing to zero the gap between the global moral disposition and its manifestations in particular acts (pp. 52-53). But first, what would become of immoral acts in the *past*? Since no future act can affect the ethical quality of former acts, either corrupting them or atoning for them, a man who has even once committed an immoral act cannot attain virtue, no matter how long his life lasts. This consideration makes the postulate dispensable. If it is true that we cannot attempt becoming *more* perfect unless we have the assurance that we can become *fully* perfect, no moral progress will be possible at all, since the postulate of immortality cannot provide this assurance. And if, on the contrary, man can work toward his moral perfection even without believing that he can become actually perfect (attain virtue), then the postulate is superfluous.

In addition, virtue is defined as "moral disposition in conflict," not as a "holy will" (*C2*, V:84/87). It entails the constant overcoming of the incentives of the natural will, and so the attainment of virtue

fore, that what the postulates involve are not just innocent-
ly "undecidable" cognitive propositions. What these propositions transcend are not only the limits of knowledge as
determined within the system, but the limits of the system
itself. Taken in itself, their status is irrational rather than
simply nonrational; for they are not only ungrounded in
any cognitive science, natural or metaphysical, they *conflict*
with the very theory of knowledge and with the critique at
large.

Yet the method of practical postulation proclaims the
acceptance of these propositions as rational; and it should
be noticed that what is thereby sanctified as rational is not
only *acting as if* these propositions were true, but actually
affirming them as true. Without this, Kant could not have
provided a "moral proof" of the existence of God, freedom,
and immortality. But for the same reason, he commits himself to a form of inference from ought to is, namely, to deducing certain aspects of the real world from purely moral
premises.

We are already familiar with the structure of this inference. The first and absolute premise is that there is a moral
duty to act in certain ways: this is a "fact of reason" or of
moral consciousness, admitted as unconditionally and irrev-
ocably true. The second premise, also the result of moral
analysis, is that duty entails the ability to do it (*sollen* implies *können*). The conclusion is that man, the subject of
duty, is able to perform it. Now, since ability is an ontologi-

---

will require the immortality not only of the pure soul but of the empirical self, the body, as well!

There are two ways to reinterpret the postulate of immortality if one
wishes to make it functional. One is to read the postulate as saying
nothing of its official subject, indefinite existence, but (in analogy with
the "existence of God") as only providing the bare assurance that whatever the mystery involved, the individual can after all attain moral perfection. The other way is to regard the postulate as referring to the
species, not the individual, such that the "virtue" in question will be
reinterpreted as attainment of the ethical community included in the
highest good. But clearly Kant himself takes neither of these ways.

cal concept, presupposing a certain makeup of the universe, Kant goes on to affirm certain aspects of the real world as adding up to this ability: there is positive noumenal freedom; there is a common ground for nature and morality (God); there is immortality. Thus we have passed over from the pure analysis of ought to a form of is. Having started with the structure of moral consciousness, we now make *a priori* claims about the structure of the world.

Objectionable in itself, this passage from ought to is violates Kant's own rigid distinction between fact and value, on which his ethical theory hinges; and it also commits the "critical" fallacy of learning something about real existence from pure concepts of reason. Setting its own rule to itself, this form of inference has no other grounds than Kant's overriding optimism. The world, Kant ardently believes, *must somehow* be structured in a way that makes moral action possible. Therefore, by discovering the preconditions of moral action it is possible to learn something *a priori* of how the universe is made. If we look closely, this is a tacit and illegitimate extension of the Copernican revolution, as if the structure of *moral* consciousness gives us another source for determining *a priori* the structure of the world and prescribing ontological conditions for its possibility. But first, moral consciousness is pure reason, and reason cannot of itself determine the world; this is only the task of the understanding, defined as the function that unifies the manifold of sense-impressions and as *limited* by them. And secondly, while the synthetic–*a priori* status of the categories is given a "deduction," i.e., a justifying argument, from within the system, here we are left with an arbitrary dogma that transcends the system. Why should the world correspond to the necessities of moral action? This is certainly *demanded* by moral consciousness, but why should the world comply? Since the critique construes the universe as alien to reason, how can we know *a priori* that it does not defeat man's moral interests, even making the concept of duty itself meaningless? Suppose even that moral consciousness itself, with its inherent concept of obligation and its ideal of the highest good, is just another metaphysical delusion that a proper critique should rather set aright? (A similar line was taken, indeed, by Nietzsche.) We certainly have such moral consciousness, and it would be undermined in the absence of freedom. But it cannot *of itself* guarantee that it is not so undermined, and that freedom exists.

Except for Kant's compelling conviction to the contrary, there is nothing in the system excluding this ominous possibility, for no legitimate link is available between pure reason and the ultimate foundations of the universe. Even the doctrinal sense of the primacy of pure practical reason, as included in the architectonic of reason, cannot help in this respect, for (again) all this doctrine refers to is the structure of *pure reason* as such; but as long as man is finite and there is receptivity, reason does not create the world in its pure image but confronts its material elements as given. Therefore, even after we have studied the pure architectonic of reason and know all about its inner interests, forms, and demands, we have still no knowledge of real existence and have gained no passport permitting us to move from the structure of pure reason to that of the actual world in a merely *a priori* way.

In the final analysis, Kant's methodological use of the primacy of pure practical reason is an extrinsic dogma. It rephrases a presystematic intuition, a compelling conviction no less absolute and arbitrary than that of a religious devotee. Indeed, if we look in Kant for a form of deep religiosity, a religiosity without God, we shall find it in this moralistic conviction that, bypassing the concept of God and replacing it with absolute human morality, makes the latter the legislator not only for the will, but also for the ultimate foundations of the universe.

The Historical Antinomy as a Variant of the Problem of Dualism

Underlying most of the problems we have encountered, including those of the postulates, is Kant's radical split be-

tween reason and nature, itself a derivative of the duality
of spontaneity and receptivity.[17] This duality is the most
fundamental principle of the critical system. Without it,
the Copernican revolution will make no sense, and there
will be no transcendental science and no necessary and universal foundations for knowledge and ethics. Also, without
this duality, reason cannot be subject to a critique that defines and restricts its boundaries. The split between spontaneity and receptivity expresses the finitude of man, his
being a "limited rational being." As such, man is no *intellectus archetypus* but is bound by sense-perceptions in
knowledge and by natural appetites and desires in action.
These, however, are particular and contingent elements,
which cannot of themselves provide a rational—that is, a
necessary and universal—basis for knowledge and action.
The possibility of the latter presupposes that, in addition
to the empirical constituents, man has also an independent
or transcendental faculty, producing of itself (spontaneously) the supreme laws of both fields and subordinating
the empirical constituents to its own *a priori* rules. Any
mixture of these two sources will deprive the transcendental element of its *a priori* status and thus annul its capacity
to provide the required necessity and universality. At the
same time, the pure elements are not self-sufficient, but must
impose themselves on the empirical constituents in the form
of a synthesis, in which the transcendental rule is applied
from without to something merely given, putting it in intelligible relations and imparting to it the form of necessity
and universality. The concept of synthesis must therefore
be construed by Kant as *an external reunification of the
heterogeneous.* Just as neither of the elements being con-
joined is derived from or explicated by the other, so they
cannot mediate or penetrate each other when being put to-

[17] This goes also for the PPR, especially its methodological use,
which is specifically designed to overcome the reason/nature dualism.
Its doctrinal sense refers more directly to another feature of the critique
—the finitude of man and the limits of knowledge (which it attempts to
overcome in the field of praxis); but fundamentally, the limits of knowledge are also determined by the duality of spontaneity and receptivity.

gether, but must remain alien and mutually exclusive even in their *syn-thesis*.

There is no need to stress the great difficulties that this dualism generates for Kant. Known as the problem of schematism in the broad sense, it penetrates all the parts of his system, expressing itself as the unbridgeable gap (or unintelligible correspondence) between the categories and sense-perceptions, the form of duty and its particular content, virtue and happiness, reason and nature, the phenomenal and the noumenal, the empirical self and the rational self, and—in the case at hand—empirical history and rational history. Indeed, the difficulties we have noticed add up to the systematic *untenablity* of the concept of rational history, which on the other hand we found to be genuine and *indispensable* in terms of the system; and so we are faced, in the last analysis, with an antinomic situation. Both the thesis and the antithesis of this historical antinomy are grounded in the logic of the system, but I do not claim that their incongruity can be resolved. Rather, as matters stand in Kant, we are left with a theory of rational history which is not fully coherent and accounted for. But this should not serve as a basis for dismissing the genuine character of this theory, no more than other, more readily recognized Kantian theories (like the thing in itself) can be dismissed just because they entail insoluble difficulties. As I noted in the Introduction, were we to reject as non-Kantian all the concepts that give Kant trouble, especially those related to the problem of schematism, very little might indeed be left.

Aufhebung by Hegel

Without blurring the systematic differences between Kant and Hegel, we have noticed throughout the book important similarities between them, some of them usually unrecognized. Generally speaking, Kant anticipates Hegel's attempt to place the principle of reason within a historical context. But Kant comes closer to Hegel in a number of more specific ways, sometimes suggesting—in embryo and without dialectical logic—a doctrine normally associated with Hegel.

In the theory of the highest good Kant breaks away from his narrow concept of a rational will that wills itself directly and subjectively, in separation from the actual world that confronts it. He now construes a concept of rational will that wills itself as *embodied* in the course of the world and as being reflected to itself from it. The object of the rational will in the narrow sense is the good, namely, a certain subjective shape it gives itself in the act of moral willing; but the object of the will in the enlarged sense is the *highest* good, i.e., a certain ideal kind of world which it has yet to create. The will demands to recognize its rational norms as realized not only in its own mode of volition, but also in the global shape of a world to come.[18] It is true that Hegel derides Kant's attempt as self-defeating because of its underlying dualism and the conception of reason as an external ought; but this underlines rather than mars the proximity of their interests. Had Kant not tried to reunite *Tugend* with the *Weltlauf*, Hegel's acute criticism would not even be relevant.

An even closer anticipation of Hegel is found in Kant's theory of the history of politics, religion, and philosophy; for here a principle of reason is supposed to emerge from the empirical history itself by a certain dynamic of antagonism or antinomy.

When studying culture, Kant anticipates Hegel's famous doctrine of the cunning of reason—which must, however, take in Kant the form of the cunning of *nature*. It asserts that even when a truly rational intention is absent, an objective form of rationality is produced in the social domain by the very opposite of reason—passions, violence, and self-interest—such that raw nature transcends itself by a teleo-

---

[18] Cf. *Phenomenology of Mind*: "The Moral View of the World" (VI, C, a); "Dissemblance" (VI, C, b); "Virtue and the Course of the World" (V, B, c), and numerous other places.

logical principle of its own. Yet this form of rationality must be branded by Kant as merely "legal" or external, not as genuine rationality; and it can contribute only to political progress, which is *not* for Kant the supreme practical end.[19]

A more pronounced if less apparent affinity to Hegel we discovered in the history of religion, where the one religion of reason is embedded in the norms of the many religious cults, imparting to them a unifying or totalizing pattern. As cruder forms of religion give way to purer ones, their essential content is preserved, each time assuming a shape closer to the *a priori* paradigm of rationality. The history of religion differs from that of politics in that it is no longer confined to external institutions, but involves the evolution of subjective consciousness—maturing to the full recognition of its own moral structure; yet this process, too, is construed as taking place *within* empirical history and as inevitably mediated by it. But perhaps the most striking proto-Hegelian idea we found in the history of philosophy, where all great doctrines of the past form a latent organic totality, each expressing one-sidedly and under sensuous cover some aspect of the single system of philosophy. And, proceeding by antinomies, revolutions, and a final synthesis, this mode of the history of reason again takes place as reason's *self*-explication from within the empirical history of thought.

However, as we have seen, *the closer Kant anticipates Hegel, the more antinomic his own position becomes.* Hegel can develop the Kantian themes on history more comprehensively and more coherently because he overcame the Kantian dualism—and thereby the historical antinomy—within a new *Aufhebung*, using his own view of rationality. In this view, the rational is necessarily mediated by its "other" (the empirical, the element of Being, etc.) and con-

[19] For Hegel, the supreme practical end *is* political; but the practical end itself is only a subservient moment of the historical end proper, which is *speculative* (absolute knowledge). For Kant no absolute knowledge is possible, and its place is taken by the absolute of praxis—morality and the highest good.

stitutes itself *qua* rational only in and through this other. The rational *as* rational must have empirical existence and be realized through it. It is not an alien principle imposed on the world from without, but an immanent principle manifesting itself in the various forms of the empirical world, assuming even the lesser degrees of reality and the mind, and actualizing itself as truly rational by their necessary mediation. Among other things, this view rejects as an abstraction the construal of reason as pure and transcendental. The notion of "pure" reason presents the principle of reason as no less abstract, unreal, and devoid of self-sufficient status than its opposite—the contingent elements of perception and all items having merely empirical *Existenz*. Regarding either of these opposites as actual and self-sufficient is a common metaphysical error,[20] shared by rationalist and empiricist metaphysicians alike; it is the typical standpoint of the "understanding," confusing rationality with an abstraction and actuality with a mere shadow. A *dialectical* critique of reason should overcome these metaphysical abstractions by canceling the mutual exclusion of the rational and the empirical and viewing them as *mutually constitutive moments* of a single dynamic totality— that of actuality *(Wirklichkeit)* and eventually of the Concept *(Begriff)*. This does not blur the difference between the two opposites but rather establishes it adequately for the first time; for only their dynamic unity can confer their proper distinction on the rational and the empirical, now conceived as interdependent moments and not as independent principles. Hegel thus retains the duality of the empirical and the rational while sublating their *dualism*, i.e., their being totally heterogeneous and self-sustaining, each in its proper domain.

Hegel's *Aufhebung* of dualism also overcomes the Kantian historical antinomy in both its aspects, concerning time

[20] Of course, the term "error" is here understood in the dialectical sense, as an element of truth appearing in distorted form and with a one-side pretense for exclusivity.

and concerning schematism in general. Time is no longer a subjective "form of intuition" but an aspect of being, the externalization of the Concept; and reason can actualize itself only within this externalization. In other words, the intermediation of the moments applies also to reason and time. Reason, the supratemporal, must constitute itself as such by way of its temporalization; and only as developing in historical time can it emerge as absolute and eternal. This eliminates one aspect of Kant's historical antinomy; for whereas Kant's theory of history cannot account for the temporalization of reason, Hegel's dialectic cannot admit of reason otherwise. In addition, schematism in the Kantian sense becomes unnecessary, since each of the opposites now mediates the other as a condition for its own constitution, with no need for a *tertium comparationis.* Kant needs an external bridge between the opposites, since he conceives of them as initially alien and independent; but in Hegel neither is independent per se, but each is initially constituted through the other, such that their unity has logical precedence over their difference and makes it, too, possible. Hegel does, therefore, ascribe a common principle to the rational and the empirical, although this principle discloses itself only at the end, by way of its actualization.

We have seen that Kant must conceive of schematism as an external representation *(Darstellung)* in which the principle of reason is reproduced in a lower domain while each retains its proper and mutually exclusive characteristics. In Hegel, however, the principle of reason gives the empirical manifestation to itself, assuming the various shapes of the world and history, alienating itself in them and finally recovering itself as genuinely rational (that is, actual) within its adequate empirical manifestation. Reason does not need, therefore, an external principle to schematize it; it grows and is explicated from within the real world and does not impose itself upon it from without.

Hegel's *Aufhebung* of the Kantian dualism enables him to view rationality as *embedded* in the lower forms of culture, politics, religion, etc. and as explicating itself from them, and so he can accomplish more coherently what Kant failed to do: he can unite empirical and rational history in a single dynamic whole. This also gives a systematic foundation for making the cunning of reason the prime mover of history, prompting the ascent of rationality and freedom by the force of ambition, passion, and violence; and this, in turn, enables Hegel to develop more coherently the Kantian idea (implied in the highest good) of a rational will that wills to realize itself not just subjectively, but through its embodiment in the actual world. At the same time, since the rational will operates in the disguise of its "other," without the guidance of a moral ought or an ideal world to come, this eliminates the utopian element of Kant's philosophy of history and breaks the necessary link between the rational and the *moral* will. Indeed, while Kant's passage from the first to the second stage of praxis is a move from subjective morality to moral history, in Hegel the move to world history transcends the sphere of morality altogether, leaving it as the realm of pure subjectivity and of merely *individual* self-consciousness.

Needless to say, Hegel's dialectic also forgoes the need for external postulates and admits of no transcendent God. God is not some particular entity beyond the world, but the totality of the Spirit, actualized in human history and within its immanent domain. Moreover, the genuine medium of the absolute Spirit is not practical but speculative. The final end of praxis, which in Hegel is political, not moral, is not itself—to use Kant's language—"the final-end of all creation," but a subservient moment of it. The ultimate end is actualized by *speculation,* as the totality produces its own self-understanding through the philosophical self-consciousness of man, attaining the stage of absolute knowledge and thereby constituting the dialectical unity of being and thought, object and subject. Thus Hegel gives primacy to speculation over praxis, although he makes the latter a dialectical condition or moment for the former.

Hence the immense importance of the history of philososophy in Hegel's system. For Hegel, the history of philosophy is not only the self-explication of the rational subject alone, but equally of his object; it is the history of Being itself, in its varied substantial forms, as it conceptualizes itself and attains subjective self-consciousness. In Kant, on the other hand, the history of philosophy remains the self-explication of the rational subject alone, as *facing* an external reality and not as mediating its own development. Thus a fundamental antagonism between Hegel and Kant remains, despite the quasi-Hegelian theory we found in Kant concerning the history of philosophy as totality.

To elaborate the full scope of these differences, and to discuss the nuances and inner difficulties of Hegel's own *Aufhebung* would require a new book where a sufficiently long one has just ended. But let me say in conclusion that if we wish to locate the crucial rivalry between these two systems, we need not stop at Kant's critical dualism, but take a further step back toward the doctrine of human finitude in which his critical dualism itself is rooted. Indeed, if Hegel succeeds in building a more coherent theory of history, it is by abolishing the finitude of reason and making man—collectively, in his history—the medium whereby absolute knowledge is attained and the Absolute as such is produced. This, however, is much too great a price to pay. Is the Hegelian absolute Spirit the only alternative to Kant's dualism? Can we not conceive of history as an intelligible process while renouncing both? Can history not be viewed as a move towards emancipation, both practical and mental, even if we do not attribute to it an inherent metaphysical teleology—or a guiding moral ought? And can we not preserve the basic finitude and limitations of reason while construing it, in a Hegelian fashion, as a concrete principle, penetrating the totality of human life and interests? Between the Kantian failure and Hegel's overachievement, the idea of history must be questioned anew.

SELECT BIBLIOGRAPHY

Adickes, Erich. *Kants Opus Postumum.* Berlin, Reuther und Reichard, 1920.

Beck, L. W. *A Commentary on Kant's Critique of Practical Reason.* Chicago, University of Chicago Press, 1960.

————. *Early German Philosophy: Kant and his Predecessors.* Cambridge, Mass., Harvard University Press, 1969.

Bruggen, Walter. "Kant und das höchste Gut," *Zeitschrift für Philosophische Forschung,* XVIII (1964), 50-61.

Cassirer, H. W. *A Commentary on Kant's Critique of Judgement.* London, Methuen, 1938.

Daval, Roger. *La Métaphysique de Kant.* Paris, Presses Universitaires de France, 1951.

Delbos, Victor. *La Philosophie pratique de Kant.* Paris, Alcan, 1905.

Despland, Michael. *Kant on History and Religion.* Montreal and London, McGill-Queen's University Press, 1973.

Döring, A. "Kants Lehre vom höchsten Gut," *Kantstudien,* IV (1898), 94-101.

Düsing, Klaus. "Das Problem des höchsten Gutes in Kants praktischer Philosophie," *Kantstudien,* LXII (1971), 5-42.

Eisler, Rudolf (ed.). *Kant-Lexikon.* Berlin, Mittler und Pan-Verlag, 1930.

England, F. E. *Kant's Conception of God.* London, Allen and Unwin, 1929.

Fackenheim, Emil. "Kant's Concept of History," *Kantstudien,* XLVIII (1956-57), 381-398.

Galston, William. *Kant and the Problem of History.* Chicago, University of Chicago Press, 1975.

Goldmann, Lucien. *La Communauté humaine et l'univers chez Kant.* Paris, Presses Universitaires de France, 1948. (rev. ed.: *Introduction à la philosophie de Kant.* Paris, 1967; Eng. trans.: *Immanuel Kant,* by Robert Black. London, 1971.)

Guttmann, Julius. *Kants Gottesbegriff in seiner positiven Entwicklung*. Berlin, Reuther und Reichard, 1906.

Hassner, Pierre. "Les Concepts de guerre et de paix chez Kant," *Revue française de science politique*, XI (1961), 642-670.

Kelly, George A. *Idealism, Politics and History: Sources of Hegelian Thought*. Cambridge, Cambridge University Press, 1969.

Kojève, Alexandre. *Kant*. Paris, Gallimard, 1973.

Kroner, Richard. *Kants Weltanschauung*. Tübingen, Mohr (Siebeck), 1914. (Eng. trans. by John E. Smith. Chicago, University of Chicago Press, 1956.)

Krüger, Gerhard. *Philosophie und Moral in der kantischen Kritik*. Tübingen, Mohr (Siebeck), 1967 (1st ed. 1931).

Lübbe, Hermann. "Philosophiegeschichte als Philosophie," *Einsichten: Gerhard Krüger zum 60. Geburtstag*, ed. K. Oehler and R. Schaeffler. Frankfurt am Main, Klostermann, 1962, 204-229.

McFarland, J. D. *Kant's Concept of Teleology*. Edinburgh, Edinburgh University Press, 1970.

Martin, G. (ed.). *Allgemeiner Kantindex zu Kants gesammelten Schriften*. Berlin, Walter de Gruyter, 1967-69.

Medicus, Fritz. "Kant's Philosophie der Geschichte," *Kantstudien* 7 (1902).

Murphy, Jeffrie G. *Kant: The Philosophy of Right*. London, Macmillan, 1970.

Nahm, Milton C. " 'Sublimity' and the 'Moral Law' in Kant's Philosophy," *Kantstudien*, XVLVIII (1956-57), 502-524.

Oehler, K. and R. Schaeffler (eds.). *Einsichten: Gerhard Krüger zum 60. Geburtstag*. Frankfurt am Main, Klostermann, 1962.

Reboul, Olivier. *Kant et le problème du mal*. Montreal, Presses de l'Université de Montréal, 1971.

Ricoeur, Paul. *Le Conflit des interprétations. Essai d'herméneutique*. Paris, Editions du Seuil, 1969.

Rotenstreich, Nathan. *Experience and Its Systematization*. 2nd enl. ed. The Hague, Martinus Nijhoff, 1972.

Schweitzer, Albert. *Die Religionsphilosophie Kants in der Kritik der reinen Vernunft bis zur Religion innerhalb der Grenzen der blossen Vernunft*. Freiburg, Mohr, 1899.

Seth Pringle-Pattison, Andrew. *The Idea of God in the Light of Recent Philosophy*. New York, Oxford University Press, 1920.

Silber, John R. "The Copernican Revolution in Ethics," *Kantstudien*, LI (1959).

———. "The Ethical Significance of Kant's *Religion*," Introduction to Kant. *Religion within the Limits of Reason Alone.* New York, Harper and Row, 1960.

———. "The Importance of Highest Good in Kant's Ethics," *Ethics,* LXXIII (1963), 179-197.

———. "Kant's Conception of the Highest Good as Immanent and Transcendent," *Philosophical Review,* LXVIII (1959), 469-492.

Simmel, Georg. *Kant.* Leipzig, Duncker und Humblot, 1904.

Strauss, Leo. *Persecution and the Art of Writing.* Glencoe, Ill., Free Press, 1952.

Unger, Rudolf. " 'Der bestirnte Himmel über mir': Zur geistesgeschichtlichen Deutung eines Kant-Wortes," *Festschrift zur zweiten Jahrhundertfeier seines Geburtstages.* Leipzig, Dietrich, 1924, 239-263.

Vlachos, Georges. *La Pensée politique de Kant.* Paris, Presses Universitaires de France, 1962.

Walsh, W. H. "Kant's Moral Theology," *Proceedings of the British Academy,* XLIX. London, Oxford University Press, 1964.

Ward, Keith. *The Development of Kant's View of Ethics.* Oxford, Blackwell, 1972.

Weil, Eric. *Problèmes kantiens.* Paris, Vrin, 1963.

——— et al. *La Philosophie politique de Kant.* Annales de philosophie politique, IV. Paris, Presses Universitaires de France, 1962.

Weyand, Klaus. *Kants Geschichtsphilosophie. Ihre Entwicklung und ihr Verhältnis zur Aufklärung.* Cologne, Kölner Universitäts-Verlag, 1964.

Wilkins, B. T. "Teleology in Kant's Philosophy of History," *History and Theory,* V (1966), 172-185.

Wood, A. W. *Kant's Moral Religion.* Ithaca, Cornell University Press, 1970.

Yovel, Yirmiahu. "Bible Interpretation as Philosophical Praxis: A Study of Spinoza and Kant," *Journal of the History of Philosophy,* XI (1973), 189-212.

———. *Kant and the Renovation of Metaphysics.* Jerusalem, The Bialik Institute, 1973 (Hebrew).

Zeldin, M. B. "The *summum bonum,* the Moral Law and the Existence of God," *Kantstudien,* LXII (1971), 43-54.

INDEX

156, 253-254, 257, 297; Copernican revolution of rationality, 4, 12

Cosmic provincialism, 177n.

Counterproductive action, 217n.

Criminal justice, 66

Critical period, 128

Critical philosophy (or system), 30, 83, 91, 92, 104n., 116, 127, 135, 141, 227; basic rules (or assumptions) of criticism, 274, 276, 287, 294; critical philosophy of history, x, 125

Critique of teleological reason, 159, 161

Culture, 75-76, 81, 138-139, 141, 146, 156, 176-178, 193, 194n., 256, 268; culture of skill, 182-184; culture of discipline, 184-185; culture distinguished from history, 181-182 (*see also* Civilization)

Cunning of nature, 8, 9, 31, 126, 140-153, 161, 168, 173-175, 186, 190, 194, 277-279, 301

Cunning of reason, 301, 304

Dasein (Ger., Heidegger's sense), 291

Darwin, C., 170

Deduction, 5, 164, 250, 259, 260, 262, 265, 267, 297; metaphysical deduction, 265; transcendental deduction, 22, 260, 265, 267n.; moral deduction, 276

Deductive method, model, 250, 253, 262-264, 266

Deferred satisfaction, 68

Definition, 264n

Deity, 29, 105, 109, 119 (*see also* God)

Demiurge, 78, 82

Derived a priori concepts, 261-262

Descartes, R., 3, 100, 260, 262, 285

Design (hidden), 8

Desires, 65

Despair, 109, 114

Despland, M., xi, 213n., 215n.

Despotism, 150, 167; despotism of reason, 204; spiritual despotism, 205, 208; transcendent despot, 204

Destiny, 193, 270, 271

Determining ground of the will, 34, 52, 55, 57, 60

Deus ex machina, 100, 109, 144, 272, 275

Deviations, 53, 197; deficiency of the will (or an act), 112

Dialectic, 8; dialectic of practical reason, 32; dialectical self-overcoming, 145, 185, 187; dialectical logic, 23, 24, 237, 277, 301; dialectic of master and slave (Hegel), 110-111, 149, 183n.; dialectical technique (in arguments), 214; natural dialectic, 159, 168 (*see also* Cunning of nature)

Disinterested pleasure, 162

Disposition(s), 8, 47, 66, 76, 112, 194

Divine, divinity, 205-206, 210; divine commands, 205-206; divine guarantee, assistance, 87, 95, 95n., 99-100

Dogmatic, x, 8, 18, 30, 118, 127, 140, 154, 155, 239; dogmatic rationalism, dogmatic metaphysics, 20, 73n., 211, 253-254, 256

Dualism, x, 21, 23, 60, 88, 273, 294-295, 298-300, 303, 306

Duality, 86, 93-94, 303; duality in the moral will, 43-48

Duty, 47, 61, 64, 67, 140, 273, 280, 296

INDEX

318

defaultOmnipresence, 92
Ontological conditions, 252, 297;
ontological import, 8n.; ontological guarantee, 78; ontological commitment (lack of),
161-162
Open-mindedness, 211-212
Oppression, 182
Optimism, 121, 257, 297
Ordo cognoscendi (Lat.), 265-266,
267
Organic world (or phenomena),
159, 162; organic individuum,
145; organic system (or whole,
totality), 10, 227-228; organic
unity, 233-234; weak and strong
organic model (for philosophy), 234-235
Original mother species, 170
Other (or next) world, 30, 72
Ought, 48, 56, 80, 271, 274, 279,
280, 296, 297, 301, 305, 306
(see also Sollen)

Pascal, B., 100, 130, 132
Passion, 8, 73; social passions, 110
Peace, perpetual (or true), 187;
distinguished from cease-fires,
56 (see also War, World-Con-
federation)
Personal highest good, 51-61
Personality, 52
Persuasion, persuasive techniques, 202, 212, 213
Philosophy, 6; Scholastic definition of, 231; definition as
"world concept," or wisdom,
232n.; pseudo-philosophy vs.
genuine philosophy, 233, 235-
236; philosophy as science (or
scientific), 10, 261; end of
philosophy, 225, 237, 239, 268-
269, 286; learning philosophy,
243-244 (see also meta-philos-

ophy, method of philosophy,
history of philosophy)
Philosophizing, 10, 234-244; phi-
losophizing history of philosophy, 245n., 247-251
Physics, 6, 238, 253, 262, 266, 267
Pietism, 208n
Plato, 3-4, 12, 21, 237, 144n.,
164n., 291
Political community, 111, 173-
174, 194
Political (or "legal," Kant's
sense) institutions, 8, 47, 75,
138, 172, 278, 283
Political technology, 188-190
Political totality, 183, 183n.
Popkin, R., xii
Postulate, 21, 81, 96, 103, 108,
116, 126, 221, 274-275, 287-288,
291
Potentiality-actuality, 82, 96,
121, 142
Praxis, 6, 91n., 134, 136, 137, 140,
201, 289, 293; infinity (open-
endedness) of praxis, 260, 268,
274
Prediction, 278
Pre-established harmony, 66, 77,
134, 275 (see also Harmony)
Prestige, 149
Priestley, T., 236n.
Primacy of pure practical reason,
20, 21n., 89n., 91, 91n., 104,
114, 221, 232n., 259, 276n., 288-
298; as doctrine, 289-293; as
methodological principle, 269,
294-298
Primitive terms, 263
Priority (of formal law over material), 33-35
Privation, 17-18
Processuality (pure, or non-temporal; distinguished from
time), 22-23, 284-285

Productivity, 101, 102
Progress, 127, 140, 144, 151, 166,
193, 194; political progress,
170n., 186, 187-188, 278; moral
progress, 74, 197 (see also
Moral history)
Projection (of moral goal by sub-
ject), 18-19, 79-80, 178-179
Projêt fondamental (Fr., Sartre's
sense), 52
Promotion (dist. from realiza-
tion) of highest good, 96-98
Proof from design, 156
Property, 76, 138, 139, 148, 184,
196, 261; Property as Juridical
postulate of practical reason,
184n.
Prosperous sinner, 63n
Protestantism, 208, 209
Providence, 94, 97-98, 161, 168,
215n., 295
Prudence, 216
Punishment, 261
Pure practical reason, 84
Purposiveness, of freedom and of
nature, 49 (see also Teleology,
Finality)

Quantification, 266-267

Ratio cognoscendi (Lat.), 58n.,
88
Ratio essendi (Lat.), 58n.
Rational will, 8, 58n., 65, 127,
273; Rational beings (or, creatures), 65, 69, 132, 144; on
other planets, 176n.-177n.; rational history (see History of
reason); rational faith (see
Faith); rational scholarship,
246; rational historiography of
philosophy, 245n; rational plan
without rational intention,
143; rational interests (see un-

der Interests of reason) (see also
Reason)
Rationality, dual condition of,
203-204, 208; model of, 13;
constitution theory of, 12, 19;
Copernican revolution in, 4, 12;
growth, rise, ascent of, 3, 212-
213, 285, 305
Rationalism, 3, 4, 108; rationalists, 287, 303
Rationalization, (a) making rational, 274; (b) producing ex-
cuse, 92
Realization of morality, 29; distinguished from promotion,
96-98
Reason, historization of, 3-4, 14,
18, 225, 227-229, 236-237; temporalization of reason, 271, 282,
304; becoming, processuality,
development of reason, 4, 16,
227-228, 249, 264n.; reason as
goal-setting activity, 14; reason
as interest, 14 (see also Interests of reason); reason as self-
sufficient teleological system,
14, 19; reason distinguished
from intelligence, 190, 192;
erotic side of reason, 9, 15, 24;
reason as self-assertion, 211-212;
self-explication of reason, 9, 14,
223, 225, 262-263, 286, 302, 306;
finitude of human reason, 11,
13-14, 17, 24, 88; essential ends
(or, immanent tasks) of reason,
14, 17, 230-232, 235, 253, 289
(see also under Interests of
reason); accidental (or, external) ends of reason, 14, 17, 235;
architectonic unity of reason,
12, 19, 20, 21, 232, 238; "need,"
"aspirations," etc. of reason, 16,
32, 91n., 105, 254, 257; autonomy of reason (see under

State (political), 71, 91n., 150, 152
State of humanity (*vs.* state of animality), 190, 190n., 194
State of law, 148, 150
State of nature, 110, 150, 152
Statutory laws, 205, 207; statutory religion, 204, 206, 211, 213
Stratification, 168, 182
Strauss, L., 215
Subject, human, 13, 19; rational subject, 271; empirical subject, 60; thinking subject, 12, 204; willing subject, 273; concrete subject (Hegel), 23; super-subject, 276, 277n.
Sublimation, 192, 278n., 291
Sublime, 73n., 130-132
Sublimity (in religion), 209-211, 275
Substrate (or Substratum), sensuous (or empirical) substratum, 73, 280, 282; supersensible substratum (of creation), 60, 90, 96, 118
Subsumption, 279
Suffering just, 63n.
Sukale, M., xii
Supersensible(s), 258; supersensible world, 49; supersensible substratum (*see under* Substrate)
Suspension of judgement, 94n.
Synthesis, 6, 31, 36, 37-39, 42, 45, 51, 56, 68-72, 74, 74n., 79, 81, 84, 139, 194, 254; practical synthesis, 37-39, 68-72 (and most of pages above); cognitive (empirical) synthesis, 86, 262, 267; synthesis of the manifold, 284; a priori synthesis, 40; internal synthesis, 100; external synthesis, 100, 299-300; comprehensive *vs.* fragmentary

synthesis, 75; historical synthesis, 27
Synthetic logic, 155, 159, 258, 267, 282

Taste, 147
Technology, technological, 75, 76, 133, 139, 183, 196, 232; political technology, 188
Teleology, 128-132 (*see also* Finality)
Tenner, E., xii
Tertium comparationis (Lat.), 100, 304
Theocracy, 207
Theodicy, 78n., 145, 194n.; Moral theodicy, 55
Theology, 215, 232, 253, 294; theological import, 121; theological dogma, 203; theological knowledge, 203
Thing in itself, 5, 12, 19, 23, 79
Time, 5, 21, 72, 79, 86, 239, 282-285, 286, 303; time distinguished from pure processuality (or *tempus vs. duratio*), 22, 23
Tools, 138
Totality, 31, 99, 164, 170; moral totality, 7, 31, 138, 141; totality of wills, 65n.; total object of the will, 36
Totalization, 6, 19, 29, 36, 40, 51, 74, 79, 102, 138, 202, 273, 290
Totalitarianism, 204
Transcendent (use or application), 93, 115, 121
Transcendent world, 30, 72; transcendent master lawgiver, 211, 280; transcendent postulate, 274; transcendent explanation, 136
Transcendental functioning of the mind, 12; transcendental

Library of Congress Cataloging in Publication Data

Yovel, Yirmiahu.
   Kant and the philosophy of history.

   Bibliography: p.
   Includes index.
   1. Kant, Immanuel, 1724-1804.   2. History—Philosophy.
I. Title.
B2799.H7Y68   193   79-84024
ISBN 0-691-07225-6